CONFIDEN

T0270343

"Suzanne Worthley's skill in multidimensional energy healing and protection for people, places, and the natural world is unsurpassed. In *Confident Empath*, she has created a comprehensive and engaging guide that reveals, step-by-step, how to understand, navigate, and truly thrive in this amazing multidimensional universe of energy in which we all live. Now, perhaps more than ever, is the time for the 'bold and sacred rebels' to whom Suzanne has dedicated this book to become adept at the skills needed for not only their individual transformation but also the planetary and collective one."

~ **Annie Wilder,** author of *House of Spirits and Whispers*
and *Spirits Out of Time*

"In my vocation as a professional chiropractor, I interact daily with clients who struggle with anxiety, worry, and exhaustion, typically due to some level of empathed energy. In this book, Suzanne brilliantly lays out the information that allows the reader to be guided through the world of unseen energy all while being supported by insightful, tactical ideas to maintain their health and wellness. *Confident Empath* will definitely be a reliable resource for me as well as a consistent referral to my client base."

~ **Jill Friedrichs, D.C.,** doctor of chiropractic

"In this time of awakening you are being called to embrace your gifts and self-empowerment. Suzanne's incredible insight and amazing wealth of information will help you through this process. Being an empath and practitioner myself, this book has helped me expand my level of consciousness and understanding to the next levels. The vast amount of material covered and the simple tools offered are invaluable for the beginner to the advanced healers. Suzanne's experience and knowledge is a gift to you and the world. I encourage you to embark on this beautiful journey of self-discovery."

~ **Michelle L. Warner, CCST,** certified craniosacral
therapist/instructor and certified medical intuitive

"Having the tools to know the difference between empathy and empathing has made such a difference in the quality of my work as a massage therapist over the last 23 years. I am thankful to have Suzanne as a personal mentor when it comes to the energy dynamic of holding empathetic space in healing and my personal life. Suzanne has a way of explaining the unexplainable in a clear, concise manner. Readers will establish better boundaries and experience a much happier, healthier way of life while gaining the skills of how to live in love versus fear!"

~ **Stephanie Tennessen,** master DeepFeet Shiatsu sports massage therapist, ACE certified group fitness and personal trainer, sports nutritionist, and psychedelic therapist

"*Confident Empath* should be required reading for all therapists, coaches, bodyworkers, medical professionals, caregivers, and anyone operating in the healing space. Only when we learn how to discern, care for, and manage our own energy in the world can we create a truly sustainable and ethical healing practice that uplifts all those we seek to serve. In her highly relatable, readable style, Suzanne provides a practical pathway to do just that."

~ **Jane McCampbell Stuart, M.A., LMFT, CPCC,** licensed therapist and certified coach specializing in the healing of trauma and PTSD

"In an age where language and labels are infinitely predominant across all genres, none seems more so than the moniker 'empath.' *Confident Empath* is a must-read for anyone who truly seeks to understand themselves, their fellow humans, and the energy exchanged between them. Having the privilege of being the archivist for the Patrick Flanagan Library with access to many lost and long forgotten books bridging science, spirituality, and consciousness, *Confident Empath* is a modern-day description of lost enigmatic knowledge. Suzanne's incredibly unique gifts have given rise to this powerful guide for anyone who believes they understand, as well as for those who have no understanding of, the label empath. She presents a highly transformational tool and body of wisdom not only for the divine human but for humanity itself! This guide is a must for every library, including the Akashic!"

~ **Gisele M. Bonenfant,** archivist for the Patrick Flanagan Library and crystal bed facilitator

CONFIDENT
EMPATH

A Complete Guide to Multidimensional Empathing and Energetic Protection

Suzanne Worthley

FINDHORN PRESS

Findhorn Press
One Park Street
Rochester, Vermont 05767
www.findhornpress.com

Text stock is SFI certified

Findhorn Press is a division of Inner Traditions International

Disclaimer
The information in this book is given in good faith and intended for information
only. Neither author nor publisher can be held liable by any person for any loss
or damage whatsoever which may arise from the use of this book or any of the
information therein.

Cataloging-in-Publication data for this title is available from the Library of Congress

ISBN 978-1-64411-755-2 (print)
ISBN 978-1-64411-756-9 (ebook)

Printed and bound in the United States by Lake Book Manufacturing, LLC
The text stock is SFI certified. The Sustainable Forestry Initiative® program
promotes sustainable forest management.

10 9 8 7 6 5 4 3 2 1

Edited by Michael Hawkins
Illustrations by Mary Schaubschlager and Damian Keenan (p. 77)
Text design and layout by Anna-Kristina Larsson
This book was typeset in Garamond, Comfortaa and Ubuntu

To send correspondence to the author of this book, mail a first-class letter
to the author c/o Inner Traditions • Bear & Company, One Park Street,
Rochester, VT 05767, USA and we will forward the communication,
or contact the author directly at **www.sworthley.com**.

I dedicate this book to all of the beautiful and brave souls
that made the conscious choice to embody as a human being
on this planet during an amazing time of chaos derived
from multidimensional transformation and change.

Many, embodied during this time, have signed on for a soul
mission, to move our planet and its human inhabitants forward
to align in a new and higher vibration of unity-based love and light.
Navigating the challenges of being an empathic human vehicle of Source
takes courage, tenacity and patience as the energies ascend across
dimensions, time, and space. It does not come with a "How to"
manual detailing the steps on how to proceed; therefore we
have become a confused and unhealthy race of beings which
in turn affects our planet and our cosmos.

I dedicate this book to the current flood of spiritual
awakening moving through those that are open to it,
anchoring light within not only their individual transformation
but also the planetary and collective one.

I dedicate this book's message to bold and sacred rebels willing to
challenge beliefs and let go of the things that no longer serve and
I offer gratitude and support to their mission.

And lastly, *I dedicate this book to* those empathic readers willing
to do the work of embracing and utilizing their empathic abilities;
to energetically protect themselves so they can live an empowered
life and contribute in a responsible and meaningful way to
creating a more positive, life-affirming reality.

Contents

PART TWO

Building Sentient Awareness

PART THREE

Practicing Discernment

Appendices

Introduction

Confident Empath: A Complete Guide to Multidimensional Empathing and Energetic Protection is your guide to the realm of unseen energy. Its purpose is to help you find and ignite your inner light of true human compassion and empathy. There are many books out there on the topic of empathing, but I have found none written from a professional energy healer's perspective that explain in detail the difference between true *empathy*, which is love-based, and the process of *empathing*, which is fear-based. That is why I wrote this book, so I can share my professional experience with anyone that struggles with this concept.

Compassion is often a reflection of our own suffering; therefore, instead of using our birthright of true, love-based empathy, most of us consciously or unconsciously "empath" the chaos of the energetic world around us. Right now, our world is oversaturated with fear, anger, and desperation, *none* of which offers our body, mind, and spirit anything positive in the way of healing, health, and wellness. As energetic beings, we are designed to own our personal truths, to self-heal, and to assist others. As a divine being of Source, we are gifted a human physical vehicle, an earth body, to experience this. My book is a clear, step-by-step guide to energetic self-empowerment.

Through my years of practice as an energy practitioner I have witnessed how our empathic behaviors are connected to the health of our human energy field. There are many auric reasons why we empath and many ways we humans empath individually and collectively, which directly impact our life here on this planet. In my client work, I have found most empaths are not often aware that they are empathing energy. Or conversely, I have many clients who own the word *empath* as an overused, yet misunderstood, label to explain why they are so stressed out in life. Typically, an empath is not present as to what they are encountering in the way of energy and what it is doing to their body, mind, and spirit, nor do they have any idea they can change it. Most of us are unaware of our connection to this invisible world of energetic upheaval within and around us—though it indeed does affect us. Yet when we learn how to become present, we can connect to our divine energy and inner light for personal healing, planetary healing, and assisting humanity as a whole.

The information in this guide will help you identify ignored nudges or misunderstood signs from your inner guidance that, when recognized and honored, will support your health and well-being. The messages within can assist you in remembering you are a divine being, a vehicle of Source love and light embodied in a planetary experience by use of a human body. When we are energetically unplugged from our inner guidance, we move through life asleep to our surroundings. We become disconnected, frazzled, perhaps even depressed or exceedingly driven and obsessive. Without a true connection to our own container of personal fuel that ignites our inner light, we live life from an exhausting false-fueled sense of self where we not only become inauthentic to ourselves, but to others. *This is the empath.*

We can only learn to manifest our inner purpose and remember who we truly are and what we came to do on this planet when we learn self-discipline of not just our physical earth body, but our divine, love-filled energetic ones—and this book will show you how to do just that. It will walk through the chakras and auric fields to learn the critical skill set of discernment and protection. It will introduce numerous planes of reality that each hold unique energy and information to shed light on how this can either help or hinder your journey. It will examine energy from the highest perspective of the soul—soul contracts with others and the Akashic Records and Library—to illuminate a grander plan of guidance from your Higher Self and Source. Actual client case stories will illustrate for you just how limitless this world of energy is and offer you advanced strategies to harness its infinite power to heal yourself and others.

As a full-time energy practitioner, every day is a new opportunity to offer my clients tools and resources to support their journey and align with and own their true energy, to burn their divine fuel, to ignite and shine their inner light offered from Source. I have taken over a decade of experience through my professional practice and the knowledge built through thousands of client sessions, to share with you a perspective for remembering that energy is everywhere. We can neither deny it nor run from it. We can absorb it from another human being, place or space at any time. Energy can come from within or upon our planet or from the cosmos and beyond. The information in this book can assist you in learning how to identify the different kinds of energy affecting every breath and every action you take as a human being. My purpose as an energy healer is to assist others in finding divine alignment in their energetic world and connect them to their authentic fuel of Source. This book is here to remind anyone reading it that Source abundantly flows, offering energy that is consistent, pure, and true. When we learn how to access it, we can recharge and heal our heart, mind, and body at the deepest levels. We can remember we came here to utilize the gift of our human experience in a physical vehicle, to be the eyes, ears, heart, and mind of Source. To hold and experience the love of oneness by use of the miracle designed as a human body. Only then can we learn how to give that love away to others unconditionally. We cannot live our higher purpose if we don't know who we are.

You are meant to be here right now, to bring love and light to this planet. But you can only do that through effectively fueling yourself first and using our human birthright of compassion and empathy, not by overextending your humanness through imbalanced and exhausting efforts of empathing energy from other people, places, and things.

As we grow spiritually so does our inner light, but the condition and strength of our container that holds this light is vital to how we share it. The goal of this information is to help you grow both inside as well as outside as a divine human vehicle, a container of Source fuel. The empath can learn to retrain how they give and receive fuel to effectively share spiritual light as sacred healing space and when this happens, the spirit of energy becomes our best friend. It is constant, reliable, and unconditionally loving not just for ourselves, but for others. It is the glue of oneness, the invisible world of energy that connects us all and enhances our human relationships and our planetary and cosmic connections.

I invite you to open your hearts and minds to the perspectives shared here and take what resonates and toss the rest.

PART ONE

Shedding What We Have Been Taught

✦

Chapter One

We Are Feeling Beings

If somehow you have made your way to finding this book, maybe you're drawn to it for a good reason. And just maybe, you are *supposed to* read it!

Possibly it was the title that caught your eye, and you recognize the word *empath* as something you resonate with, or maybe it was a family member or friend who suggested you learn more because they view you as one such *empath*. It could be you have simply felt the need for setting healthy boundaries but don't know how. You might be stuck in a toxic relationship, a job you hate or a caretaker position that feeds off of your energy, running you ragged and leaving you constantly worried. You may be the one people label as too sensitive, too delicate or emotionally complex. Perhaps you are just plain exhausted, worn-out, and sick and tired of being resentful of everyone taking advice, time, and energy from you, all the while never feeling like you get anything in return in the way of help, attention, acknowledgment and appreciation.

Most of us have been taught early in life that we are here to help others, and indeed that may be a truth for you. But these constant energy exchanges we experience throughout our day can leave us physically, emotionally, mentally, and even spiritually overwhelmed and exhausted. No one really taught us that in order to effectively assist another it is crucial we help ourselves first in terms of energy. So what does energy have to do with the idea of the empath?

As we humans traverse life each day, we exchange energy with people in a variety of experiences, situations, and thought forms from a simple hello, hug, or handshake to high-fives or fist bumps, to participating in a heated meeting at work or cruising the bar at happy hour. Most of the time we don't even have a clue these energy exchanges are happening, but they are, including vibrational interchanges through our texts, phone calls, voice and emails, blogs, apps, and whatever the newest social media craze may be that we use to tell our story and form connections. The more we can become aware of these continual energy interactions and how they affect us, the better we can also become at managing our energy within and around our own field to maintain a balance of health and wellness.

Energy moves between us when we communicate, when we laugh, when we cry, when we have sex, when we worry and when we pray—all as unseen vibrational frequencies hard at work surrounding and interpenetrating us individually and collectively. Depending on your current state of mind and body, you may be surprised at what is actually energetically filling or draining you each moment of your day.

When any human being connects to others, it creates an exchange or transference of energy, sometimes for the betterment of self, and sometimes not. As a professional energy practitioner, I work with clients every day who are challenged with some form of energy interchange that, if left unattended, can result in not just emotional distress but also physical ailments and dis-ease in the body. Recently, this idea of being an empath has become almost a popular label as I have witnessed a dramatic increase in clients branding themselves as such, and yet most of them have no idea as to what the label entails. This is one of the reasons I chose to write this book. I have direct experience in this field from an intuitive-energetic perspective as an energy practitioner. *I am also an empath.* However, I am a professional empath, and therein lies a vast difference. I have diligently trained myself over years of practice to use my psychic-sensitive abilities of empathing to do my work and to live my life as an intuitive. I know how to turn it on and off. Most empaths do not. Therefore, my goal is to offer you knowledge and skills to be able to navigate the world of the empath based on information gained from empirical experience combined with over a decade of professional client work.

I document encounters from my healing work for my own personal learning, but now I share this information to assist you in realizing the myriad of frequencies that envelop us each day, some taking us to places and spaces we never dreamed possible and others that can be dangerous. In the chapters ahead, you will read personal and client stories that illustrate the typical empath experiences as well as some that reveal just how wild this world of energy can be, including a paranormal home clearing where I encountered intermingled timelines from the 1800s, to a healing investigation where I walked through the holographic history of a 100+ year-old brothel still active with ghosts and memories, to client stories of past life experiences that continue to affect their physical bodies.

You may or may not have had crazy energetic experiences, but in some ways we are all empathing subtle to dramatic interchanges with energy just by living our lives whether we realize it or not. I include these stories as knowledge as much as entertainment. I do believe knowing how dangerous, trapped energy can threaten and harm our physical bodies and emotional hearts is just as important as knowing how glorious omnipresent energy can fill that same body and heart with the joy and passion of being human. This book, therefore, is about being aware of energy. Learning to be present. Taking personal responsibility for how we interact. Energy can help, harm, educate, and heal. The words on the pages of this book are here to expand the focus of your mind as well as your heart. To magnify infinite possibilities, to entertain the ideas of just how much we do not know about energy transference. It is also written as a tactical toolbox of ideas to self-heal and grow in love and light.

Further into the book, I introduce how energy works after we die, where we go and what we do in between lives. As always, I am not here to claim anyone's truth, only to offer potentials to ponder and to break down how our soul and our Higher Self has the ability to heal our DNA and adjust our lineage to stop abuse and heal hearts as well as bodies. We can change the world, but it can be a difficult task if we do not understand the energy that is either working with us or against us. Energy overall is neither good nor bad, it just is. But sometimes it feels differently for the empath.

I personally am not aware of any books that energetically explained empaths when I began my intuitive work in 2001 and still haven't found one that presents this concept from a psychic energy practitioner and healer perspective. This book is written from my personal experiences not only as an intuitive empath, but from lessons learned mostly on my own by trial and error. Some of the information I present addresses concerns of negative energy but just as much, if not more, highlights the gifts of positive energies that surround and support us. Finding the balance in life is key, and it is the same with energy. My goal is to present encouraging optimistic tools and ideas to incorporate into your daily spiritual journey while at the same time sharing some of my more difficult past experiences so you can learn to protect yourself and not encounter traumatic events like I did along the way. No one told me about protection when I began this work. No one really explained how the energy remained if it was not cleared, and this ignorance landed me in the emergency room from an "accident" that should have resulted in my death.

Years ago, I did an energy healing on a young man who was very misguided and lost for several years, finding himself homeless and addicted to drugs, all of which depleted his divine energy and replaced his field with negative darkness. After the client session, he felt better but I left my space unaware I was in trouble. Back then I was not mindful of or trained in energy transference. I did not fully clear my healing room following that session and simply shut off the lights as we left. I was a newbie who ignorantly thought if I was working with love and light, all was OK. I was wrong.

The following morning I went upstairs to do a short personal meditation. Because I was untrained in reading the energy of the space, I was clueless to the residual malevolent energy still lingering from the night prior. Everything seemed OK during my morning meditation but as I turned to leave my healing room, my body was violently launched down 22 stairs ending up on the concrete floor below where I believe I should have been dead or at least paralyzed. I inherently knew this was evil I was dealing with, so I instantly began to work on myself energetically commanding love, light, and release from what was still lingering and causing harm. Even though I was terrified, I somehow found the courage to crawl across the yard where my son found me crying out in extreme pain. Later, while in the emergency room of the hospital I could hear the physicians talking about my case outside my door trying to figure out why I was not completely broken or even paralyzed from the outcome of my plight. It took some time to physically heal from that experience, but much longer to emotionally and mentally heal and release the fear.

This experience set my healing career on a new path, one of presence and protection of my space, my body, and my mind. I began to study and introduce protocols of locking down my healing room, some of which I still perform any time I do work in that space. Now I am a diligent, skilled worker but more importantly I am a diligent, skilled empath. I use my body to read the space of my surroundings at all times and I am consciously aware of my energy, the client's energy and the room's energy. Obviously, most people will not encounter the level of negative energy I did in this story, yet each of us exchanges energy constantly even though we may not be aware of it. Some of this energy may be negative and some positive, but for anyone who is additionally sensitive to their surroundings, either form of energy can become overwhelming and exhausting, especially for the empath.

I work with many clients who proudly wear the empath label as a badge of honor, and just as many who feel it is a curse they wish they could shut off. I see it as neither but more so something we might choose to understand and appreciate, plus I see it as an opportunity to develop and implement distinct boundaries to stay healthy and safe. It is important at all times to be aware of your surroundings and your personal boundaries as us humans can absorb just about anything we come in contact with, from other humans to animals, to spaces and places, to inanimate objects, to sounds and smells, to nature, to thought patterns and even controlled programming frequencies from on- and off-planet. Depending on the environment, our human container will align with the known or unseen frequencies and vibrations of its surroundings, much like a sponge soaks up water, and we begin doing this at a very young age guided by the beliefs we are taught from our families, societies, and world messaging. We will see later in this book just how much beliefs influence the way we interact with all forms of energy in either a positive or negative manner.

One of the biggest belief-messages we receive is to trust our think-center versus our feel-center. True feeling takes time and effort to tune into your own body and listen for the truth of the situation, the words or the messages, yet our species is trained to find validation outside of ourselves and then react accordingly. And most of us react the way we are told we *should* react. When we use our think-center the feelings resonate within somewhat disconnected, almost automated, versus when we use our true feel-center, we fully connect to own the embodiment of the message. Many families create feel-related boundaries by setting limitations through words like "toughen up, don't cry, behave, follow the rules, don't, can't, should, have to" and so on. We validate our children at home, in schools, in sports and more for following the rules and berate them for acting upset or showing frightened reactions and unbridled emotion. We encourage using the brain and discourage sharing our feelings. That's why

I've made it my life's work to help people learn about the energy centers of the body to assist them in finding ways to connect their head to their heart. The beautifully designed human body is an incredible map of information, and this book can help teach you how to find that information and trust in it.

I cherish the wealth of opportunities I have each day as a professional intuitive energy practitioner to experience and observe the map of energetic information stored in my client's body, and it is always interesting to watch how they settle into the chair as a session begins. I witness them physically begin to relax the moment they align with the high vibrational energy that permeates my healing room. Each session begins with a client intake or verbal interchange to determine their needs and much to their surprise many find themselves already "feeling better" even before we do the healing work on the massage table. Why is that? It is because I am a trained empath and have already begun the work the moment they arrived in my office and stepped into my energy field.

I have trained my personal body to professionally tap into their energy as an intuitive and telepathically adjust their fields resulting in healing and wellness within their body, mind, and spirit. This energy exchange begins the moment of their arrival and ends days or even weeks later. How do I do that? I give myself permission to feel what they feel. I allow and skillfully use my body to become theirs for a limited amount of time so that I might be able to fully know what it is like for them to hold the pain, anger or fear prompting them to book a session to heal their physical body, emotional mind or broken spirit. I simultaneously scan their body with mine to identify discomfort and dis-ease by incorporating not only my clairvoyant skills but also by using my own personal vehicle to first merge with and then become theirs. I intentionally empath their energy. I take their field directly into my body to create change. I can feel if their chest is tight because mine becomes tight. If their back holds stiffness, mine will as well. I can even tap into their psyche and know things like their struggles growing up with a sibling or abuse experienced by a grandfather. I can feel the sadness of a miscarriage as I merge with the trapped agony of loss and grief. For a brief amount of time, our lives and bodies become one to allow for not just empathy but *empathing*, a transference of the actual energy.

Even before we move to the healing table work, I visually witness an immediate transformation right before my eyes as their shoulders drop, their breath slows, and the pace and rhythm of their voice softens. I intentionally hold this full empath-connection throughout the healing work done on the table, then the moment I finish, I purposefully release myself from them and their story to fully return to being just Suzanne. It is a professional, conscious, sentient connection and release process.

We Are Sentient Beings of Consciousness

We humans yearn to be heard, to be acknowledged, and to be understood. Since birth, we are wired to look for connection with others. When we're having a bad day, we find ourselves craving another human to talk to, to share our experience with and to share how we are feeling. Feeling heard and understood is a basic human need yet most of us struggle with the mechanics of how to truly feel much less connect with the feelings of others. This is why many people end up in the offices of energy practitioners and healers, massage therapists, chiropractors, counselors, and various models of therapy. Their voice needs to be heard. Their body needs to be heard. Their heart needs to be heard. If we are not heard, the unvalidated, disconnected energies can become stuck within our bodies and eventually manifest as dis-ease and even disease. Energetically-based healing modalities are designed to assist with this re-connection, to rewire the communication and alignment of body, mind, and spirit resulting in the client feeling validated that what they are experiencing is real.

One of the most natural and moral rights of being a human is to experience our feeling-senses, not only for ourselves but on behalf of others. In order to experience the value of human life, our body, mind, and spirits must experience *feeling empathy* as a true core essence of every human's highest potential. Empathy is the gift of sensing other people's feelings or emotions coupled with the skill of stepping into their shoes, so to speak, to further embrace what they may be going through. Empathy communicates a message that "I am with you in this, and you are not alone" and it is what bonds us as a human race.

As a practitioner I look at the world through the eyes of energy from how the human body works to how it interacts and co-creates with all other embodiments of Source energy on the planet and beyond. From the time our energy centers activate *in utero* to the time they shut down during the death and dying process, we have the gift of being here on this Earth as a full, sentient being or embodiment of Source consciousness. When we incarnated, we chose the divine human vehicle of a human body to experience life on behalf of Source. We are the eyes of Source. We are the ears of Source. We are the hearts and minds of Source energy all designed in a divine human vehicle. Our human bodies are physically, emotionally, mentally, and spiritually designed to feel. We are uniquely created to be sentient. This sentience is part of our blueprint or our cellular DNA instruction set, and our ability to feel and discern our feelings is what makes us different from any other container of Source-consciousness. It is what makes us uniquely able to have empathy. It is our tool for oneness.

Our body is made up of multiple layers that hold this sentient energy as physical, emotional, mental, and spiritual fields or templates that directly link us to not only other humans but all other consciousness containers. Sentience encompasses the consciousness of all living things, both with and without form, which can include various energetic forces that make up our multidimensional existence or reality. It is difficult to get our heads around the idea that we are all truly one, from every living thing on this planet to the wheeling galaxies of the cosmos and beyond time and space.

Each and every thing, in our reality is made up of energy and we can use our sentient human body to connect to the world around us—from human loved ones, to strangers, to plants and animals, to planets and stars and Mother Earth herself. We pass through countless fields of energy each day completely unaware of the exchanges taking place. How are we to know what is good for us and what is not if we are not even taught this energy exists and the exchange is real? Think of the subjects we teach our children in school. We put importance on things like knowing the name of each state capital and yet we do not introduce the concept of energy. We still learn Christopher Columbus discovered America when we know historical evidence tells a different story. We learn with our ears and our brains instead of learning to trust in our bodies and our hearts. It may be time to shed some of the things we have been taught—ideas and concepts that we automatically embrace as truths. Again, use your own discernment as you read this book as well because no one can hold our truth for us, it is our responsibility to align to what resonates as divine for us, and the first step in doing this is to reactivate your gift of true sentience through self-discovery. Although the path of self-discovery and spiritual growth looks different for everyone, I tend to see clients move through three distinct stages in their journey to include:

- shedding what we've been taught;
- developing sentient awareness;
- practicing discernment.

Shedding What We Have Been Taught

As children we are born self-aware and self-involved yet are immediately trained to put ourselves second as we are told to share our toys, put others first, and find external validation for DO-ing. We are a culture of human doing machines, over-filling our days with tasks while checking them off our never-ending "To Do"-list only to draft another list. Many of us fill our days with the goal of being the helper, being the one to fix the problem or being the one in charge of diverting conflict altogether making sure the boat does not rock for anyone. Helping others is part of the true nature of the human experience, to support and care for one another but it is the belief behind the effort that drives the action in a non-integral way, and yet many are not aware that this narrative is even driving the action. The hidden belief is some version of "I am good because I DO" which can quickly become a never-ending cycle of conditional behavior of how I do, when I do and where I do. We seek our reward by way of validation from others, and this is how it becomes a never-ending process. And all the while we are busy do-ing, we are unaware of the energy and emotion exchanging along the way until we find ourselves at the point where we are full of anxiety running on overdrive, resulting in exhaustion and resentment.

The human-doing machine is just one example of how our belief systems set the groundwork for how we fuel our daily activities and invite empathing behaviors that create imbalance within our energetic systems resulting in stress, anxiety, and eventually dis-ease and disease in the body, mind, and spirit. Growing up we are not taught the skill set of discernment to maintain healthy boundaries and validate our truths. We are not taught to be present and aware of what is beneficial and supportive to us for our own positive growth. We are not taught to energetically put ourselves first.

We are not taught to trust our feel-centers and communicate with our own bodies to learn what is good for us or not. We are not taught we are sentient beings. So as we continue to grow, we also continue to lose our spiritual sentient awareness as we instead continue to buy into the physical, emotional, and mental societal belief systems that surround us in our world each day all centered around DO-ing.

As I work with thousands of clients each year, I am continually reminded we are all spiritual beings with innate sensitivities and intuitive gifts many of which are untapped and lie dormant. For some, their gifts have been shut down or turned off at a young age due to negatively positioned belief systems learned through family, politics, religion, education and more. The spiritual-based energy of sentience never really goes away, it just lies dormant because of our lack of understanding and mostly our inability to trust our feel-centers. Just like a snake needs to shed its old and outgrown skin in order to move forward and grow in size and strength, I believe we humans are designed to shed beliefs and truths that no longer serve us in relationship to our world and the life experiences it offers us. One of the first stages I witness clients move through as they embrace their energetic journey is to examine and shed old beliefs that no longer align with their personal container of truths. For the empath who is looking to harness and own their energetic gifts, learning to trust in what feels like truth or not is a first step. This process is followed by a continuing journey of peeling back deeper and deeper truths much like an onion with a multitude of layers and beginning to wake up to our sentient awareness.

Building Sentient Awareness

Just like we have become a culture of doing-machines, we humans are also trained, encouraged, and validated from a very young age to also be thinking-machines. While our incredible human capacity for intelligent thought and intellect is certainly a gift to be valued, our focus on the mind has devalued the role of our feel-centers. We are created to be intuitive beings, constructed with a design intelligence to feel and experience with great sensitivity, offering oneness with all things manifest. As stated earlier, we are conceived as a divine human vehicle, an embodiment of Source energy that is capable of giving and receiving love from all embodiments of Source, from the forces of nature, to our planet, to the animal and plant kingdom, to our human species, to the cosmos and beyond, all by use of our sentience. We are all one. But this idea is quite difficult if we only "think" it through versus *feel* it. Thinking love and feeling love are two distinctly different things. Our body, mind, and heart connection are designed to be intuitive with great sensitivity and capacities to feel the experience of life itself, but too often our dormant feel-centers divert our experiences to the monkey-mind of over-processed, over-thought actions and reactions. We are unable to feel the signals from our bodies designed to help us discern and remain in alignment, truth, and well-being.

When working with any client, one of my main tasks as an energy practitioner is to assist them in getting out of their head and into their feel-centers and to remind them that they are a divine being of love and light experiencing life in a unique and amazing human vehicle. Most of my empathic clients believe their problem is they actually feel too much, however, I find that what they are playing out is an overactive mental-center disguising itself as overly emotional. We are trained to think-feel. We do not feel-feel.

When we think-feel, we experience a loss of control and the mental mind triggers and overreacts, offering an outcome of exacerbated emotions like panic, tears, shaking, dizziness and more. For example, when I encounter an overactive think-feel client their mind is constantly running, they are overextended and too busy, they cannot possibly do all this, they feel as if they have no help, which turns into anger, panic, stress, exhaustion, and resentment. However, if we train ourselves to get to the true feel-center, we can examine what is actually triggering that mental tirade.

Anger usually indicates a think-feel state where fear sheds light on the true feeling. The true feeling is a fear-based sense that there is not enough. There is not enough time in the day for me to get all this stuff done. There is not enough help from anyone, and it is all up to me and I feel alone and scared. All of this equates to the anchored feeling of "I am not enough." The true feeling is fear. The true fear is *not enough*. Remember, the think-feel stops at an angry outburst of resentment that no one helps me, and I am not loveable enough to receive support.

Think-feel and true feeling are two distinctly different forms of working with the energy churning throughout your body, mind, and spirit. When I say feel, I actually mean tapping into the vibrations held within our own divine human vehicle/body, being truly aware of them and having a relationship with them including conversing. How we learn to converse with our body is a personal choice, but I encourage many of my clients to learn how to body scan, inviting them to shut off the mind chatter and not just feel what it is like to be each body part but trust the information and messaging that comes forth. I describe a body scan in detail later in this book to help demonstrate how you can learn to practice this type of effort whether it is done in a deep meditative state or while standing in line at the grocery checkout. Over time, as my clients become proficient at communicating with the vibrations of their own body, they can then begin to trust how to move through life critically aware and able to discern what is and is not theirs, allowing them to be effectively present for another with no conditional energy attached.

Again, most humans do not really listen to their body nor do they treat it as a unique divine vehicle of Source energy designed in love and light. We listen to our heads instead, the egoic mind, which houses our mental field of programmed beliefs that can trigger exacerbated emotional response. We all get to learn to trust the body and its true feeling instead of the mind-based think-feel but for the empath it is even more important to use discernment skills that are honed at the individual level through knowing and owning personal emotions and beliefs. Only when personal feelings are authenticated can you begin to experience things in a more objective manner as the observer by learning to see and feel how deeply your view of others is connected to your feelings and choosing to separate what is yours or not yours. The more your true emotional nature comes into your sentient awareness and daily life, the more your discernment emerges as your natural state of being.

Practicing Discernment

Why discern? When we fail to discern, we carry others' truths and energies as our own and allow them to influence our thoughts and actions. By building skills of discernment, we move into and even beyond awareness to actively determine what is and is not ours and then make critical choices to realign our energetic fields to command health and wellness. Becoming highly attuned to the sources of energy that surround us daily can assist us in determining what is positive fuel and what negatively drains us as fear fuel.

Grounding and upholding our personal auric boundaries and applying consistent discernment towards all things we come in contact with allows us to manage our consciousness and life-force energy to determine when it is safe to share, or not, more effectively. The idea and skill set of discernment comes when one chooses to commit to some form of personal practice that offers spiritual maturity and the ability to align to your inner truths without judgment and what others may think of your choices. This is not about religion or dogmatic principles but more a committed personal spiritual framework to help you develop disciplines to release old negative programming and limiting behaviors that hold you back from being the highest version of your Source-self, including your birthright of empathy, compassion, and forgiveness.

Spiritual awakening and personal journeying can assist a person to grow and perceive levels of awareness beyond the 3D survival-based need of self-preservation and fight or flight. Only then can we begin to open to the larger collective where we are all interconnected, which again increases and expands sentience. As we continue to increase our human sentience and overall omni-connection to the whole we find the value of empathy for all we are interconnected with from the tiniest insect to the vastness of galaxies and beyond.

This discernment includes the ability to see the situation as another sees it to the best of my ability without judgment or bias, based on my own beliefs and communicating that support and understanding using empathy versus sympathy or compassion.

Empathy can have many different definitions that encompass a wide range of emotional states, such as sensitively taking on the role of caring for another, wanting to help someone out, pairing up to another's emotional state, harmonizing with what another person is thinking, or feeling another person's sensations.

Technically speaking, no one can actually feel what another truly feels in the form or way they feel it because our body, mind, and spirit awareness is running through a matrix of programming, memories, and experiences housed or stored within our own personal consciousness container. Each multidimensional layer of a person, whether physical, mental, emotional, or spiritual, encompasses sentient information that is energetically unique to that individual. Our feel-centers perceive through our exclusive lens that works in relationship with our divine human vehicle of Source, the physical body and our brain. The way each of us experiences our truths is completely unique and individual yet in principle we can use our birthright of empathy when we want to sense or align to what another may be feeling as a support for them in their experience. But remember, we are still using our own beliefs, feelings, and senses to project ourselves into the other person's situation to get a feel for what they may be experiencing and yet this is all energetically happening separate from one another.

As any practice or spiritual journey allows you to continually learn, accept and live as who you truly are, you will learn it also allows others to be exactly who they choose to be without conditionally taking on or having the need to empath another's energy hoping they will change or heed your advice. A sense of spiritual maturity is fostered through the desire to feel and discern the body's resonance to any and everything you come across and concentrate on, knowing one's inner self, owning one's truth, and when discernment is diligently practiced it will allow one to move beyond selfish 3D dramatic actions such as judgment and anger, and open the higher heart to true compassion and empathy for oneness within not just humanity but for our planet, the cosmos, and beyond into collective awareness.

Sadly, our collective consciousness field is currently filled with fear, which clouds discernment. When our human vehicle is working with fear-based fuel, the sensations churning through our physical bodily container confuses our brain and neurological messaging, which puts our mind-matrix on high alert and scrambles our inner narrative resulting in us feeling lost, confused, and alone. We lose what is known as our inner spiritual compass or guidance system that leads us to safety and allows us to make the best choices for our higher good. Each one of us is responsible for learning to overcome our fears, which depletes our energy fuel tank and sets the stage for us to empath and steal fuel from others or psychically vampire another to serve our 3D ego. When we are no longer controlled by fear-based belief systems and impulsive programmed reactions, we can begin to find inner peace individually and co-create it collectively. Then we are working in true empathy.

✦

Chapter Two

What Is Empathing?

We have all grown up with a multitude of belief systems that may or may not want to be shed when it comes to how we give and take energy to better understand empathing, empathy, and sympathy in our relationships with others. Empathing is actually neither good nor bad—it is simply a tool or capacity we have as sentient beings, but what is it from a perspective of energy? This is where we can begin to determine a good or a bad factor in the way we maintain and hold onto the energy that comes into our life, body, and fields.

Empathy is often characterized as the ability to "put oneself into another's shoes" or in some way experience what another person is feeling. When we offer empathy, we create the space for another to share their experience and feelings while responding from a place of compassion. While we may be stepping into their shoes, so to speak, we are not actually becoming the other person or taking their experience as our own. When we experience empathy, we can connect to another's energy or emotions yet still maintain a boundary between our respective energy fields, allowing ourselves to understand the other while maintaining our energetic field or auric bubble of self.

Empathing is different. When we empath, we emotionally and physically *experience* what another person is going through and then take on those emotions or physical sensations as our own. When we empath, we basically steal the energy. We actually *feel* what another person feels, and then we ourselves take those feelings and allow them to influence our own circumstances. From my perspective, empathing happens through a transfer of energy from one source to another. As we'll examine in future chapters, our bodies are a hub of life-source energy, taking in energy, holding energy within our fields, and releasing energy. When we empath, we *embody the energy of an emotion, situation, or a place*—and sometimes we can even take one another's physical attributes including sickness, pain, and dis-ease. We human beings can empath almost anything through our energetic relationships with all kinds of sentient life, from family and friends, to complete strangers, to pets and nature, to land and buildings, or even the cosmic planetary systems. Not only can we empath the energy of the emotions and physical attributes of those who are near our energy field, we can also empath energies from a distance, and all of this can cause great amounts of strain and stress on the body, mind, and spirit.

Many of my clients, across the gender spectrum, empath to various degrees, and yet I find many of them are oblivious to the levels of energy exchange and its connection to their sense of well-being. Honestly, I believe we all are empaths in some way or another, but the true empath believes they are helping, assisting and fixing others, all fueled by an inner belief that they "should." This should-belief is something I look for when I meet with a client to determine the level of empathing that is manifesting in their life as stress, exhaustion, and overachievement efforts.

When I meet with a client, I begin each healing session by talking about how they're doing and what prompted them to book an appointment. It is important to remember at this point my client has given me permission to merge into their field for their healing—it would not be ethical for me to enter their field without expressed permission. While I am psychically paying attention to their energy field, I am also telepathically scanning their body and listening carefully to their language. The words my clients use tell me a lot about their behaviors and actions, and any person who consistently incorporates into their story's key phrases of "I have to, I need to, I should" will strongly indicate to me an overdriven sensitive empath. I monitor how many times these types of phrases naturally flow into their conversation and note how that physically alters their body as well. I can psychically follow energy cords or blocks that trigger their breath or posture simply by using words that drain their fuel and deflate their fields and I can sense where these cords and blocks attach themselves to or within the body, further indicating the trigger patterns.

Empath clients tend to also talk about not having enough time in the day and overextending themselves in most areas of their life. This type of client struggles with huge amounts of self-worth issues surrounding the narrative of *not enough*. Not enough time in the day. Not enough help. They are simply not enough. This negative self-talk is often not even apparent to the person, yet it can be amplified from outside of themselves by others in their family or close circle, causing additional problems of judgment and blaming. I have seen this happen with many of my caregiving clients through a family member's journey of sickness and death, lasting well into the end-of-life arrangements including funerals, estate arguments, financial disagreements and more.

The overall current health crisis of Alzheimer's, dementia and long-term sickness has dramatically increased the number of clients I see who find themselves juggling some semblance of caregiver duties that put great strain on their own personal health and mental wellness. Most of my caregiver clients struggle with being empathic. Even though they may be only one of several siblings or family members available, they will often position themselves as being "the one" typically responsible for the parent or person in need, a form of codependent. They ultimately end up in my office searching for a way to handle the stress manifesting as mental anxiety or physical exhaustion and sickness. Caregivers are not only found in scenarios of dying and death but everyday life of running errands, raising children, going to work and school, and juggling all of the balls for self and others. In terms of language used, the belief system of being "the one" will reveal itself consistently through the use of the word "but" . . . for example: Yes, I have other siblings that can help *but* they are never available, or *but* they do not do the meds correctly, or *but* they are too busy with their own families and I am the available one. Yes my spouse can do it *but* he or she has a real-job and my job is the kids, and so forth. The use of this transitional word "but" will flip the responsibilities back into their own arena where they will continue to run the narrative that they are "the one." Additionally, their body language, actions, and behaviors reveal how they move throughout their day driven by the belief they are responsible for others, not only in terms of doing, but also for carrying emotions including worry. The majority of empaths struggle with ongoing mental chatter or rumination of how they could have done things differently or better, most often coupled with perfectionism tendencies that fuel, then drive their thoughts and actions. Again, trigger words and behaviors I look for when scanning stressed, depleted, and exhausted clients.

After my client has finished talking through why they showed up in my office, I typically invite them to participate in a body scan prior to the healing work to allow them to identify and own any stuck energy their divine vehicle of Source energy or human body is holding onto. This stuck energy comes from repeated mental and physical stress. Most empaths will hold and store deep emotions within their belly and lower back, including feelings of guilt, shame, not enough and more. This will dis-ease the digestive tract oftentimes resulting in not just a bad belly but also discomfort in the esophageal tract creating heartburn, difficulty breathing and a tight chest plus a feeling of a backpack on the upper neck and shoulders and base of head.

Another indicator of an empath is found in the energy field surrounding the body, showing up as rips and tears to the auric bubble or egg. An empath will basically have an extremely weak, torn or even non-existent aura that has been compromised by energy leaks and negative energy transference to and from others. Additionally, outside of the aura, I will psychically see a myriad of chaotic corded energies swirling around the client. This can also psychically be seen as what is better known as attachment energy that looks like a lot of dark and dense blobs or the sensation of a heavy blanket covering the client. Confused auric energy lies at the base of the back of the head and skull where I find old programming that has been instituted in the client's thoughts and feelings from childhood and beyond. The level of density here will be directly related to how much the person is running on personal truths from within or automated programs outside of themselves. Such weak auric fields will also cause this type of person to lose track of things easily and feel flakey and ungrounded, much like taking two steps forward then ten back or feeling stuck in the same place. This can further cause feelings of frustration, despair, exhaustion and loss of hope.

Empathing does not only have to do with a caregiver situation or those who feel overly sensitive to the world around them. Through my experience working with thousands of clients and studying the human energy field, I believe all human beings empath. All of us are in relationship to others in some form or another whether we are a parent, a partner, a sibling, a child, a co-worker, a pet owner or a friend. Through my work, I tend to observe three different levels of sensitivity when it comes to empathing. These levels are not good or bad. There is no value attached to any of them—they just are. Some of my clients even find they can at times tap into any level depending on the situation, location or relationships involved—or by using the skills they've developed through their own personal energy practice.

Qualities of an Empath

The qualities of an empath can change over time as one grows through personal experience, gaining knowledge and honing skills. Some of the qualities below may be present in your life now or have been in the past. Some may show up in the future. If you recognize yourself in the following descriptions, you may choose to learn more about why you take on energy by observing if there is a pattern to your belief systems and actions to better understand your way of empathing.

- Inner knowing: knowing, feeling, and sensing things others do not.
- Feeling overwhelmed or emotionally drained in public places or certain situations without knowing why.
- Nerves often frayed or affected by noise, smells, or excessive talk.
- Picking up others' physical symptoms or feeling others' emotions, at times without awareness, taking them on as one's own.
- Fear of becoming engulfed by intimate relationships.
- Discord creates unpleasant feelings.
- Endeavors to settle conflict or confrontation as quickly as possible, preferring to avoid it all together.
- Watching violence, cruelty or tragedy on TV or online feels unbearable.
- Feeling weighed down and anxious by clutter.
- May carry extra weight without necessarily overeating.
- Often overscheduled and commonly tired and exhausted.
- Good listener and others often share their troubles and problems.
- Strives for the truth, always looking for the answers and knowledge.
- Likes adventure, freedom and travel.
- Need for solitude to recharge.
- Creative and loves to daydream, finding routine, rules or control, imprisoning.
- Lover of nature and animals.
- Drawn to healing, holistic therapies, and all things metaphysical.

General Empaths

Many of my clients are general empaths. They may identify with a few qualities of empathing, such as feeling overwhelmed by public spaces, being a good listener, or finding joy in eliminating clutter in their house, but their experience of empathing doesn't often affect their day-to-day life. They are generally oblivious to the idea that there is other energy they are connected to or involved with. Some may find themselves occasionally taking on the stress of a bad interaction with a stranger or feeling a certain sensitivity in certain spaces and places. Others may feel the overwhelm of collective anxiety at times of great stress in our world, but they typically don't hold onto this energy for long or they have developed healthy habits (knowingly or unknowingly) that allow them to easily pass through or release energy after an exchange. General empaths may have a natural way they process the energy of others and maintain their own field, or they may be severely blocked from their feeling centers and have shut down most empath abilities.

Nevertheless, general empaths become more sensitive during times when they let their energetic guard down, so to speak, or their energetic fields become more heightened. Especially during times of trauma—such as breaking up with a partner, caretaking for a dying family member, or losing a job—general empaths can find themselves moving into the realm of sensitive empaths.

Sensitive Empaths

A sensitive empath is someone who has many empathic traits or they may have a few that are extremely heightened. Sensitive empaths often find they have a difficult time repelling environmental or external energy and therefore have to be much more aware of how to self-assess what they can and cannot handle in terms of energy and vibrational frequency overload. Being in crowds or large groups can be challenging as other people's thoughts, feelings and emotions can mistakenly or automatically be absorbed or held as what is known as an attachment. A sensitive empath could also find they have a hard time letting go of the emotions experienced by family and loved ones. For example, if their partner is stressed after a long day at work, a sensitive empath may find that they themselves become stressed as well. Not only do they take on this stress from their partner, but they often will find they continue to carry that stress long after their partner has let go of that energy themselves. This style of empath often will be triggered by belief systems of their own or others and this will compound the amount of unhealthy emotion or feelings within their system either mentally, emotionally, and even physically.

When I first meet a sensitive empath, I find they are generally unaware of their sensitivities on a conscious level and have limited knowledge of their energy field. There is no judgment about this. It's not often I meet someone who was taught about their energy field as a young child, so it is perfectly normal for a sensitive empath to have or experience:

- A lack of awareness about personal boundaries and the energy field that surrounds the human body.
- Little knowledge about using and strengthening the energy field.
- Trouble being or staying grounded.
- Feeling constantly overextended and overscheduled in most areas of life.
- Fatigue or a physically weak or ill body.
- Areas of weakness or vulnerability in their energy field when interacting with others, allowing for rips and tears in auric fields, which creates energy transference.

Not only can sensitive empaths take on the energies of others, but they can also easily have their energy drained. They often find themselves over-committing to activities and relationships to the point of not having any energy left for themselves. Typically, they move through their day on autopilot with routines that are all about just getting things done. They wake up, run off to work in a rush just in time to give energy all day to others, only to come home exhausted, find a bit of family or "me time" just before crawling to bed in order to wake up and do it all over again. They run to appointments for themselves and others, do chores, pay bills and juggle finances, drop kids at practice, and walk pets. Humans overschedule everything and everyone. This constant drain makes them particularly easy marks for emotional or energy vampires, which are people who manipulate the empath through their own energy field and deliberately drain energy through dominance and control. And at the very same time, the sensitive empath may find themselves the one who is the energy vampire, continually sucking fuel from others just in order to survive whether they know it or not.

Sensitive empaths also can develop heightened sensory abilities that are not limited to emotions and physical pain. For example, sensitive empaths may have a more developed sense of smell, where they become overwhelmed or experience sensory overload through a reaction to things like essential oils or perfumes or a range of aromas including chemicals and molds. I personally have found it difficult at times to walk through the cleaning supplies aisle at large stores due to the dizzying combination of fluorescent lights and chemical smells. I also am extremely careful in antique stores due to the mold-filled aroma coupled with old energy attached to the artifacts.

Each empath is unique as one may feel relaxed and emotionally supported by aromas, fragrances, and surroundings while the other feels assaulted by the experiential smells. It is important for the sensitive empath to become aware of what sort of places are toxic for their fields, and this only comes with being present throughout our day, making clear choices that benefit us versus powering through like the proverbial Energizer Bunny automatically placing one foot in front of the other until our batteries finally wear out. Empaths can experience sensory overload through any of their five senses—sight, sound, smell, touch, taste—through different developmental levels in their sensitivity. Typically, these types of empaths were very open and psychic as a child and have most likely shut down their sixth sense skills, leaving the other five in overdrive. When empaths begin to experience sensitivities beyond the five senses, they move into the level of psychic empathing.

Psychic Empaths

Psychic empaths are gifted with functioning levels of energy receivers and transmitters that not only connect to others but feel *beyond* what others can. Through their psychic-empath gifts they connect to another's energy and can receive information, emotion, and feeling through the energy itself. Psychic empaths can perceive physical sensitivities and intuit spiritual compulsions, as well as grasp motivations and intentions of other people through their natural skills of higher sensory perception or psychic knowing.

For psychic empaths, crowded spaces often hold a lot of negative energy build-up that can feel like a direct assault on the physical, emotional, and mental body leaving it feeling drained, depressed, or burdened with heavy energy or toxicity. When an empath is stressed, it is common for their psychic skill set to become even more heightened, all while their personal boundaries lessen, creating a situation where emotional sponging happens even more easily.

For many, this extrasensory gift can feel more like a curse as the empath's life is unconsciously influenced by others' feelings, emotions, passions, desires, wishes, thoughts, and moods as they are barraged by external energies from many different environments from this world and even beyond. This can cause empaths to override their own needs and maintain poor personal boundaries because they psychically sponge what is outside of them and, for this reason, many experience chronic fatigue, environmental sensitivities, or unexplained aches and pains making it harder to accurately feel what is inside of them. Psychic empaths are also susceptible to overwhelm in their spiritual field causing psychic spiritual misery, disconnection, and mystical depression as many are approached by spiritual beings from the other side looking for assistance or communication, and if the person is not aware or educated in this realm, this can feel extremely uncomfortable and sometimes scary.

While the extrasensory gifts can be challenging to navigate without awareness or practice to harness those skills, the psychic empath can find that by building their knowledge and developing personal practices, they can live in a more balanced state—being able to tap in and use their psychic gifts while protecting their boundaries and operating from a state of empathy versus empathing. Most of us do not grow up in family structures that embrace the idea of being psychic. We think this is reserved for a select few, for "those people" and yet this is a birthright of being a human. The skill set of heightened awareness is something most of us shut off in our inner navigation systems quite early in life unless we have a support system surrounding us early in childhood. We are all designed to be psychic. We all have skills that can indeed be activated, re-activated, heightened or shut off. Even when shut off, the amazingly gifted human vehicle we embody continues to have experiences that interpenetrate the body and energy fields and this is the exact reason I encourage my clients to get in touch with the feel-centers to ensure the energy they encounter is to their benefit and not their detriment.

The Gift of Empathy

We all are feeling beings who have the gift of empathy to be able to connect with other sentient life. The challenge for us as humans, as we are learning, is it can be hard to separate ourselves from the energetic connections we make through our feeling-bodies, taking on what is not ours. This is the difference between empathy and empathing.

Empathy is the ability to share, understand, or feel another's emotion and what they may be feeling or experiencing from within the other being's frame of reference. Remember, it is often characterized as the ability to "put oneself into another's shoes," or in some way place oneself in another's position or experience. Empathy creates understanding, an energetic connection and resonance with the emotions and feelings of someone you interact with, resulting in a supportive closeness. It does not take on another's situation as our own nor does it embody another's emotions or physical pain. It is not about believing that our ideas, care or support will change people or about doing things for them. True empathy is *gifting others energy with no conditions attached*. It honors the other.

Empathy is the truest sense-organ of the incarnated divine human vehicle, but it cannot properly function through the individual ego— only through the collective, unconditional energies. As a birthright, our empathy offers us the ability to align and harmonize with every energetic thing on the planet and throughout the cosmos. We are a genetic DNA pattern within much greater genetic DNA patterns of Source energy and embodiments. This means our existence is partially here to find unconditional collective oneness with not just humans but with all Source offers us from the forces of nature, to the plant and animal kingdom, to humanity, to the cosmos filled with stars and planets within multi-universes. We are genetically designed to be one, making us a holographic microcosm of the entire cosmos as fractal patterns of Source repeating themselves as one.

Embracing the idea of feeling and being one with everyone and everything as a collective nature with no strings attached is quite difficult as most of us are only aware of our individual self. When I choose (either consciously or unconsciously) to take on your feeling, your emotion, pain, fear or your situation in an individualistic way, I have now fueled the energy with conditional fear instead of unconditional love of oneness. When I empath, I shift from the collective observer into the conditional judge of the other or the situation, and then take from the other's energy and make it my personal affair.

Let me remind you most empaths are not taking another's energy in a malicious or dominant way (although some do). Instead, they feel as if they are helping the other person by fixing, offering solutions, or taking over completely. However, these empathing behaviors still hold fear-based conditions or judgments on the exchange. When we experience energy in a truly *unconditional* collective manner, it is a love-based fuel that allows every other energy to *just be* their individualized version of Source. If I work in love and honor my individual energy, all while honoring the other's individual energy as is, then there are no conditions attached, but if I work in an egoic, fear-based fuel I am actually empathing versus using my gift of empathy.

Even though I say empathy is a birthright, it is a learned skill. To sense other people's emotions coupled with the ability to imagine what someone else might be thinking or feeling takes practice and diligence. And to move to a place of unconditional oneness, feeling what another feels with no conditions attached, takes even greater skill. Relationships offer many different ways to feel and experience empathy, so not all empathy looks and feels the same. Just like empathing, there are different kinds of empathy based on what kind of connection we're making by use of our energy bodies. As we understand more about empathy, we can learn how to use these different forms in our own relationships and exchanges to protect ourselves and others from unhealthy energy exchanges and become more skilled, aware empaths.

Cognitive Empathy

The concept of cognition is all about simply *knowing*. Therefore, cognitive empathy is based on the energy of thought and means we simply *know* how the other person is thinking, feeling, or emoting. This style of empathy allows you to use your own emotional feel-centers to align to the situation while also demonstrating the knowing and understanding from an intellectual level. Although cognitive empathy provides a way to connect to another's experience, this form of empathy can feel somewhat shallow or disconnected because cognitive empathy responds to a situation with brainpower, for example it strives to *understand* pain as a think-feel, yet that is not the same as allowing yourself to truly *feel* the pain of another. However, sometimes cognitive empathy may be best for a situation from a protection standpoint when you want to get inside another person's head to do your best to understand their situation but not get fully inside their emotions and pain body.

Personally, my traits and psychic skills highly revolve around cognitive sensitivities, and this has not always been easy for me. Throughout most of my life I have been seen by others as insensitive. Over the years I have had family and friends comment and even joke that I have no compassion or show no heart in many circumstances and this has been hurtful many times throughout my life. I have always felt a sense of shame that my body was somehow broken and not able to perform like others when it comes to matters of the heart. Because of this, I often feel different, alone and "not normal" when my energy works in this manner.

Intuitively, I have an extremely heightened cognitive nature, simply knowing things, and always have since childhood. My knowing can come off as arrogance or present itself as thinking I am superior to others, but that is not the case. Like others whose cognitive energies are most heightened, my entire essence simply knows things. I also fully know when something is not mine to own and, therefore, I do not engage either energetically or mentally. Even though this is seen by others as non-feeling or non-caring, I perceive it as the opposite. I simply "know" when something is not mine and I will step back and remove myself from the situation, the idea, the person, the place because it allows the other to simply be, as well as protects my own energy. It protects my truth. It protects my field of personal fuel. I "know" when I do not have the right to take from another in terms of pain, feelings, emotions, and even situations. Even though I continue to struggle with others' judgment of this knowing, I choose to hold strong in my truths as best I can. I know it honors them and their truth if I do not engage by empathing.

Emotional Empathy

Unlike cognitive energy, which enters our field in the form of thought, emotional empathy happens when we physically feel the emotions of the other person in order to offer support for their pain and suffering. Our human meat-bodies have an incredible way of connecting to those we deeply love and it is a natural reaction to feel that pull on your heartstring to help another in need. This is our deep-seated, fully human response to emotionally connect and form a bond.

Although it is helpful to identify with another's pain, it can be challenging to separate oneself from the emotions of another when we open up our energy fields to feel what they experience. The downside of emotional empathy occurs when people lack the ability to manage their own distressing emotions, which shifts emotional empathy into the stage of empathing, moving from unconditional oneness back to the individual ego of needing to fix the situation, "be the one," or take control. Without proper practice or intent, emotional empathy can become overwhelming or inappropriate in certain circumstances when the supporter fully takes on the physical, emotional, and mental states of another. Feeling too much of something that is truly not yours can make even small interactions feel overwhelming and lead to exhaustion, anxiety, or full burnout and physical health challenges.

Compassionate Empathy

When using compassionate empathy, we combine the energy of thought (cognitive empathy) with heart-based feelings (emotional empathy). Thoughts of the brain and feelings of the heart are not opposites but more so intricately connected and provide a more holistic picture of understanding. By *knowing* the situation and having a sense for the *feelings* experienced by another, compassionate empathy honors the natural union of head and heart to achieve a powerful balance.

The majority of the time, compassionate empathy is ideal as we want to be able to cognitively understand why someone is feeling or experiencing a situation or emotion and at the same time also offer emotional comfort to pain and suffering. However, we do not want to take the person's pain-energy and make it our own as in the case of empathing. We are designed to be one, but only unconditionally. Unconditional means no conditions attached. We expect nothing in return for the actions given to another.

True compassion and unconditional empathy towards others can only happen when we are in harmony and the right relationship to ourselves, first. This combination of compassion and empathy is something I have chosen to train myself in over the recent years as I learn to trust my divine human vehicle of an earthly body more. As I stated above, I inherently default to using my cognitive skills when engaging with others but have learned that my feel-centers combined with my physical container can expand my capabilities as a psychic and a human.

At this stage of my life, I have begun to understand just how important it is for me to maintain a sense of presence with me. To take the time and have the passion to be all about me first in terms of my energy. To do my personal work and gain skills of discernment. If I am not a fully fueled, balanced, and harmonized Suzanne first, I am no good to anyone else no matter how hard I try to "do" for others. I hope these perspectives may help you see how the word "selfish" may not necessarily look like what we were taught and how critical it is in terms of essential energy to fuel self-love and align with Source within oneself *first* so that we can then be able to give love to others without fear, conditions or cords attached. Only then does true compassion and empathy naturally bridge us in selfless unity with others. This can be directly opposite of what many of us have been taught growing up in families that teach, hold, and maintain belief systems surrounding the idea of doing for others, so it may be time to re-examine what you think you know versus what your body truly knows.

The Challenge with Sympathy

Many people think they are extending empathy when they are actually projecting sympathy or a sense of feeling sorry or having pity for the person or the situation. This happens because the initial connection to the energy of the situation and the person's story can often trigger old programs or unresolved issues within the person who is listening to the story or experience of another, again stemming from our initial beliefs. Our own past occurrences can interfere when we energetically connect to another person, unearthing trapped emotion that can alter the perspective of the situation, which can either minimize or maximize the experience. Once an unresolved emotion or belief is triggered, it can be difficult to show true empathy or be present in a genuine way and the end result becomes sympathy instead.

Empathy energetically creates a supportive and love-fueled connection that comes from the activated resonance between people creating a bridge of understanding between the two fields that strengthens trust and honor. However, with sympathy the energy is anchored in fear-fueled judgment held either consciously or subconsciously, which creates a disconnection and separation leaving out the bridge of understanding, trust, and especially honor. This is easy to illustrate in everyday occurrences. For example, someone shares a challenge they are facing, and we find ourselves being the listener. Possibly they have lost their job, have a sick relative, or have no money to pay their mortgage. Maybe their car needs an extensive repair job or they had a horrible fight with their partner or are experiencing health problems. Whatever the challenge being shared, you might find yourself to be the chosen listener whether you are open to it or not. Lots of times when we are not fully vested in the listener-position we mindlessly articulate some version of "Oh, I'm sorry about . . ." While at times this action and articulation may be completely appropriate for the situation, other times it may be an attempt to shut down or minimize their experience or it can prompt the reverse reaction where you then want to fix the other person's feeling or circumstances and maximize their experience.

Sympathy has limitations. When we half-invest, put up with another's story and truly do not want to be involved yet continue to listen, we can become resentful. When we try to fix another, we ultimately do this because we take on the discomfort of the situation and feel the need to fix it ourselves, which is when resentment may also arise. In either situation, it is us who will feel better if their situation is resolved, yet we are not responsible for that change nor do we get to determine for them what "resolved" looks like. As we can guess, sympathy can often be the unconscious response of the empath who either wants to block themselves off from the overwhelming feelings of another's emotional distress or they overcommit themselves by taking on the situation or the problem as their own.

Due to this unconscious response to block or fix, my empath clients often see themselves as a magnet for others to spill their guts, tell their woes, point out their pain patterns whether it is the random stranger, the co-worker, or their best friend from the 5th grade. These attention seekers seem to come out of the woodwork the moment they enter the room. And when they engage in the situation not only do they give advice, but they go the extra mile by offering solutions from sharing websites, to suggesting products to telling everyone exactly what needs to be done, even if the advice is unsolicited.

Offering Empathy versus Sympathy

It is common for people to think they are empathizing when they are actually reacting with sympathy. Because we have not been taught how to use our feeling centers, we often don't know how to be the empathetic, collective observer and instead turn the focus to our own discomfort. If someone is sharing their hardship and we think, "I can't listen to this (or them) because they are so sad or hurt" or "I've got to fix this for them," we are instinctually reacting with sympathy. What is happening beneath the surface energetically, however, is your own need to feel good because you helped them change their outcome, sometimes allowing yourself to be saddled with an end result of taking their pain or discomfort. The responses given through sympathy are essentially focused on you and rooted in your feelings, all while packaged as helping another.

Again, it takes awareness and practice to approach our relationships and energetic interactions from a place of empathy—honoring the other and their experience by responding through compassion without judgment or conditions. Fully embracing the fact that whatever they are facing, feeling or experiencing is exactly what they are supposed to be doing holds honor for them.

If you react to someone else's plight as the observer, honoring how to create a compassionate space for this experience and this person, you are then working with your gift of empathy from an observer standpoint that will ultimately inspire an energetic compassionate connection of spirit. Many of us have been taught to always put others first, ultimately creating a "don't think about yourself, go take care of others first, fix it for them" empath situation instead of working with observer empathy. One may not experience true states of love, compassion, and empathy until these underlying belief systems are examined at the surface and they begin to connect with their true Higher Self, which works with no conditions attached to any energy transferred.

Let's look at two examples showing you how you may choose to react to a situation offering empathy versus showing sympathy.

Example #1

A co-worker shares with you she is having difficulty with her child. You half-listen to her woes much longer than you would like while secretly resenting her for taking up your time. Nothing is going to change as a result of the interaction, in fact it is not even a true conversation.

Sympathy: "Well that pretty much sucks. I don't know how you do it, I am so glad I don't have kids because I would never know what to do or how to handle them."

- It acknowledges pity for the situation without really addressing any underlying feelings or connection.
- It shows you do not find any common ground with this person or scenario and might be feeling like it is headed toward an unpleasant conversation that you want to move away from.

Empathy: "It sounds like your child's behavior is really making you feel sad and disconnected. I know that you put a lot of time and effort into your parenting, are you feeling hurt?"

- This statement expresses some understanding of the experience.
- Your response does not pass any judgment onto your friend or her child nor does it add an opinion or try to offer a fix.
- Asking the open-ended question allows for honest reflection and an open space to talk further if she chooses.

Example #2

A dear friend has been emotionally hurt by one of his family members and has come to you to vent his frustrations. This has been an ongoing situation for your friend, and he is upset and completely obsessed about being ignored by his family. You have tried offering him various solutions, ideas, and concepts but his story never seems to change. Each time you get together with him, new scenarios of the same situation continue to surface, and at this point you would do anything to shift or adjust the subject. For whatever reason, your friend is not finding resolution.

Sympathy: "It breaks my heart to watch your family treat you so poorly."

- This statement expresses *your* sadness and hurt presuming your friend feels the same plus mingles your feelings with theirs.

- The situation just became about your judgment of the friend and their family rather than acknowledgment of the original frustration and helplessness.

Empathy: "That must feel really frustrating and disappointing for you. I know how important your relationship with your family is and it must really hurt to go through this."

- This statement accurately mirrors your friend's emotions while affirming how important family is to your friend.
- The compassion expressed to your friend can help them to ease their own inward judgment and struggles of not being heard (if they chose to) because it addresses the actual hurt that hides under the frustration.

Empathy provides an authentic sounding board for another to process their experience. It takes practice because every situation and person is different, requiring active work and authentic responses rather than rote reactions.

Practicing Empathy-Based Responses

Difficult, pain-filled situations can make everyone involved uncomfortable. Even though it is less about what you say and more about showing up and listening, we all strive to say the right thing so here are some examples of empathetic responses that may help when a friend or family member shares something difficult with you. Putting ourselves in the other's shoes is more about being there instead of doing for or fixing the one in need.

Show Genuine Interest
"How are you feeling today about your situation?"
"Can you describe for me what this has been like for you?"
"What I'm hearing you say is ____ . Is that along the lines of what you are feeling like?"
"Is there anything else you want me to know about, or you to share?"

Acknowledge Their Suffering, Discomfort or Pain
"I'm sorry to hear this is happening to you."
"This must be scary."

"Your situation seems really difficult and challenging."
"I can see how sad this makes you."

Share How You Feel
"I am so sad to hear your news and I really don't know what to say."
"I can't imagine what you must be going through."
"My heart is hurting and I wish I could make it better but know I can't."
"It makes me really upset to hear this happened to you."

Be Supportive and Encouraging
"Please know that I am always going to be here for you, happy to listen."
"Can you tell me what you need or how I can help?"
"I love you and I am so proud of you."
"You will know what to do when the time comes and I will support you."

Show Gratitude
"I am glad you came to me and shared today, thank you."
"Thank you for allowing me to hold this space for you."
"Thank you for trusting me, it means a lot."
"It must be difficult to open up and talk about this, I appreciate you doing so."

Because empathy is all about putting yourself inside the human, feeling experience of someone else, it is always good to remember it is not a "one size fits all"-style effort but more an organic process depending on those involved.

This calls for self-awareness. This means it is important to be confident enough in your own sense of self to set aside your opinions and emotions for a moment to truly be present to another's experience and peer into their unique perspective. It requires a sense of self-confidence to be able to discern your own feelings combined with the ability to set aside your own judgments and your need to fix things or fix others.

Three Tips to Determine If You Are Offering Empathy or If You Are Empathing

Healthy empathy means honoring whatever another person is facing, feeling, or experiencing, which creates the space for a compassionate connection of spirit. Empathing, on the other hand, is fear-based and operates from a place of believing you need to fix the other person. Here are a few examples to help you determine if you are offering healthy observer-based empathy or if you are coming from a place of fear-based empathing:

Know Your Intention

Empathy: Is your intention simply to do your best to understand, connect, and support? *Healthy.*

Empathing: Is your intention to stop your friend's ill feelings so they do not make you uncomfortable, or are you holding on or waiting to see if they heed your advice or change their actions because of your input? Do you go home ruminating about their experience, lose sleep or find yourself worrying? *Not Healthy.*

Monitor Reactions

Empathy: Does he or she calm down, slow their anxiety, become centered during conversation? *Healthy.*

Empathing: Does his or her emotions escalate during the interchange along with your own? Do you feel yourself beginning to feel anger, sadness or pain that was not there prior to the conversation? *Not Healthy.*

Release Corded Energy

Empathy: Did you feel connected during the conversation with the other person, yet allow yourself to be free from them and the outcomes of their situation completely? *Healthy.*

Empathing: Do you find yourself judging your own self-worth by the result of the conversation depending on how the friend chooses to move forward or not. Do you feel you have the right to own or hold onto any piece of the scenario or the energy surrounding it even after the interaction is finished? *Not Healthy.*

+

Chapter Three

The Connection between Beliefs and Empathic Behaviors

Empathic behaviors can be driven by many outdated and even false belief patterns that we hold within our subconscious minds and sometimes we are not even aware this drives an inner narrative that fuels our actions.

Growing up in a family of six siblings I was labeled one of the big kids who took care of the little ones. I fully accepted this role for many years with no resentment or worry. When I was 15, my father lost his funeral home business. I remember standing in the kitchen watching strange men I did not know take things from our home and drive away in our family car. It was devastating to have my sense of safety crushed while I watched pieces of my life walk out the door, leaving me confused about what was really happening. In this moment, I remember telling my 15-year-old self I would never allow this to happen to me because I will always be *the one* in charge—instilling a core belief narrative in myself that I embraced and fed for many years to come.

To others, my adult life seemed to be one amazing accomplishment after another. I was the mother of four small children as well as the corporate executive flying around the globe. I was the hockey mom, the field trip mom, the sibling who hosted all family gatherings and who was sure to have the appropriate festive napkins that matched the plates and both green and black olives placed in the correct trays. I had no idea that in the process of being *the one*, I was actually sucking the life-force out of my entire family as I screamed at my small children and husband like a drill sergeant to make sure the house was perfect for company at every occasion. Hours of this behavior filled up my energy tank all while draining theirs, only to prove I was the one within the family who could "do it all." Sadly, over the years my extended family and friends bought into this charade and supported me as the one . . . the one to turn to for advice, the one to make the plans, to schedule everything for everyone. We all drank the Kool-Aid so to speak that Suzanne was in charge or in control. I had created this as my reality. I believed it was real.

This belief system of needing to be in control also seeped into my professional career as a marketing executive, and my belief in the false narrative continued to grow. When walking through a crowded trade show floor I was managing or a bustling airport I was passing through, the sea of bodies would seem to part as I made my way through the space.

At the time, I thought it meant I was in control and skilled at my job as I made my way through the masses—seeming to be in command of the crowded event floor or airport corridors. But what I did not realize was just how powerful my energy field was and how much I was taking from everyone and everything just to make it through my day. When I found myself exhausted and depleted, I would unintentionally seek out another person to help bring me back up again, either in a positive or negative manner. Back then, I was completely uninformed about the concept of energy, much less empathing, so I had no idea of just how invasive my fields were.

As my ego grew so did my hidden exhaustion, but I would never admit this to anyone because it was useless to ask for help because I could do the task faster and better than others so why bother—this was my mantra. I fully remember feeling like the pink Energizer Bunny on the TV commercials, terrified that if my batteries ran out, I would not get back up again. Yet I kept this all a secret because that would only show others I was weak and not capable. I was dying inside and no one knew, not even me, because I just kept going like that damn bunny putting one foot in front of the other. I sucked energy daily from my children and my husband to fill my egoic needs not even aware of it as I justified my actions as being a strict parent and capable spouse. I did the same at work with employees and clients. I drained the energy of my friends and family when I would make phone calls to them and offload my horrible day looking for compliments on how amazing I was, just to refill my ego tank, again ignorant to the motivation of the underlying energy exchange happening.

All of this unintentional empathing behavior came crashing down one day when I buckled under the pressure of it all and reached out to one of my sisters saying I was done "being the one." I remember her responding with some semblance of: "But Suzanne, if you're not the one, we are not sure what we'll do" and boy was that unnerving. Because I was still naive to ownership of energy, I projected this as anger to my family claiming I was not going to even host the next family holiday. I said I would only show up elsewhere at another sibling's home and not even cook, only bring a store-bought pie because I was sick of it all. When that holiday approached, I arrived at my sister's with my store-bought pie and a huge chip on my shoulder.

I will fully admit here I secretly wanted the holiday to be a failure and to have everyone be miserable in my sister's small house, therefore validating I was indeed the one with the better space and was the better host. Well, low and behold, the exact opposite happened. Everyone was on top of one another in that tiny, cramped house, yet everyone was fully enjoying themselves. The kitchen was busy and chaotic with barely any place to put the food, and still my sister and her husband were beaming and excited at the opportunity to be "the one" for the first time for our extended family. This scene took me to my knees.

I was utterly, totally embarrassed at my behavior, and even more disgusted with the way my egoic belief of being the one had robbed so many of them of having the opportunity to be. All those times I was in control of being the one, no one else got to shine, got to make mistakes, got to experience any of it for themselves. I literally left the kitchen to go out on the porch and cry at how selfish my actions were for the years I had robbed others' energy and forced limitation and control just to fill my own depleted tank. That was my awakening. Yes, they allowed this limitation as well, but my ability to overpower and command their energy was the vital ingredient in this recipe of codependent behavior. I was so ashamed. That day I vowed to change, and it started with changing my core belief system. I realized being the one does not make me safe. I am safe. I am worthy, no matter what. Now I get to *choose* to be the one, if I choose, how I choose, when I choose, with no conditions attached.

I learned about energy fields after this experience, but changing my belief system was the beginning of that journey. It also took a lot of work to forgive myself. I spent a lot of time healing from this core belief I anchored at age 15, taking energy from a childhood situation that was never mine to own in the first place. Do not get this wrong here, yes my 15-year-old perspective on what happened to my family through my own eyes was mine to own, yet the entire truth of the overall situation of what happened to my family was not. Taking the time to feel the difference is important and results in how the belief is anchored. Looking back at that entire situation even so many years later opened my eyes to the connection between my beliefs and my empathic behaviors and I certainly value the lesson learned.

Learned Beliefs

Our beliefs create the stage for the behaviors we use to navigate and play out our days. Beliefs are the core of who we are, how we behave, what we do and how we show up for life itself. When we traditionally think of the idea of beliefs, it most often brings to mind a form of mental representation of conscious thought, meaning what we *consciously* decide is truth. However, beliefs can also be held *unconsciously* as inner convictions. Either way, a belief provides a certainty about what something is or means in our reality, which causes us to act upon that belief or against it.

So where do beliefs come from? We form our beliefs based on what we're taught by others or learn through experience. Beliefs are narratives we accept as truth, often shaped by our morals and values. We often accept these narratives on the grounds of an apparent authority. However, beliefs do not have to be based on actual facts, and most often they are tools for social conditioning rather than expressions of our inner realization or universal truth.

Most beliefs come from messaging we observe or receive during the early informative years of childhood offered or forced upon us from parents, grandparents, siblings, extended family, teachers, coaches, and friends. As we grow, these beliefs serve as guiding principles to provide direction for our actions and meaning in life. In this way, beliefs can be viewed as preset, organized filters we use to perceive the world (external and internal) that work much like internal commands to our brain. They originate from what we hear, see, watch, and experience mentally, emotionally, and physically throughout life beginning in childhood and prior, as I have found messaging ingrained in my clients since being *in utero*.

Our beliefs become the very essence of how we see ourselves, other people and the world, and are continually fueled by our life experiences and events. Because they form the foundation of how we see the world, beliefs are usually rigid, strongly held and inflexible. They not only create our mental filters through which we process the world but also our automated emotional reactions. We typically maintain these beliefs by focusing on information that supports the initial ingrained belief while ignoring evidence or information that may contradict it. This is exactly what I did as I continued to fuel my perception of myself throughout the years, building a sense of false safety and control.

Supporting energies for our beliefs come from our environment, events, knowledge, past experiences, visualization and more, which seem foundational to our reality, but beliefs are actually a *choice* and are very *changeable*. We choose our beliefs based on a variety of validation methods or mental processes:

- **Credibility:** We trust the source of a belief versus the substance itself.
- **Assignment:** We acquire beliefs from family, culture, religious background, and therefore are assigned for us rather than chosen.
- **Blind Faith:** We have total faith in a narrative without any questioning.
- **Doctrine:** We accept beliefs to serve our programs, agendas, and traditions.
- **Dissent:** We choose a belief because it deliberately opposes conventional and established beliefs.
- **Alignment:** We carefully consider the options and then choose the belief.

This concept of choice may seem difficult to realize because beliefs are subconsciously held for many of us and intertwine with our emotions, which is why we often feel threatened or react with aggression when our beliefs are challenged by the words or actions of others. However, if we take time to actually examine our beliefs, we will find the truth as to how we choose them and can evaluate them from a conscious perspective.

I am personally going to tell you this is not easy work. It is humiliating and humbling. There is a lot of shame and sadness connected to this type of inner-healing, yet I believe it is imperative to examine what no longer serves us. This is our own responsibility, and no one else's. But sadly, our Western culture does not support the examination of our belief systems nor teach us how to do this work. After my family holiday experience, I had the luxury of spending a long weekend at a cabin in the woods in silence with myself meditating on what I truly believed and did not. You do not necessarily need a cabin escape to do this but you may choose to get quiet with yourself to go within. This is not a one-time fix, however, it is an on-going process because we oftentimes don't even realize how many ordinary beliefs we hold each day as involuntary aspects of the mundane and of our expected existence. But it is through the power of our beliefs that we do create our reality and this is what directly or indirectly causes things to happen throughout our day. The energy we put into those beliefs determines how we show up in life either with deep conviction and energetic power or as a walking zombie going through the motions.

Though our empathing behaviors can be driven by many false beliefs, there are a few key belief patterns I find in my client work that most often influence empaths.

Worry

Years ago, I was sitting in the kitchen with my daughter who was dealing with a health situation. We were in discussion about her going to the doctor the following day for some tests when a long-time client arrived for a healing appointment. Overhearing our conversation, he jumped in and expressed concern for my child's welfare and unknown condition. While the support was appreciated, he attached a high level of fear to his concern that did not match how my child and I were feeling about her health. Given what little information we had at this point, his fear-based worry seemed unwarranted until she saw her doctor.

We left the conversation and my client and I moved on to my healing room for his appointment, but immediately following the session my client once again returned back to his worry for my child. I reassured him I was not worried, nor was my child, so maybe he could also let go of his concerns, especially until we all knew more. Later that evening, I received a text inquiring how my daughter was doing. And again, the following morning, there was a voicemail where I learned he had not slept all night over concerns for my child's well-being. My daughter did go to the doctor, received her tests and found her situation could be resolved with a simple change to her health routine. All of that extended worry and concern my client took on which affected his own body, mind, and spirit turned out to be completely unfounded, plus the situation was never his to take ownership of in the first place.

Whether we consciously or unconsciously take on the energy of another's situation and worry over the potential outcome, we choose this behavior because somewhere deep within we hold the belief that worry shows love and is the responsible thing to do. This is a typical belief system for most human beings that is heightened when we empath the feelings and physical symptoms of others. Whether we are male or female, we are all trained in various ways to mother, to care for and assist others. This is what played out with the client and my child's health issue—concern equals worry which equals showing compassion or love.

Our belief tells us if we keep worrying long enough, it will somehow lead to a solution, alter the outcome, or prevent further problems. We then get stuck in a mental cycle, ruminating and continually replaying the thoughts, images, emotions, and actions of a negative outcome in a repetitive, uncontrollable manner. Because we internalize this worry for ourselves and others, the negative mental spiral can actually lead to dis-ease in our bodies in the form of anxiety, panic attacks, depression, and fatigue, plus manifest physical symptoms. My client lost an entire night of sleep due to his worry about a child that was not his who turned out to be just fine. Such strong reactions to others may ignite from a habit or ingrained belief pattern but it might also indicate a similar deep fear in his subconscious that may need further attention and healing.

The vibration of worry can also come from many packages beyond family, friends, and those we encounter in our everyday life. Many of us unknowingly take on the vibrations of humanity, Mother Earth, and the future of our planet. With every news headline and social media post, we find ourselves running on the hamster wheel of worry as we continue to scroll through the headlines consuming more fear-based messaging. This behavior again is driven from the same belief system that our worry is productive. By engaging in the behavior of worrying, we empath the external situation as our own and believe we are assisting with a solution. While we believe we are working towards a solution that will change others or fix the planet, we are ultimately most concerned in relieving *ourselves* from the suffering we have now empathed. In this way, we again flip from observing with unconditional compassion to judging with conditions, requiring a resolution that relieves our pain and discomfort.

It becomes tough to break this empathing pattern if we believe our worrying serves some positive or productive purpose. In some instances, concern may be justified but subconsciously allowing the energy to drain our fuel tank through worry is not beneficial for anyone. The rumination of worry in our mind on behalf of helping others or the collective does not offer or show love and is not the empath's best tool for working the energy of a thought pattern. It is exhausting and holds no solution to the situation, only reinstating the fear that we cannot do anything to make change.

Worry ignites the fear there is not enough of me to go around, the fear that I am not enough. It is an action that offers the potential for harming our energy systems and physical body, especially exhausting the one doing the worrying.

When we overwhelm our system with worry, it can often have the exact opposite result of what we intend and will take a toll on our health and well-being if we continually allow this subconscious narrative to chip away at our spirit, mind, and body. This can lead to similar beliefs of: I am too tired. I am too stressed. Ultimately the belief of not enough. Not enough time. Not enough of me. I am not enough. This confusion can cause scattered energy lines that result in feelings of anxiety, loss of control, and ultimately triggers a belief of not feeling safe.

Anxiety

While worry ignites fear there is not enough, confused, scattered, and distorted energy can additionally trigger a sense of loss of control within the mental and emotional bodies. When we do not feel in control, we ultimately do not feel safe in our physical body. A belief of not being safe can activate multiple physical and emotional symptoms experienced as anxiety. Experiencing some level of anxiety is a normal part of life, however, there are people with disorders that experience far more intense anxiety and for far longer periods of time than would be expected in most typical situations. Oftentimes anxiety disorders involve repeated episodes involving sudden feelings of intense anxiety, fear, or even terror that within minutes reach a peak known as a "panic attack" which can additionally ignite flight-mechanisms.

Symptoms of an anxiety attack can include intense, excessive, and persistent worry and fear about everyday situations which can interfere with daily activities due to a feeling of losing control or going crazy, increased heart rate, palpitations or chest pain, feeling like you're going to pass out, or trouble breathing.

When overwhelmed with stressful emotions or taking on the thoughts and feelings of others, empaths can experience anxiety, depression, fatigue and may even show physical symptoms of a full panic attack such as an increased heart rate and headache. Remember, this is because they are internalizing the emotions, feelings, and pain of others without the ability to discern and distinguish it as separate from their own. Over time, empaths can become predetermined or encoded to avoid external stimulation as a self-preservation tactic and in some cases this can then lead to feelings of isolation and depression and if symptoms begin to show up as feeling numb, with an extreme loss of interest in normal activities, life-threatening trouble eating and sleeping, decreased energy and decreased self-esteem. Sometimes empaths or psychic-sensitives may develop compulsive and addictive behaviors (food, drugs, alcohol) as their outlet for the expanded feelings outside of themselves. You may want to seek professional medical assistance as addiction, suicidal ideation or thoughts of self-harm are also possible and may warrant emergency care. On the flipside, it is important to also note that it is not unusual for people with sensitive-psychic empath abilities to be falsely diagnosed with anxiety, depression or other disorders, so it is important to have professional assistance to determine the difference.

Service to Others

One of the hardest beliefs to navigate as an empath is that of serving others before ourselves. For whatever reason, the female human, more so than males, has bought into the idea that everyone else comes first. I am sure this is due to eons of collective programming, social and family beliefs from outdated times when the mother was responsible for caring for the home and raising the children while father had other duties. This in no way diminishes the struggles of the father position as many now choose the stay-at-home position themselves, and fathers can also struggle with their own form of guilt and feelings of not enough. I personally still see so many mothers working inside or outside of home feeling overextended. We have turned into taxi services, teachers, and coaches. We fill our schedules until there is no room to breathe and yet rarely do we schedule in the "me time" first.

Why do most of us put everyone else first? Why are we so concerned with being the perfect host or being the one everyone comes to for help? Where does this push come from in the human? And you may ask, why is that bad?

When examining this behavior of serving others, it's important to consider our motivation behind the behavior. While human nature has an ordinary impulse to ease the suffering of other living beings, the beliefs we inherited during childhood from family and society set the stage of how and why we value serving others first. Most true empaths have been raised in a family structure that supports fueling the ego through actions for others. In this way, when we commit to acts of altruism, we may actually be doing so because it makes us feel better about ourselves. Some of the indicators to this behavior are thinking we are the only or best one who can help the situation or that we *"have to"* spend our time doing or we *"can't"* leave or *"should"* visit whomever how often. As we explored earlier, these words and phrases are indicators that our belief is rooted in fear-based ego.

When we consistently put others ahead of our own well-being, we often do so because something within us does not feel complete, whole or good enough without action that gains outside validation from others. Empaths often run on fear-based-fuel driven by the messaging of *"I have to, I need to, I can't, I should,"* striving to replenish their self-worth through outside actions and accolades. These words indicate an energetic lose-lose situation where the empath and the other are ultimately depleted by the action. This creates a loop pattern that is never-ending—there is never enough. If the empath changes the thought and word pattern to *"I get to"* and *"I choose to,"* the very same actions can be driven from a love-based fuel with no conditional cords of energy attached to other people or their situations. This is an energetic win-win situation. There is enough. I am enough.

Additionally, when we fill our days helping or fixing others, we have no time left for ourselves. This behavior can be a protection mechanism most empaths use as an excuse to not look deep within to find that inner voice that says there may be some work needed to examine self-validation and learn that important messaging that I am good enough just for being me and not because of what I do for others. It is sometimes easier for the empath to work for and on behalf of others before working on themselves.

Generosity, acts of kindness, altruism, and charitable gestures are all wonderful ways to connect to others as long as they are not feeding an egoic program belief system of worth. Though many of us were taught that *if I help everyone else, then I am wonderful,* the truly balanced human knows *I am already wonderful and get to choose* to assist another with no conditions attached to the outcome. If you find yourself compelled to be of service to others, I invite you to scrutinize the driving force behind your impulse. Examine your motivations to see if you are working in a fear-based fuel, or a love-based one, anchored as a core belief about yourself.

The Need to Be Right

The need to be right and prove it to others is so deeply embedded not only in our current culture but within our physical, mental, and emotional belief system that makes up our collective psyche. Everything in our reality structures supports the fight of right versus wrong, and we learn this message from an incredibly young age through our educational systems which promotes the value of being right, from rewarding correct answers on a test to celebrating athletic accomplishments. So why *do* we as a culture fight so hard to prove right? Again, it comes down to our core beliefs about self-worth being validated by others, which is the initial primal programmed fear of the human.

There are some real fears behind this messaging of wanting to be right and one of them is the fear of being wrong or *failing*. As a practitioner I work with failure programming every single day and I cannot tell you how this takes a toll on the body, mind, and spirit. I have young school-age and college-age clients who are terrified to disappoint their parents. They live a secretly miserable existence taking classes and doing sports they have no passion for and yet it is the fear of failure that drives them. School or sports is not their vision or goal, it is their parents', and this need to do it right, to be right is drilled into them from day one so they stay the course as they continue to dis-ease emotionally, mentally, and even physically. Failure is not tolerated in many families and yet how silly it is that we do not look at this from another perspective—as another opportunity to do it differently, to experience it another way. We work so hard to meet someone else's vision of right, often losing ourselves along the way.

Another reason we strive to be right from any and all external sources is because we have no connection to our inner truth and instead seek validation from others. If I maintain I am right and someone or something validates it, then it proves it. Validation proves I am right. And yet, the reality is we are *all already right*, in our own individual lens of reality and perception. We just do not have the courage or the wisdom to know we do not need validation from others or outside resources. And for the empath, this need to be right will morph into various behaviors and actions that end up depleting Source energy, such as vampiring, control and victimization—all discussed in Part Two of this journey.

Programmed Beliefs

From our first breath on the planet, we are taught how to survive, what to fear, and how to be safe through the stories of others. We see and watch, we hear and listen, we experience and feel. We are drawn into the stories of others and then use their experiences to then create our own.

As children we initially allow others to influence our experience of how to survive and be safe because no one has informed us of anything different. We are vulnerable as young children and rely on those around us for our survival, and naturally we learn from their experience and make it our own. By the time we are old enough to consciously choose for ourselves, our survival beliefs are often so ingrained that we don't realize they are there guiding our behaviors. We don't necessarily know we have the capacity to question their validity and truth. When we grow and have children of our own, we subconsciously then pass on these beliefs to the next generation. I view these as programmed beliefs, at a deeper level than our learned beliefs, because they are ingrained in us on a more subconscious level and are more collective to our shared human experience.

Our behaviors become programmed through our beliefs in many ways throughout our days, throughout our lives, throughout our generations. Whether we know it or not, most of us are told what to believe and the messaging comes from numerous outside sources such as religion, politics, medicine, finance, education, societal and legal structures and more. The information can be presented with an agenda-riddled spin-factor that nudges individuals to see, act, and live the way these outside sources want, ultimately affecting communities, nations, and an entire species for generations.

As a collective we continue to reinforce these beliefs of how humans survive, what we should fear, and how to be safe. Amazingly we do this by either paying attention or not. Generation after generation, we pass down the same human programming which ultimately creates the human reality structure we find ourselves living in—like our current patriarchal top-down systems of limitation and greed. This is all programmed. So how do we as individuals allow these programmed beliefs to ultimately influence our instincts on the most subconscious level? Because they trigger primal wounds held within the DNA of every human body.

Perceived Separation

It is common for us humans to feel a deep sense of longing or separation that we can't quite explain. Much of our art, music, and written works express this feeling of having a hole or void within that our human body longs to fill. Many of us are not even aware that we yearn to fill ourselves up while others will do just about anything to ease that longing using things like work, relationships, food, substances and more to fill what might be missing. Who or what is missing is a mystery yet it holds an underlying sense of separation that instinctively drives us to survive and connect to someone or something to feel safe and have worth. This feeling can be seen as a *primal wound* of perceived separation, or a collective belief wired into our DNA from birth and programs our sense of survival, suffering, and separation.

This primal DNA messaging has been a part of the human DNA structure for eons as we fought for every breath just to eat, stay warm and survive. It remains as a blueprint within our original cellular structure directly affecting our fight or flight mechanisms. Yet the true disconnect is not our separation from a person, thing or even Gaia but more so a sense of separation from life itself, from its totality, from the birthright of oneness with all Source.

While *in utero,* our DNA along with this primal wound programming incubates as the fetus hears, senses, feels, and knows its surroundings from within the womb. Using these outside messages and sensations, the fetus begins to form a matrix of reality. The fear program of separation and fight for survival is also experienced the moment we are born into this world and are physically cut and separated from the only source we are aware of—our biological mother—as we fight for our first breath. As we grow, this primal wound messaging or belief of separation runs within our subconscious and creates the sense of deep longing we experience into and throughout adulthood.

Most humans are unaware of this inner narrative of separation and because of this ignorance we begin to look outside of ourselves to fill the yearning for connection and purpose. We look to consumer culture and the material world to help us feel connected. We fill our schedules with activity after activity to give us a sense of purpose. We constantly feel the need to be of service to others or demonstrate our worry for others to receive validation and acceptance. Ultimately, we are trying to find something to connect with, something to heal this separation sensation as we seek to experience oneness again with all things and especially with each other to connect with our true birthright of empathy. We may not know why we yearn for seeking this connection and purpose exactly, yet it seems almost instinctual. It feels like the natural thing to do. The only problem is there is a hidden sensation of lack of resources in where to find it or how to get it plus an inner feeling that there is never going to be enough to satisfy us. This perpetual and innate hunger is built into all human beings and it is what drives all human progress. But this human progress is expressed as outer material or even societal progress and little to do with true inner human spiritual awareness.

This deep unrest within the human body drives us out into the world to try to find something or someone that can bring an end to the hunger or to play that perfect character as we hide behind the perfect mask. This hunger drives all human experience from money, drugs, food, sex, religion, business, science, and even war and more. It partners with another form of programming—*impatience programming*—that fuels our hunger.

Impatience programming is something we have all created and accepted as a norm in our current society. We expect life to give us what we want 24/7 in the fastest and quickest ways possible from overnight shipping to online payments. This pushes us to hunger for more and more, faster and faster. As our hunger then fuels our impatience, it all becomes a classic biofeedback loop that keeps us operating in a never-ending cycle.

We are a hungry and unfulfilled species. We are a species that expects and demands instant gratification. We do not know *what* we want, but we want it now! However, nothing outside of us, nothing external, can bring clarity much less an end to our DNA-rooted suffering or yearning for connection and our search for purpose. And because every human is challenged with this same primal DNA-wound, the programmed beliefs stay just that—*programmed*.

This primal survival-wound of separateness has run throughout humanity for eons. Because most individuals do not take the responsibility or understand how to clear out personal programming, our collective consciousness as a humanity continues to align with the wound of perceived separation. As individuals and as a collective, our reality continues to co-create and align to the programmed messages of material things, stuff, and people that will offer us safety, connection, purpose, and worth. This perception of reality grows into a core belief that *I have to DO to be loved and accepted,* hence why we are a human race of DOing machines. No one teaches us that we are safe, we are worthy, we are loveable just because we are here, so, sadly we just keep searching. We keep searching to find purpose and validation and we are never satisfied because the true primal wound is never addressed so instead we search through our behaviors outside of ourselves to find a cure for our deep separation. Healing this can only be accomplished when an individual awakens within and realizes they have a choice over their beliefs and begins to look inside to align their beliefs with their actual personal truth.

Controller Programming

As mentioned previously, we are taught to look outside ourselves for security, safety, and worth from a young age. We go to schools to learn what is right and what is wrong, what is important or not, what is valid or real. We watch the world news each night to see how and what our government is doing to protect us from the enemy, whomever or whatever that may be. Then through the creation of wars, we are shown how the military protects us. How our elected officials know what is best for us. We are taught to look to organized medicine as the final authority over our health and well-being. We rely on our politicians to create laws and policies designed to keep us safe or protected and expect others to implement them on our behalf. We envy and emulate the lives of the famous who have achieved material wealth and recognition because we believe this is what creates purpose and worth. We attend churches and synagogues to atone for our human behavior and ask for someone or something outside of ourselves to forgive us and make us worthy once again. These societal structures are all designed in some way to align the average human mind to believe authority and control comes from outside ourselves.

Controller programming from our social and cultural structures is what keeps most people "asleep" in the victim mode and a prime target to become human doing machines. There are many top-down structures of control in human society, which include but are not limited to:

- Government
- Military
- Intelligence agencies
- Religious groups
- Education
- Legal systems
- Economic and financial systems
- Medical practices
- Mega corporations
- Media, entertainment, and celebrity culture

Because of these controller systems, humanity has become a society of people who are afraid. Added to this are the ways messages from these controller systems are sent and received 24/7 through our modern communication platforms, all designed to keep us asleep and in a state of fear. Each of us can choose (or not) to believe in the idea of outside control, but regardless of our level of knowledge or ignorance it continues to assist in creating our current realities. If I see the experience of *life is tough*, life will be tough. If I hear *I am not safe*, I will create "not safe." If I see I have to *fight to survive*, I will continue to fight. These combined messages develop and then root within us the primary belief about our loss of control, driving us to behaviors where we are either giving away our power or grasping to take control ourselves.

Our belief about control dictates if our behavior is driven from external forces or our own inner guidance. People with an external focus feel their fate is not within their direct control, settling for how things stand yet not happy with the current situation. Diminished external control beliefs gives power away crediting fate, luck or outside circumstances with the energy of the behavior. The belief in external control has a fear of failure which leads to task avoidance or non-action overall because the idea of not succeeding generates for the empath a negative emotion such as guilt, doubt, and humiliation and it just becomes easier to avoid the behavior instead.

Having a strong belief in external control is a trait of an emotional empath, a prime suspect for giving away their power and being controlled by others, becoming the *victim*. Over time, the victim may become depleted and either shut down, moving into depression, or they may constantly look for an external source of blame for their perceived challenges. We can see how common this is as many people go to work each day hating their tedious jobs yet do nothing to change it, or staying in toxic relationships thinking someday it will change.

Conversely, those who believe in an internal focus of control own their personal power and feel in command of the world around them. This type of person believes they can orchestrate their life including career, relationships and more as this internal focus acts as a catalyst for personal development, attaching and owning their responsibility and accountability to their successes as well as their failures. However, having an internal focus of control represents the degree of importance one places on the completion of tasks as a value of self and can result in positive behavior but also negative. If a person measures their worth and intrinsic value only by how much they *do* it can become a dangerous core belief. This creates the *control freak*, the person who makes a list for their lists, constantly going and doing because ultimately the task directly connected to the completed behavior is intertwined with the person's self-worth and personal value. This is the empath who never stops, never feels like they have done enough and will keep on going to the detriment of their health and self-wellness. Yet if the individual genuinely enjoys doing the task without personal value attached, the concept of doing can be a healthy belief to drive behavior and empathing does not result because the work is coming from a place of unconditional love versus conditional. It is all about true balance.

Poverty Consciousness

I would like to specifically explore a common belief about money because it is one of the most challenging outcomes of various controller programs I see not only in my client work but also in my personal life story. The human monetary system is a massive controller-narrative taught to us as the solution for our safety and survival. Many people have an abundance of material things and yet they feel deep anxiety pushing them to accumulate even more. Growing up, we are shown and taught by our families and the greater human culture that the accumulation of money and material possessions creates safety and security. Therefore, we humans have a deep fear of lacking money or material worth, driving us to consume more and more. This belief, known as *poverty consciousness,* has been designed and programmed over countless generations as an enslavement tool to trap us in the cycle of materialism and consumerism.

Near the beginning of this book I shared my personal story of when my father lost his business and how that created a core belief of being "the one" within me at a young age. This devastating event created another deep belief in me and my family—one of poverty consciousness. One day I felt safe, living life in a home filled with things, food and joy, and in a flash our family was struggling to put food on the table to feed a family of eight. Little did I know that almost the exact same scenario would become a part of my own life-script many years later.

Both my husband and I were corporate executives by the time our four children were born. We had good salaries, 401K's and a savings account. In terms of monetarily "doing things right" we felt we were on track for a safe and secure future. I was just coming into my own learning about healing and energy and both my husband and I decided that it was safe for me to leave the corporate world and have the faith to physically, emotionally and, especially, financially jump full time into self-employed healing work because he would hold the position of the "responsible corporate one."

Within months of making that leap, my husband was blindsided as a company takeover quickly removed him of his corporate position, now leaving our family high and dry with no guaranteed paychecks between the two of us. We had four kids, two mortgages, typical bills for a family of six and no way to see what the future held—needless to say it was terrifying and reignited poverty conscious programming as I found myself reliving almost the same scenario I experienced as a child, watching almost everything I knew and loved as security be taken away including my savings, 401K, and the belief that I could feed our children. Three weeks later we were standing in a food stamp line struggling with the idea of how did we get here?

Old wounds of shame, guilt, and fear smothered me daily. The stress level in our home affected not just our marriage but our parenting and, I am sad to admit, I know I passed poverty consciousness programming to each of our children in individual ways that can still challenge them in adulthood if they allow it. The programming of poverty consciousness runs through all of us, it does not discriminate or choose favorites. Goodness knows I never believed I would repeat my childhood nightmare within my own family and yet I did because little did I know it was a gift from a higher aspect of myself; I had inner work to do that I was not even aware of. In many ways this inner work continues even today for me and that is OK, because it is all part of the ongoing journey of self-discovery.

Poverty consciousness is a trauma-based disease that exists within the minds of the spiritually bankrupt (not the financially bankrupt) and triggers deep fears over personal security, safety, and self-esteem. Many people feel terrorized by obsessive thoughts of poverty and homelessness even when it has not happened to them in their lifetime. Even if they do not hold fear to that extent, most people do feel that something is not right with the world economy and monetary system, yet we are not clear on what it is that is scaring us. However, when we look at this control program on a planetary level, this sickness of poverty consciousness continues to produce separative beliefs perpetrating the cycles of violence, ignorance, hatred, victimization, and enemy patterning between the people of the Earth.

It's important to note I tell most people I grew up in the "Brady Bunch" where my life was truly easy and filled with wonder and magic. It was not abusive. It was not scary. We as a family experienced a wonderful life in so many ways together and yet my programmed narrative told my subconscious otherwise. On an individual level, poverty consciousness has nothing to do with the amount of money, physical comfort, or material possessions we have acquired—it is deeply rooted in human fears of victimization, survival, insecurity, and limitation. For a long time I was not even cognizant of how this narrative was playing out in my own life because I had not cleared the energy held within a story from youth of not feeling safe and especially not feeling a sense of true worth. As the months and years progressed in my adulthood, it became clear to me I had work to do within my own soul and heart with regard to my childhood insecurities and recreating my story.

Humans Create Their Story

Our collective story of humanity begins as a whole with our primal separation of Source. As human beings, our very first experience in life is separation from our biological mother, the source of life itself and this creates the context for our entire reality, which we experience as one of *separation from the Source of ALL Life*. It urges us as individuals to create a story for our validation for being.

The details of the story we create for ourselves and show off for others are formed by the beliefs and messages found within our family, society, religion, community, and so on because our core beliefs are the very essence of how we see ourselves, other people, the world and its future. Yes, some elements are found within our actual DNA and drive our path in life according to what our lineage and soul-history offer as life lessons, but many beliefs are given to us in childhood and continue to develop over time, fueled by significant life experiences and our continued searching for acceptance, connection, and purpose.

Remember how *I chose* to believe I needed and then wanted to be *the one* in my family structure from a very young age. This then set the stage for me to continue this inner narrative and it was *me* who continued to feed that story line into my adult years with validation from my position at work to my reputation amongst friends and family. It was another form of vampiring energy as I continually searched for outside validation to feel good and make sure everyone knew it. Many of us do this daily without awareness of the belief behind the action.

The energy behind our beliefs is a powerful force when it comes to our mental processes and turns into the narratives we tell ourselves about who we are and what we can and can't do in this life. These mental narratives can drive the empath's daily actions in harmful and negative ways driven by false truths which become mental loop patterns run through the mind to create the story. *I'm too old to make a career change. I'm not smart enough. I'm just not creative. I never have enough money. I can never lose weight. I'm not lovable. We just don't do that in our family. I'll never have the things I want. We will never be out of debt.* These false narratives of *"Have to, need to, should, and can't"* are all fueled by fear-based energy we hold in our core beliefs about our safety, self-worth, and disconnection.

But just as powerful as these learned and programmed beliefs are over our mental processes and behaviors, we humans have an even stronger capability we can use to change them: our consciousness. If we remember we are sentient beings of consciousness, we recognize we are incredible energetic beings whose birthright is our connection to every living thing on this planet and beyond. Using our gift of discernment, we can develop a skilled mind and begin to identify the boundaries of truths and untruths. This starts with taking time to get quiet, to be still and go within to listen to the current story we're living. *Who do I believe I am? What narratives do I constantly run inside my head? Are they true? Where do they come from?* Confronting our deep beliefs is part of the skill set of discernment which allows us to dismantle the narrative each time we feel triggered by anger or fear:

- What deep within me is causing this reaction?
- Who originally taught me this way of thinking and at what age?
- Is this thought still a sound and rational idea today?
- Is it absolutely factual or is it programmed?
- In the deepest part of myself, do I believe it's true?
- What does it mean about me if I choose to release this idea today?
- What idea can I replace it with that will truly empower me?

As you make the time to stop, listen and determine what the message, sensations and feelings mean to you, remember to do so without attaching any ownership to them. From this place of observing without judgment, you can more easily uncover the belief, evaluate its merit and determine if you will continue to choose it for yourself. When we move to the role of observer, we can also show more kindness and have empathy for our own self, providing the nurturing we need to release old patterns of thinking and begin telling a different story.

Through self-love, self-worth, and connection to Source, the energy stored within the shadow of hunger is released into the human who knows *simply being is enough*. Instead of the shadow being squandered outward in the world to be validated by being a human doing-machine, we can recognize we humans are designed as a BEing, not a DOing. This idea and unconditional way of living is such a difficult concept for the empath but it is possible and it all begins within oneself. Living and giving unconditionally to ourselves and others increases the love vibration, which not only makes us happy but aligns us with that connecting tissue underlying all creation, that universal oneness we yearn for that heals the story of separation. This magical adventure happens when the human spirit decides to break free from the mind, its programming, and the crazy controller storylines we create and play out with others.

I am here to honestly tell you this is not easy work, especially for one that is an empath. Going through my own personal soul work of embracing and releasing not only poverty consciousness but also the need to be right, releasing learned beliefs and programming is probably the most difficult thing I have done and it continues to be a work in progress. And this process has affected my relationships in all areas of my life. When you choose to change, your energy changes, which then affects others because we live in a collective reality.

We are always going to be assaulted with programs, with memories, with energy that is not ours and that is one of the reasons I wrote this book: to let you know you are not alone in this and you can choose to live differently, or not. One of my next steps in creating a foundation of knowledge included learning about my own human energy fields—my energy vortexes, chakras, auric fields and more. In the beginning of my learning curve, I had no idea just how critical this information was to overcoming my struggles as an empath especially when it came to my auric boundaries. This was completely foreign to me back in my corporate days, but looking back now I intuitively knew this information in some manner was already held deep inside me. I just needed to remember what I knew— what I believe we all intuitively know somewhere within.

✦

Chapter Four

Our Human Energy Field

Many of us have had the experience where we meet someone for the first time or bump into a stranger and it makes a distinct impression even if few or no words are exchanged. Perhaps we feel somehow drawn to this person like we already know them or want to get to know them or maybe instead we feel repelled or a sense of friction, though we can't pinpoint exactly *why* we feel this way. In these encounters, what we are experiencing is a coming together of two individual human energy fields, each holding its own vibration.

Every human being has a unique vibration or resonance called our *energy field* and when we interact with another human, these fields merge and because of this we all are prone to empath others to some extent. Our human energy field is how life-force energy manifests through our human body and how others subtly experience us in our interactions. From birth we have a baseline resonance that is our unique vibration, but our energy field can also shift as we go about the experience of life. Throughout a typical day we may extend out or shrink down our energy field depending on the events or interactions. It can shift vibrations or frequencies along with our moods, health, or experiences. It is a tool we are constantly using to sense the world around us and navigate life yet most of us do so without awareness. But what creates this field? What is this energy and how is it connected to our bodies? And how is this helpful or harmful with regard to empathy and empathing others?

In my book, *An Energy Healer's Book of Dying*, I often refer to the concept of using psychic energy eyes to describe what I experience at an energetic level when working with dying clients. In the same way, I use my intuitive skills, or psychic energy eyes, each day in my healing room while working with clients who have come to heal and repair areas of their energy system to prevent dis-ease and disease and maintain a healthy flow of energy overall. During these sessions I telepathically and empathically scan their body to locate areas of stress, breakage, blockage, or attachments and cords. The descriptions found on the pages ahead are what I see on a psychic-energy level and also align with what most light-workers or energy healers see in their practice. I believe with learning and practice, these psychic-intuitive skills are available to *all of us* as sentient energy beings.

Source Energy

Across religions, traditions, and belief systems, there is recognition of a universal energy that flows through and interconnects everything throughout our cosmos, our Earth, and our human bodies. It co-creates the details of our day and how we see, experience and understand ourselves and our world. There are different ways humans express the concept of this omnipresent energy. Some call it God. Others call it prana or chi. In my healing practice, I choose to call it Source energy or life-force energy.

One way to look at Source energy is by understanding conscious-ness. Consciousness has been defined as sentient awareness or the ability to experience and feel. But what makes us consciousness beings? From my perspective as an energy practitioner, consciousness is the life-force energy flowing through our bodies. Source energy itself is omnipresence and does not have a container or body. It just "is." Our bodies provide this intelligent life-force energy with a container to live out the human experience.

There are a multitude of containers for Source to embody, for example a body of water, a plant or an animal, a rock or a tree, a star or a planet, each created as a vehicle to give Source energy form to play out its co-creation of consciousness in matter and experiences. Each of us humans have chosen a divine human vehicle as our individual container for experiencing our current life. Not unlike an automobile, you need a vehicle to move through life, gas to run it, and a tank to store the gas. Life-force energy is the gas used to fuel our Source vehicle. When your vehicle is running in top shape, fueled with good gas held in a healthy container or tank, you can fly down the road of life in an easy and synchronistic manner. If you have no gas or a faulty tank, the vehicle begins to break down and will eventually die.

So how does our human-body vehicle work? How do we ensure we keep our vehicle fueled and intact? Life-force energy interacts with our body and keeps it running through essential energy structures called the dimensions of light, the chakra system, the meridians, and the auric fields.

Dimensions of Light

We humans know we're part of the third dimension, but most of us don't stop to ponder what that means. If we remember back to our schooling days, the third dimension offers us the ability to experience the world in three dimensions: length, width, and height, etc. In the third dimension, we use our 3D bodies to experience the world using our basic five senses. Scientists believe there are many dimensions to our universe and beyond. Energy is frequency, and everything in our universe consists of layers of vibrational frequency creating different dimensions or planes of reality. But it is certainly a challenge to wrap our 3D minds around this concept of multidimensions, much less open to the idea that we are born with much more than simply our five senses.

We often think of another dimension as being "out there" or in a different place that is not here. However, all dimensions are right here all the time, but most of the time we only have abilities to experience the third dimension as our reality. Though we may not have the ability to perceive these other dimensions with our five senses, we are constantly surrounded by their frequencies with higher and lower vibrations or densities. A dimension can be seen as a plane of reality, but it is also energy that is intelligence.

There indeed may be hundreds of planes of reality or dimensions of light, like a layer cake of consciousness. Dimensions with lower, denser energetic vibrations (like the third dimension) are towards the bottom of the cake. Dimensions with higher, lighter energetic frequencies are toward the top of the cake. Yet we are each a part of every dimension in all time, place, and space as we experience this unique individual incarnation in our divine human vehicle of Source.

All energy is intelligent, and when you put this intelligent energy into a human body, we experience it as human consciousness with the natural ability to evolve and expand our levels of sentience. Our third dimension is a particular resonance and vibration of the *physical, measurable* universe and yet is an exceedingly small portion of the universal spectrum. There is overlap between dimensions, but as humans we are currently based mostly in the third dimension while other forms of life or containers or vehicles of spirit are based in other levels and sometimes, under the right circumstances, they can interact with our world.

Those who are sensitive or psychic empaths often navigate frequencies lower than 3D and higher than 3D, opening up to additional planes of reality without awareness. This means we pick up or empath frequency vibrations from many different Source vehicles, human and more, outside our own personal containers and take on many different emotions and feelings beyond our own bodies because this energy still exists even if it is not made visible.

In my client work, I continue to see an increase in those who are empathing energies beyond the third dimension even if they may not consider themselves to be full empaths. As higher dimensions of consciousness become more available, we can tap into the frequencies and vibrations of these higher planes. This opens up opportunities of expanding our perspective and awareness to experience more love-based fuel versus the fear-based fuel of the 3D reality we currently exist in.

Again, this is all about perspective and perception. We do not technically go somewhere else when we interact with these other planes of reality or dimensions, we lift a veil into a higher reality realm. The veils between dimensions or planes of reality are thinning and providing access to higher vibrational frequencies and additional planes of existence for us all, but the empath is directly affected. With enough personal mastery, we can indeed change our energy to resonate with different dimensional vibrations in more intentional and healthy ways. But to do that we have to understand how our energy works through our human body and the chakra system.

The Chakra System

Chakra is a Sanskrit word meaning wheel of energy. The system includes seven wheel-like spinning vortexes or energy centers that run down the center of the human body. The chakras are seen as both actual vortexes of

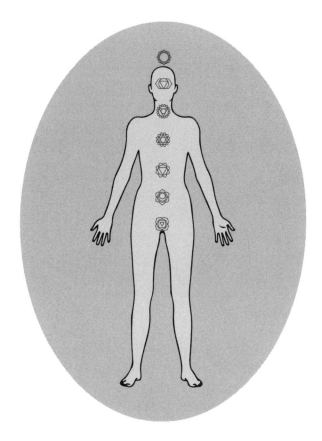

1. The Chakra System

energy as well as metaphors for the way our body, mind, and spirit works in unison.

The job of the chakra system is to push life-force energy throughout the human body and spirit much like how the hose at the station pump is used to insert the gasoline into the car. You can think of the chakras as divine fueling destination points, allowing Source energy to fuel your divine human vehicle or physical, emotional, mental, and spiritual body. They are not anatomical, i.e., not a physical part of your body. Instead, they are incredible energy centers that activate and ignite *in utero* and deactivate during the death process.

Chakras are centers of awareness in the human body. Each chakra aligns with an individual level of consciousness and dimension of light, creating a specific vortex that allows the light-energy to move and shift via intention throughout the body. Because the human body is a vehicle of consciousness itself, the chakras fuel our human organs and our mental and emotional states as well as our spirit. Each chakra has its own job in fueling the body, and when they run at optimum levels the human body is healthy, happy, and balanced. But when any chakra is not being fueled or is out of alignment, the body will be affected on a physical, emotional, mental, or spiritual level.

Any negativity held within the body will cause that vortex, specific to its body parts and organs, to become dense or blocked and the activity of that spinning wheel of energy will slow, sometimes to the point of stopping or reversing or spinning out of control. The energy of negativity can come from anywhere or anything we encounter daily from the fear, anger, judgment from people to spaces and places surrounding us. When a chakra is blocked, that level of consciousness is also blocked and cannot perform its job of creating healthy alignment within the body, ultimately causing energetic imbalance either physically, emotionally, mentally, or spiritually. If this imbalance continues unattended, the dis-connect will eventually co-create dis-ease within the vortex resulting in disease within the body, mind, or spirit. The human body energetically suffers or dies according to the imbalance of the life-force energy. When all seven main chakra centers are communicating equally and working in alliance with each other, you will feel and function at your optimum level.

These chakras break out into three planes: the first three lower chakras comprise what is known as the Physical Plane, the fourth chakra is the Bridge, and the three highest chakras make up the Spiritual Plane. More detailed information on the seven main chakras, as well as identifying chakra imbalances and practices for creating balance, can be found in Appendix 1: "Chakra Balancing Practices."

The Physical Plane

The Physical Plane chakras are the first three chakras in the system and are closest to the ground, holding a magnetic energy designed to anchor the relationship of our divine human vehicle to the earthly awareness of the planetary body. They hold our foundational beliefs, our emotions, our ego, and everything that makes up who we believe we are in this physical form. This plane influences our physical health and wellness through the design of our nerves and the glands of the endocrine and adrenal system. It also holds psychological functions of survival, desire, and will. While all humans use each individual chakra, the empath oftentimes is overextended in this plane and is affected more than the typical person in these areas.

In my client work, I find empaths have the most trouble keeping their 1st or **Root Chakra** in balance and functioning properly because it is affected by their belief system of safety and worth. Unless we do the work to examine our belief systems and choose beliefs that align with our truth, we will continue to remain unfulfilled.

The 2nd or **Sacral Chakra** is also one of the most vulnerable for the empath because it is the feel-center of our emotions and relationships. We have lost the connection with this chakra that was initially designed to allow our divine human vehicle to feel, sense, and emote. Instead, we have become more comfortable thinking versus feeling. Most of us are also programmed as to how to feel depending on that initial root chakra belief system we are running, such as *not in this family, we don't do it that way, you have to, you need to, you should,* and so forth.

The human race as a whole is out of balance in the 3rd or **Solar Plexus Chakra**. We were originally designed to have a mental consciousness that fully embraced the idea we are co-creators with Source. We, however, do not comprehend this concept much less allow ourselves true divine power, so we instead created another power: the mental state of the ego. The ego manipulates the energies of the solar plexus through being a control freak or a victim. The controller wants to continually feel they are in charge and often wants others to see it their way—they tend to make lists for their lists and the mental monkey-mind is always chattering away. The victim is at the opposite end of the spectrum, feeling as if they have no power but in truth are choosing to give their power away. Last in the physical plane, this chakra also is a struggle for the empath because it is driven by the mental chatter that validates actions and behaviors of the do-ing machine.

Overall, the Physical Plane is where we house our belief systems—from primal to learned to programmed. This, in turn, influences our feelings and relationships and plays out through our ego as harmoniously balanced actions, or not. An empath on a spiritual journey of awakening may want to spend some time on this plane of the chakra system to examine how they are or are not aligned to their own personal truths and decide if it is time to shed some thoughts, ideas, and actions.

The Bridge

The Astral Plane is the abstract realm. It is where we experience the dream state and is also known as the Bridge connecting matter of the physical plane with the consciousness of the spiritual plane. It holds the psychological function of unconditional love.

The 4th or **Bridge or Heart Chakra** connects the lower three chakras that comprise the physical consciousness to the top three chakras that hold spiritual consciousness. In this way the Bridge is the astral dimension, an in-between or dream place where we house Source itself within the human form.

This area is the Bridge connection between body, mind, and spirit that will always offer chaos to the human, and especially the empath, because it is in constant flux and affected by everyone and everything in our reality at all times. It houses collective consciousness.

The Spiritual Plane

The Spiritual Plane is composed of the top three chakras on the human body starting with the throat chakra. It holds the psychological functions of communication, intuition, and understanding as well as higher, electric frequencies compared to the dense, magnetic frequencies of the physical plane. In the higher frequencies of the Spiritual Plane, we find our connection to the realms of spiritual beings and higher vibrational bodies of Source energy and enlightenment. Here is where we can access angelics, guides, and benevolent assistance from off-planet races and beyond.

These spiritual chakras allow us to understand our connection to Source and oneness as well as extend our senses beyond the 3D physical world to discover spiritual gifts of intuition. All of us are born with these spiritual energy centers and psychic gifts, yet these abilities are quickly shut down in childhood by the belief systems of parents, religious leaders, teachers, and the larger societal controller programs. We are taught these experiences and gifts are not allowed, accepted, or safe, and as we grow into adulthood, we forget the magical experiences of our youth. However, in my work with thousands of clients, I have witnessed many people rediscovering their intuitive-psychic abilities and opening up their spiritual chakras to live out their full birthright as sentient beings of consciousness, connected to the oneness of Source.

Many empaths have strong spiritual connections, but at the same time, they have either shut down this guidance or disregard its support and assistance due to outside negative influences and messaging. Conversely, some empaths are way too open in these spiritual chakras causing them to disassociate from reality, which creates spiritual depression or a continual longing to escape 3D frequencies. But we cannot live in our daily world while wanting to be out of our 3D body. Instead, we must work to find balance within the planes.

With regard to the first spiritual chakra, the 5th or **Throat Chakra,** the empath will be either overactive in this energy or underactive, and it is always a struggle to find balance here. Evaluating our truths and consciously choosing them for ourselves, this chakra activates a sense of "you," "I" and "we" and opens us up to duality on a higher scale: that you are you, I am I, but we are all a collective we. The struggle occurs when the consciousness fully remembers we are all one, yet the lower chakras still hold the ego-related programming.

The 6th or **Third Eye / Brow Chakra** is often overlooked or on overdrive in the empath, resulting in the body feeling overwhelmed or exhausted by its experiences. This is because they are busy not only manifesting what they do want, but also what they do not want, simply because they are giving it energy.

In the 7th or **Crown Chakra,** we find divine guidance and support. Yet for the overdriven empath that is on go, go, go all day and night, it is difficult to slow down long enough or hard to trust the quiet of spirit to receive these messages.

Together, all seven main chakras form the overall components of our consciousness or energetic aspects occurring within us and around us, comprising our unique, personal fundamental basis for our individual and collective reality.

They are both transmitters and receivers of consciousness energy. The idea of consciousness is so infinite, so abstract, that most humans do not even spend the time to ponder its existence, and yet we can study and experience its manifestations in various ways.

Our unique and individual perceptions of the world we live in and believe in for ourselves and for others are composed from tiny shards or constructions of consciousness formed into matter. This is what we can then match to our physical reality to set the stage for our beliefs, which in turn create how we live out our lives with regard to survival and co-creation. These fuel-centers are vital to our connection to all things and are what offers us oneness.

Meridians

The seven main chakras are basically energy centers that channel life-force, chi or prana both in and out of our physical and spiritual selves and are considered both transmitters and receivers of consciousness energy. They work in a spinning motion to move the dimension of light consciousness throughout the system. The modalities of Chinese Medicine and acupuncture work with what are known as meridian lines to channel and move the life-force, chi, or prana through pathways as a transport system within the human body that circulates the electromagnetic energy or consciousness much like a circulatory system.

Many of the chakras parallel the meridian pathways that flow within and throughout the divine human vehicle, both affecting the subtle energy body. The degree of both chakra and meridian activity in a person's human body directly affects and creates the person's physical, emotional, mental and even spiritual health. We know that when a chakra is blocked or has no spin-movement of life-force it hampers the flow but also affects the ability for the meridian to grab that energy and transport it throughout the body. Balance is maintained when these two systems work in tandem. If there is weakness or blocked energy in any of these vortexes or pathways, illness and imbalance can occur. The energy flow through the meridians determines the vitality levels moving within the human body and when it comes to the empath, many times this energy flow level is depleted and exhausted because of the tendency of overdoing on behalf of self and others.

The Aura or Auric Fields

The final structure in the human energy system, the aura, is our energy tank, which surrounds the body and holds Source energy as auric fields. The aura helps anchor the life-force energy to our physical body by taking the fuel that comes in through the chakras and meridians and stores it in different templates called auric fields or energy bodies. Each person's aura forms a luminous body of energy that surrounds and interpenetrates the physical form with templates of energy that emit their own characteristic radiation. When you say someone has a glow about them, you are picking up on the unique vibration of the light-energy stored in their aura. Auras can be either healthy or weak.

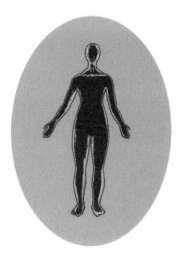

2. Healthy Aura

A healthy aura maintains life-force energy as a strong and defined energetic egg, or oval-shaped bubble that surrounds the body in positive frequency. It works in a love-based energy vibration.

3. Weak Aura

A weak aura releases lifeforce energy because the energetic egg or oval-shaped bubble has rips or tears allowing for numerous leaks and energetic seepage. It works in a fear-based energy vibration.

The aura's energy bodies or fields are not separate but mutually interpenetrate and surround each other in successive layers that suspend around the human body in an oval shape referred to as the auric egg or bubble. Our auric bubble not only holds our Source fuel within the body, it also offers protection to any energies that may not be for our highest and best good.

As a trained empath and intuitive healer, the first thing I do to prepare for each client session is to do a short ground and bubble exercise for my own auric field so that I will not take on or hold the other's energy within my field after the session. This ground and bubble exercise is found in the Appendix of the book.

A good visual is to imagine your aura as the gas tank that holds your individual light or instruction set, which is your chi or prana from Source, your reason for being, and when combined with the chakra gas together is a direct reflection of how you are living.

Each individual light dimension of consciousness that fuels the body through the chakras has its own unique template or energy body within the aura, meaning each type of fuel has its own individualized tank. The first chakra fuels the first energy body of the aura, the second chakra fuels the second energy body of the aura, and so on. As the paired chakras move upward, the partnered aura moves outward.

The physical plane auric fields are made up of three individualized templates that directly correlate to the three physical chakras. These three lower chakras and auric fields move and metabolize Source energy related to the physical world. Any of these physical auric fields, or a combination thereof can take a pretty hard hit for the empath in terms of rips and tears because this is where we not only hold our beliefs but our feelings, emotions, and relationships. And let's not forget the power center that determines the actions of the do-ing machine that drives the 3D life of the empath.

The first auric layer called the **etheric body** stores and templates the root chakra gas associated with the physical functioning of the body. The field extends from one quarter to two inches beyond the physical body and its overall shape mirrors the physical body but is composed of web-like energy lines. It has the same structure as the body including all the anatomical parts and organs. Because this energy template creates the blueprint for the actual physical tissue, having an understanding of our energy field is critical to maintaining health and balance in the actual physical body.

The second layer called the **emotional body** stores and templates the sacral chakra gas associated with the emotional aspects of being human. It extends one to three inches from the body following the same physical outline with a more flowy structure of colored clouds that vary based on specific feelings or emotions.

The third auric layer called the **mental body** stores and templates the solar plexus chakra gas associated with our mental life and linear thinking. This field extends three to eight inches beyond the body and those with psychic sight may sometimes see thoughts, ideas, and even emotions as energy blobs of varying brightness, color, and form within this field.

When practicing energy healing on an overextended empath, there is usually much repair work to be done in the chakras, meridians and auric templates of this person.

Heavy, dense energy will anchor within the fields as blockages, oftentimes in the hips, buttocks, and hip flexors when the person holds old belief systems having to do with learned or programmed parenting messaging. The father/male messaging holds on the right side of the body while the mother/female energy is on the left. Anger blocks will pull the hips back and often manifest further in the sciatica. Additionally, this will show up in the sacral area in much the same manner with the male/female information and will move beyond just parenting messaging into beliefs and emotions associated with relationships and more. In the solar plexus area, I often see the entire esophageal track stuck as the lower portion is affected by the upper planes and throat. While working with my client's energy to clear these blockages, I also look for energy cords and tentacles that intertwine and attach themselves to and from chakras and other energy points within the body and outside of it as well, which often makes a break or tear in the auric field.

The unaware or uneducated empath will be susceptible to any and all layers and levels of consciousness because they have such open hearts and believe they are here to help everyone and everything. This will show up in healings as heavy dense shields that overlay on both the front and back of the mid-body as well as cords and tentacles that twist and wind throughout the body and break through the aura.

The Empath Needs Diligence
Especially When It Comes to the Aura

As we learned earlier, each layer of our auric field directly aligns with an individual chakra and level of consciousness that allows the light-energy to move and shift through intention within and beyond our body. Just like the chakras, we can lose power and create dis-ease and disease if the aura is weak or torn, and this is how the empath experiences what is called a transference of energy. While the consciousness-vehicle and the chakra-gas are critical to our existence, the aura or fuel tank is the most important piece of the overall system when it comes to the empath. This personal boundary is what is affected when energy transference occurs or is violated when the empath is psychically attacked by another attempting to vampire their energy.

Almost every client energy session requires some semblance of energetic auric repair. Most of us are not taught that we have an energetic aura, much less understand that *it is us who is responsible for keeping this auric template or energy tank intact.* Our auric fields can be breached, torn or depleted in so many ways and for such varied reasons, all dependent on the individual and their experiences. Additionally, our aura is in constant flux, ever-changing, and susceptible to everything it comes in contact with here and beyond. Much like the chakras, the colors of the aura may become muddied when there are misaligned thoughts and feelings causing the aura to shift and hold the imbalanced energies. These diseased colors will infuse into the healthy colors causing streaks, smears and tears within the auric fields.

There are many different ways our auras can hold the energy that surrounds our physical body and beyond. A healthy aura is usually an egg-like shape; however this shape becomes altered with imbalances in energy. An altered egg shape will indicate distinct natures of how the corded or projected energy is working beyond the person and between people, place, and things. Some of these shapes can include:

- **Porcupine Quills:** Individual sharp quill-like energies that will lash out at others fields; often indicates a controller.
- **Hooks and Tentacles:** Individual cords that grab at another or entwine themselves into others anchoring into their field; often indicates a manipulator.

- **Arrows, Verbal/Mental/Emotional:** Much like the cords above, but more seen as icicle or body-projected arrows of energy moving outward attacking others; often indicates a controller/manipulator.
- **Rips and Tears:** There will be actual rips or tears in the egg shape where there basically is no template remaining in specific spots; often indicates abuse, stress, and depression.
- **Withdrawn:** This aura projects a sensation of the field folding into itself and actually withdrawing from that which surrounds it; often indicates a combination of the above highlighting abuse or lack of self-worth.
- **Outside of Self:** This is when the divine human vehicle is offset from the auric field bubble almost standing alongside it. I often see this happen as the result of a significant physical jolt, like an accident or a concussion, but I have also seen it in some clients with extreme abuse or a difficult birth process where they never really entered and anchored into their own field fully when born.

Many times I see a combination of the above mentioned imbalances in the aura, and in some cases the auric fields will also be imbalanced overall in size and shape, such as be bigger on the top and smaller on the bottom. Other times auras will show a left to right imbalance depending on what my client's consciousness container is dealing with in terms of dis-ease and dysfunction. When energetically clearing and repairing the aura, separate or concurrent work will have to be done in different templates in order to reclaim an overall balance. Remember, each auric template has its own individual tank holding the corresponding energies brought in by the individual chakra.

An imbalanced aura makes the empath susceptible to energy transference or outside energies that sneak into our own personal container through rips, tears, and wobbles within our auric fields. Because the sensitive empath does not maintain personal boundaries, their energy field becomes strained and weakened, which allows their energies to be robbed, taken, or pushed upon by controller energies seeking fuel. Understanding how energy is transferred and where we pick up and exchange energies can help build our sentient awareness and put us in observer mode to be able to better identify and protect our energetic boundaries.

The concept of chakras, meridians, and auric fields may be a lot to take in if this is new information for you, and that's okay. That's why I offer the technical details in the Appendix to allow you to return to and re-read the information over time as you continue to release old thought patterns and experience life in new ways as an energetic being. Also in the Appendix under Meditations, there is a full Body Scan exercise that can assist you in getting better acquainted with your body, chakras, meridians, and fields. I chose to go into this level of detail because I often find in my practice that lines of energy intertwine from plane to plane and chakra to meridian, because the client's belief system affects the ideas in the mental field, which in turn affect the emotions and feelings, which then affect the spirit and finally the physical body. In other words: *It's all connected.* Everything is interconnected and energies also reach well beyond our auric egg to outside people, places, memories, and even lifetimes, all of which we will discuss in detail as we journey into Part Two.

Client Story
The Ghost That Would Not Leave

I was hired by a woman who was referred to me because she had a home she was trying to sell. It was a gorgeous turn of the century house located in a great area of town, priced right, yet it had been on the market for over three years with no movement. The woman who was selling the house actually lived a couple of houses down the same block. She and her husband had purchased the home some years back with the idea of upgrading for themselves, but during the remodel, their relationship took a turn for the worse and they were now in the middle of a divorce. Hence the reason for the sale of the home. This beautiful early century home retained all the old charm, while the updates offered all the newest perks, including a wall of windows presenting a spectacular river view that should have been a top selling point. She and the sales agent were astounded that anyone touring the home rarely made mention of the remodeled kitchen or its stunning view.

The moment I entered the home, I was well aware that there was a ghost of a woman who had once lived there. She was miserable and wanted everyone else who entered the site to be miserable along with her. My client is a sensitive empath and had spent a good amount of time in the house during the remodel. As we chatted, it became clear she experienced a pretty drastic personality change during the past year that ultimately affected her relationship with her husband. She was open to the idea of ghost energy, and so I began to describe the personality of the spirit entity that was trapped within the walls of this home. Much to my client's surprise, she said I could be describing her. I explained how the ghost's husband had left her alone for months at a time as he worked on the river boats below, all while she would stand by the tiny kitchen window and wait hours upon hours to no avail, as her resentment and sadness grew. The original home had just one river view window, while the remodel presented an entirely glorious open design of multiple windows that spanned across the entire room. The ghost energy manipulated the hologram of the room to prohibit anyone from enjoying the view that she did not want to see. Even though there was an entire wall of beautiful new windows, energetically it was an angry prison with no view. It was a fascinating concept—one I had never encountered prior in clearing any home or space.

Over the year of the remodel, my client had empathed much of this ghost's angry personality traits—including a disillusioned relationship—due to the energies that had merged fields leaving my client with the sadness, depression; ultimately affecting her and her marriage.

After I cleared the home, land, and the people and the spirit energies attached to it, the house sold within days. We never know what a building, space, or land may hold, or what a ghost entity has the energetic power to control—and this situation certainly proved that.

When dealing with energies, normal or paranormal, it is important for the empath to learn how to protect themselves by commanding and maintaining clear and strong auric boundaries, and cutting all cords and tentacles, not just because of potentially dangerous or harmful energies, but to also keep their auric gas tank in good shape so that they can maintain their personal fuel and work in love versus fear.

PART TWO

Building Sentient Awareness

✦

Chapter Five

Energy Transference

I have a long-time family friend who continually struggles with not only physical pain but also emotional and mental pain. He grew up with a mother fighting cancer and within his family structure was the one responsible for assisting her in taking her medications and providing care. Accepting the role of the caregiver at such a young age created a belief that taking care of the pain for a sick and dying loved one showed and validated love. He lost his mother when he was still young, and this belief pattern continued to be supported into adulthood as his subconscious mind equated sickness = love. The sicker his body got from years of his personal struggle with his own health issues, the more energy, attention, and love he craved from those around him.

Our beliefs will ultimately provide the precedent for how we choose to navigate life. For my friend, his childhood experiences created a need to take energy from others, around the idea of being sick in order to fill that love and support void and this still validates the way he continues to live his life today, not fully connecting the old belief to his own ongoing health challenges. We all get to choose how we live. Some choose actions of worry and heightened concern as validation of love. This may also pass along the same or similar belief pattern of sickness = love from parent to child to grandchild and so on affecting family lineage. Codependent patterns of energy transference will take on a life of their own and can energetically affect everyone involved.

As humans, we are always transferring energy. Thoughts, feelings, and emotions that initially stem from our beliefs are basically blobs of energy that move to and from people through our relationships and everyday encounters. Energy can also be transferred from not only us humans but also places, things, and energy beings from beyond this dimension. Just like energy itself is neither good nor bad, transference of energy can be healthy or not. It can work in either love fuel or fear fuel. From the perspective of an energy practitioner, negatively fueled transference is the result of an imbalance or misalignment of your true self and is not necessarily driven by a negative intention or conscious agenda.

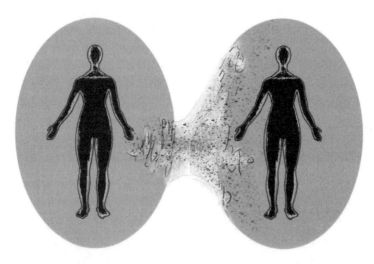

4. Energy Transference Aura

Energy transference is a stealing or robbing of another's life-force energy as two weak auras interpenetrate, allowing for additional rips, tears, and energy leakage to both fields. It works in a lose-lose fear-based energy vibration.

The energy field of our thoughts, feelings and emotions will not only affect our personal field but those people and things we come in contact with either in a positive or negative way. Our thought forms hold as stationary energy within our auric container until we are somehow triggered to release the thought or intention, which happens either by internal or external experiences or messaging we encounter throughout any minute in our day. Once triggered, these forms then begin to take on movement within the auric bubble or egg. They gain additional movement and energy through our actions and habits as well as external physical, emotional or mental validation we receive for that action or habit.

Additionally, our thoughts gain energy from what is known as the Law of Attraction. Through the Law of Attraction, like-minded energy frequencies and vibrations existing outside of our bubble or egg are drawn in or attracted to our vibrations from people, places, things, and beings. In other words, like finds like. In a way, the unbalanced field is searching out energy vibration and frequencies to assist in either balancing itself in a positive way or reaffirming it in a negative way, such as validating a fear-based narrative or belief structure that was initially triggered deep within the person's mind and body matrix. What I am saying here is that our body intuitively connects with everyone and everything around us and is continually rebalancing and refueling with outside energies that can either assist to refuel us in love to live out our truths or refuel us in fear to revalidate negative beliefs about ourselves.

The empath to some extent is always searching for ways to refuel their imbalanced belief systems by entering, transforming, and transferring energy from others' fuel tanks. Empathing happens by mirroring the neurons in the brain of the other person or the information within a holographic space and forms an exchange that allows us to fully take on the state of the other in reaction to a situation. When we fully take on another's energy and vibrational frequency, it then becomes our own and it manifests within our own personal divine human vehicle or container as well as the narrative running throughout our emotional and mental auric fields. While most empaths engage in this exchange without cognitive awareness it is important to note there are some empaths who are very well aware of the concept of transferring energy by use of control and victim tactics.

The actual energy exchange or transfer occurs when energy crosses the auric boundary and influences the fields of another. The energy of one aura breaks through the auric egg or bubble of another person, place or thing's aura wherein the energy flow or exchange is made possible. You can visualize it as two bubbles that were originally separate, then merged or overlapped, and then interpenetrated. In these situations, energy is actually exchanged or transferred between the two through the rips or tears in each bubble, thus increasing the energy content of one system while decreasing the energy content of the other system much like a syphoning effect between the two systems.

Energy comes in many forms and can be transferred from one thing to another as physical, emotional, mental, or spiritual energy and again, this exchange can be made between people as well as places or things. In some cases, the energy fields may briefly intertwine unintentionally, passing through each other and may be picking up subtly on another's vibrations, feelings, or physical aches. This could be as simple as standing near someone waiting in line and you feel a sense of tiredness, overwhelm, or change in mood that seemed to come from nowhere. In other scenarios, the energy transference is more manipulative or intentional even if those participating in the exchange are not aware of how they are using their energy fields and can be visualized more as little tentacles, hooks, or cords moving into and between the two bubbles.

I have found those who are highly empathic usually lack awareness about their personal boundaries and knowledge about their energy field which usually has rips and tears, therefore they have trouble being or staying grounded and are often fatigued or physically ill. Due to this lack of awareness, empaths tend to embody the energy of whatever is around them, much like a dry sponge takes up water. If empaths are around peace and love, their bodies assimilate these and flourish but if they are around negativity, it often feels assaultive and exhausting. And when empaths absorb the impact of stressful emotions, it can trigger panic attacks, depression, food, sex and drug binges, and a plethora of physical symptoms.

When an empath adopts the posture of another, actually feeling as another does along with taking on the distress of their suffering, it becomes dangerous to the energetic field and can begin to take a toll on the human body. However, this situation can often be confusing to the empath because of the sensations they are feeling by refueling. Because the initial taking of energy offers an immediate kind of supercharged jolt, it can be interpreted as a high or a buzz. But if it ultimately is not a match, is negative or taken through a conditional exchange, the empath will soon take a rebounding dive back to a lower frequency and depressive feeling. If the empath does not have or does not choose to use discernment and ignores the roller coaster ride of the energy transference, that individual's human brain will step in and begin to listen to the empathed narrative and will indeed find a way to attach to and then own the newfound pain or angst.

For example, if I step into an energetic field of sadness from a person or a place and did not discern it, I will find something in my life to be sad about by the end of the day as my body and mind search to bridge conflicting frequencies and information. If I took on another's fear of failure or lack of money, I would find a way to project that into my own 3D life by worrying about my job or not trusting my partner, ultimately validating the unfounded pain or angst. This creates a complex jumble of mental patterns that quickly make it hard to discern what is mine and what is true, and we begin to act on beliefs even though they are based on energy that is not ours. Unfortunately, human beings do this constantly because we are ignorant of how we empath our surroundings, but there are signs that can assist us to determine if we are an empath.

One of my goals in sharing this material is to shed light on the connection between beliefs and illness including our psychological struggles of anxiety, depression, and exhaustion. We disengage from our truths, our feelings, and our individual emotions by blocking or not trusting our own personal energy flow and its connection to our truths and to Source. This creates stagnated pools or blocks of energy including rips, tears, and breaks in our fields, which when held there long enough lead to dis-ease and eventually disease in our body, mind, and spirit. Negative energy transference is not a fix, it is much like drinking an energy drink wherein the body gets a temporary feeling of limited euphoric balance only to rebound deeper into imbalance, thus creating the rollercoaster ride of sickness and disease. And any auric bubble that has no clear, protected boundary is akin to an actual vehicle's gas tank in an old and rusted state, leaving the gasoline held within to leak out onto the ground, prohibiting movement for the car, breaking down its parts and polluting its surroundings.

Learning how to find, anchor, and protect the energetic balance of not just your vehicle but also its auric fuel tank allows the nervous system and body to find states of total relaxation, inner stillness, and that space of no stress or tension where the body is able to be comfortable, let go, and relax. This is key for health and wellness. This is why it is vital for empaths to be self-aware so that they can check in and ask: *Is this thought mine? Is this emotion or feeling mine? Is this fuel mine? Is this coming from inside of me or from outside sources?*

Energetic Cords

Beyond transferring energy through encountering one another's auric fields, we can also transfer energy through energetic cords or attachments. Much like an umbilical cord, energy cords can maintain a strong feeling or imprint between two or more people that can connect and bind us for prolonged periods of time, sometimes in between incarnations and timelines and can be either fear-based or love-based in nature. An unhealthy energetic cord is an actual linking of unresolved or imbalanced physical, emotional, mental, spiritual or karmic energy anchored within the astral and etheric (spiritual) bodies, which allow for a line of energy to tether between two or more people which can influence behavior and emotion in a variety of ways until we let go of or remove that energetic cord.

Etheric or energy cords commonly form because of connections between people, places, timelines and objects, especially when the interaction is deeply sensitive in nature. The experience of having an energetic cord connected to your field may play out as repeated or addictive emotions, an inability to positively move forward in your life or as an internal mantra repeating a message inside your mind (consciously or subconsciously), thus influencing your behavior.

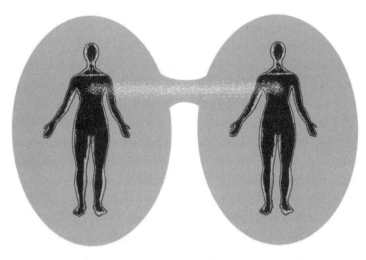

5. Energy Cord Aura

Strands of energy can cord or stretch between one individual's life-force field attaching itself to another, connecting people, places or things. Cords can be either positive or negative, working to enhance with love-based vibration or deplete with fear-based vibration.

An intuitive or psychic healer will clairvoyantly "see" these cords as long stringy thread-like cables or even ropes that attach from one entity or place to another. Remember, energy cords can run on fear-based fuel or on love-based fuel. Love-based cords resonate in a brilliant light and spread out in a feather-like way and become what is known as omnipresent love, offering unconditional energy to whomever or whatever is affected by the interchange. This is a beautiful, healthy expression of energy and needs no outside validation in any manner. Then there are unhealthy energy cords, which look and feel heavy and dense and can be seen as twisted and contorted, often tentacle-like. When cord attachments remain between people, they can become a conduit for draining energy with the dominant, vampiric person energetically sucking fuel from the other to fill his or her own tank in a repeat pattern. These cords can additionally transmit messages, sending or receiving pain, guilt, fear, and any number of thoughts and feelings that may result in actual physical or emotional symptoms if left unattended.

Cords can hold suffering experienced during different timelines playing out past, present or even future trauma from various scenarios in one's life which will fracture your energy to split off and be depleted into the source-event in the distressed timeline. I've witnessed much in the way of illness and imbalance caused from depleted energy resources due to cords draining energy from a client's etheric body and auric field, depleting the area of chi, and leading to dis-ease or disease. Lacking awareness of our personal boundaries is part of the issue. We give away pieces of ourselves energetically due to fear, guilt, conditional love and allow our personal power to be drained when we conform to another's expectations of us without allowing acceptance for who we are as an authentic being.

I have dealt with massive amounts of energy cords throughout my years as an intuitive energy practitioner, and it is clear to me that emotional conflicts left unresolved from the past will create a direct energy response in the organs, tissues, and areas of the body where the trauma is projected and stored eventually resulting in dis-ease and disease. The etheric or energy cord will anchor the trauma or suffering as a goopy clump of negative energy, sometimes held by numerous cords entangled throughout the client's body representing the original origin of the trauma. Sometimes these cords look much like a piece of licorice, a twisted rope or even an octopus with tentacles, sourced from various events or timelines that interpenetrate and weave sub-cords through the human body. Timeline and childhood trauma healing is so important because as adults we are still bound by these cords and our soul continues to fight off the pain of the experience as it shuts down various energy functions over the years that eventually develop into psycho-spiritual wounds later in adult life. Past trauma in life can be dealt with in many different ways but sometimes you don't have to go back and deal with each childhood issue, because whether you are consciously aware of it or not those childhood issues produced a vibration within you that you are still offering or giving attention to today. This stuck energy is actually what still produces the issues today— in current time. By shifting your vibration, or your point of attention and attraction, it can be a lot easier when you're dealing with today's issues, than trying to deal with childhood issues. It's the same vibration. The stuck vibration that was creating childhood issues, is now creating today's issues. Deal with it in the present time by determining which thought, feeling, idea, feels better. If these deep wounds are left unresolved and the cords are intact, the physical body starts to create further imbalance, dis-ease, and disease.

Sensual or sexual relationships that have been severed or ended poorly can result in strong energetic bonds held in any of the auric fields— emotional, mental, and spiritual—and even physical depending on the intensity and depth of the connection between the two people. This can also include past-life relationships, sexual or not, as cords traverse time-lines and know no boundary of the present time, still seeking ways to release karmic debt. As noted above, dealing with past trauma in the present can be effective because on some level there really is no time, so determine what feels best right now. When working with my clients I look for these energetic cords and tentacles in the etheric field first, knowing that the next step for imbalance will manifest in the physical body or in the emotional and mental fields.

Cords can also be formed when we allow personal power to be drained during the inner fight to conform to another's expectations of us, and this is why it is critical we become self-aware in our behaviors when driven by the belief of doing for others. If we lack awareness of our own personal boundaries, we will be easily corded and drained by an assortment of potential vampiric people and parasitic situations. A simple hand gesture of a chopping motion is a tactic I offer my clients to assist them in self-care to release energy cords. All it takes is a swift chop-motion across any part of your body where you feel the energy connection pulling to, or from outside of yourself, along with the intention of full release. It is the intention and awareness that is key. The chopping motion simply creates a tangible action of release to connect to our intention.

Because I myself am an empath, I have diligently trained my own divine human vehicle and physical container over the years to cut cords and hold strong clean boundaries. Because it is now so second nature, I sometimes find my hands automatically kicking into this chop-motion all on their own any time I sense my energy field is at risk or in jeopardy. To onlookers, I am sure this can appear somewhat funny like when I'm out shopping at a big-box retail store. When I stand in the checkout line my hands will automatically begin to swipe and chop to release anything that does not serve me so that I do not take it home. This can include things like fluorescent lights complete with the buzz sound that emanates from them, unsolicited and unwarranted judgment of others that erupts through my ego, like when I see a woman with an unruly screaming child or the overall abundance of product housed within this style of store. While I wait to pay, my hands will automatically be chopping around my entire body, head, torso, throat and more. I even caught my daughter once doing this chopping motion in line while I was doing my own chopping down at the checkout. When I pointed it out we both laughed hysterically much to the confusion of the clerk. Such a proud parenting moment!

Another version or cord-cutting routine is simply getting fresh air. I consciously use this any time I leave a hospice visit where not only the client is dying but the facility is also heavy with fear and sorrow—when I get to my car, I open all of the windows (no matter the weather) as I drive away to allow the brisk air to run throughout my vehicle for several blocks along with the intention of release and letting go. There are no rules to any of this, it is all about personal intention and choice.

As I mentioned earlier, energetic cords can also come through the energy of thought, words, and messages. So part of our awareness is not only sensing the space around us or the person nearby, but also assessing the vibrations through the stories and messages we hear. I remember attending a class presentation where the speaker was talking about someone who did paranormal work, and to me this individual being described felt unethical and held dark entity attachments—even though this person was not in the room. As the speaker continued to talk about this person, I felt the room's energy change and once again, unbeknownst to me, my hands were fervently chopping not only around my own personal field but around and throughout the room overall. It took my friend standing next to me to point it out because it is so automated, I was not even aware I was doing it.

Years ago, before I was fully aware, I had an extremely negative encounter with a powerful psychic vampire who had the ability to cord and manipulate energies remotely across the country. I was initially introduced to this gal through a mutual friend. We decided to personally meet up to discuss a potential collaborative project, but after spending time together it became clear she did not hold the same level of integrity that I look for in a business partner. I turned down the offer and walked away from the project, which highly angered this woman because without me the project would not move forward. Upon leaving she offered me an odd-feeling hug, wished me well, and I thought that was the end of it. Little did I know the level of psychic power this woman had, and I had innocently allowed her into my personal bubble through that odd-feeling hug.

It took me a couple of days to realize she had the ability to manipulate not only my surroundings but also my fields from a long distance. What the intrusive energy felt like was almost spooky, like a creeping-in sensation that would come out of nowhere much like dark magic energy you see in a scary movie as it penetrates and crawls as a moving blob of darkness across the floor. Sometimes the energies felt like a thick ooze or an impending doom gaining in momentum, moving through my home like clouds of intelligent dust. Because I was new to this kind of manipulative energy it took me a while to figure out what was happening to me, and I admit it was scary at the time. The energy could literally take my breath away. Sometimes it felt as if there was an energetic hand coming out of nowhere to choke me or twist around my neck and shoulders. Other times her vampire tactics would impede my mental mind, interrupting my day and often my sleep state, playing with me until I thought I was crazy. It took a lot of personal will and strength to stand up to this kind of vampire abuse, but I was determined to build stronger boundaries, ultimately commanding my sovereignty and freedom. Cutting and banishing her cords took several weeks, but I am fortunate to have had that experience to learn that I am in charge of my space, my mind, my body, and soul—and know fully there is no one or no thing that can hijack me, not even a powerful witch.

It is important to know when severing these energy cords or karmic debts that one of the most potent frequencies for releasing cords is love-based forgiveness. So, in addition to the chopping air techniques, I encourage clients to add the intention of forgiveness if they feel it may apply to the situation. True forgiveness can actually dissolve all of the karmic buildup, karmic cording, and karmic debt into the greater understanding of our soul lesson, accepting what has been offered and learned. That is what ultimately released me from the witch cords for good—when I found compassion and forgiveness for her. I did not condone her behavior, nor did I have to like her in any way, I just let her go because, remember, you do not have to ever accept a horrific act or the person who did it—what you are forgiving is the energy you personally carry or attach to through the energy-leaking cord. You release yourself from the scenario, person, or emotion. Any additional forgiveness steps are a personal choice. And in terms of choice, we also get to choose our awareness of these energetic cords and weaknesses in our aura. As empaths, if we are instead consumed with energy leaks and lost fuel from energetic cords, we can escalate into extreme levels of anxiety and long-term depression, and we become even more vulnerable to hitchhikers or attachment energies.

Attachments or Hitchhikers

Attachments to our energy field and hitchhikers are a different matter than corded energy and they often have to do with encountering what are commonly called ghosts or spirit entities that have not found their way to the light following their death. They can become attached to and then basically hitchhike onto earthly energies—people, places or things. For a number of reasons, they choose to reside where they should not, within our physical spaces and our human energy fields rather than progressing spiritually back to Source energy or their higher consciousness.

The uninvited or unwanted hitchhiker's energy is drawn to the empath's field by way of the person's weak aura, extreme emotional stress, and trying circumstances such as abuse, surgery, or illness. Alcohol or drug use or simply being ignorant to one's auric field or empathic sensitivity can also draw in unwanted hitchhiker attachments. The empath may consciously sense an attachment or encounter with a lower density spirit presence, often experienced as a sudden change in mood or physical symptoms, such as feeling angry, tired, depleted or just not yourself. Additional symptoms of being influenced by an energy hitchhiker can include:

- feelings of being blocked;
- unexplainable or extreme anger, fears, sadness, depression, guilt, or extreme anxiety;
- recurring dreams or nightmares;
- sudden relationship problems;
- unexplainable physical symptoms, eating disorders, sudden onset of cravings, addictions, alcohol, drugs, sex, or smoking.

From a perspective of energy and the auric field, the hitchhiker energy is its own field existing without physical, 3D form. To continue to fuel without a container, the hitchhiker literally jumps into the field of a physical being to refuel. When I see a client's aura carrying an attachment, it looks much like a person giving another a piggyback ride. It jumps on, hangs on and gets really heavy after a while, and yet there is not always an easy way to simply shake off the traveler hitchhiker or attachment. One can use the same techniques of cord cutting to assist but if a hitchhiker's energy persists it can become extremely dangerous and cause additional problems. If the hitchhiker has ailments or addictions or tendencies, the person carrying the unwanted visitor can merge and blend with this outside energy so intensely that they themselves can actually take on the attributes in a negative way. For example, you may find yourself having the urge to smoke when you never smoked before just because your hitchhiker was a heavy smoker.

Unseen spirit energy is everywhere, therefore, there is no specific place one runs into hitchhiker energy. Most of the time this style of energy attachment is short-term and fades away or falls off, sometimes within hours, sometimes within days or weeks. Usually these beings and their energy attachments just disappear on their own, but if the energy lingers and is affecting the person's life, more advanced assistance is highly suggested to remove the hitchhiker. If you find yourself with a lingering energetic passenger that is affecting you negatively, you might consider reaching out to a professional energy worker to assist sooner rather than later.

Energy Vampires

Energy vampires can be anywhere and anyone. They can be your spouse or your best friend. They can be your co-worker or your neighbor. They can be next to you at the grocery store or engaged in conversation with you at a party. Many of us encounter energy vampires on a daily basis, and we may even be one ourselves. But not everyone is consciously aware that they are doing it.

An energy vampire is a person who purposefully increases their own personal energy field by syphoning another's life-force, chi, or prana, leaving the target exhausted or drained. Often the energy vampire lacks self-love and confidence, therefore they seek out another to energetically manipulate and get their egoic needs met. In these situations, the vampire appears to suddenly be reenergized physically, emotionally, and mentally as a result of the connection to or conversation with the person they seek out, all while the person being attacked ends up feeling excessively drained, tired, or overwhelmed.

Some energy vampires are emotional vampires who intentionally feed off others, fully aware they are draining positive energy or happiness from their target. They move through life as an empty vessel in search of other's fuel, never feeling satisfied or complete. They commonly appear as a controller, victimizer, or someone who thrives on drama. Emotional vampires are experts at using mental manipulation tactics to make others feel lesser, with an ultimate goal of eroding another's self-worth for their own gain. This level of controlling always uses a form of manipulation to maintain their energetic attachments and cords to others. The energy vampire uses these energetic attachments to get things they want for themselves because they simply are not willing to do their own work to change negative habits, improve self-esteem, and eliminate parasitic behaviors. In these situations, manipulation often appears as condescending, critical, or belittling behavior as tactics to make a generally content person feel intimidated or unsafe.

At their core, the energy vampire engages in these behaviors because they feel unsafe and insecure themselves. Through dehumanizing criticisms and bully tactics, they take control of the energy of the situation by also keeping their prey in a state of insecurity. True controllers often create such uncomfortable energy that people involved feel as if they must walk on eggshells or are living with an undetonated time bomb just waiting to blow at any moment the vampire is set off. These situations inherently progress into imbalanced exchanges of codependent behavior and many times the parties involved become addicted to the transference patterns because the vampire is used to easily getting their fill and the target is fulfilling their own personal narrative of non-self-worth through the dance of co-performance or abuse.

Most of the time, these are not mutually beneficial relationships, but are one-sided, bloodsucking drains. Yet to outsiders, and sometimes even to the victim involved, these relationships can be perceived as friendly as long as the target continues to acquiesce to the control of the vampire. If either party places an unexpected boundary cutting off the energetic attachment, oftentimes one party will play out their unfulfilled exchange as an emotional tantrum which will only continue the game of controller/victim programming. Ultimately this is a form of dominance and control and learning how to identify and respond to this toxic behavior using self-love tactics will help preserve your energy and protect you from a great deal of long-term mental distress and potential physical harm.

Other energy vampires are emotional parasites who are not necessarily working intentionally in a controller/victim role but are subconsciously feeding their energy needs. In these energy exchanges, the vampire drains others through energetic attachments masked and packaged as worrying about another or showing compassion for a person's plight. This often plays out in a caregiver role of taking on another's life tasks and responsibilities but can also end up being just as much of a codependent situation as the intentional vampire.

It can be challenging to break energetic cords with energy vampires because they do not shoulder accountability and are often charismatic martyrs who have honed the skill of charming their way out of problems. In this way, they rely on guilt trips combined with giving ultimatums as an effective way to get what they want, and they often use your own good nature to drain you of your vitality. They know capturing and coercing others through shame is a great weapon against people who are compassionate and caring. Ultimately, they thrive on chaos and drama and will always do their best to one-up you and your situation and if all else fails will create a dramatic event as a last resort to syphon energy and feed their emotional demands.

Some of the most challenging cords to break are from energy vampires who use ongoing manipulation techniques to confuse others into thinking they owe the vampire or that it is the victim who is on the wrong side of the energy exchange. This is known as gaslighting, which is a specific type of abuse where the manipulator is trying to get the victim to question their own reality, memory, or perceptions. The outcome of a gaslighting energetic attack can include:

- no longer feeling like the person you used to be;
- being more anxious and less confident than you used to be;
- often wondering if you are being too sensitive;
- feeling like everything you do is wrong;
- always thinking it is your fault when things go wrong;
- apologizing often;
- having a sense that something is wrong but being unable to identify what it is;
- often questioning whether your response to your partner is appropriate (e.g., wondering if you were too unreasonable or not loving enough);
- making excuses for your partner's behavior;
- avoiding giving information to friends or family members to avoid confrontation about your partner;
- feeling isolated from friends and family;
- finding it increasingly hard to make decisions;
- feeling hopeless and taking little or no pleasure in activities you used to enjoy.

Even if you do not find yourself a victim of gaslighting, all vampiring is abusive—period. Evaluating where we may have vulnerable relationships and setting healthy boundaries generates mutually beneficial exchanges with other people. Although the concept sounds easy, it is likely you will need to change your energy patterns and behaviors to avoid and cut out toxic people, places, and exchanges. Remember, you will never change the energy vampire. You can only change yourself by adjusting your boundaries, being aware of your energy fields, and guarding your emotional capacity at all times. For some, the bottom line may be to cut the vampire out of their life completely.

While there are indeed the toxic negative energy vampires, there are also those who are not aware their actions are malicious, and I admit I was one of them. I previously told my childhood story of watching my father lose his funeral home business. I shared how I remember standing in the kitchen watching men I did not know take things from our home, crushing my sense of safety. This experience launched me into becoming a human do-ing machine to prove my worth to the world by my controlled successes. Throughout my adult life, I searched continually to be validated by others for my help, my advice, and my actions. I was completely ignorant to the idea that I was seeking validation for safety and worth and had no idea there was an imbalance of energy exchange happening. I just thought I was becoming a successful adult. And amazingly, to the outside world, it looked as if it was working. But underneath the surface, I was doing for others to feed my own insecurity, taking their energy in the process. I became tired and resentful to everyone and everything. Yet I would not ask for help because that would mean I was weak and not enough. Plus, I could do any task faster and better myself anyhow! I was not a mean and vicious vampire. I was not consciously aware I was actually sucking them dry to refuel myself because it was all masked as a productive, successful human. But a true energy vampire does not always present an evil face, and instead we are seen as simply overwhelmed and overscheduled.

I allowed this behavior to go on for years which progressed into additional vampiric behaviors because I knew no other way to behave. I controlled my household. My yard. My family. My employees. My friends. Even strangers. I commanded a sense of safety through my actions and had no idea I was such a control freak—I just thought I was organized. And to the outside world, it seemed as much.

No one teaches us to go inward. To find our value in the quiet spaces of our heart and soul. No one encourages us to find or much less validate our own sense of self-worth. I didn't believe I was actually enough unless I was busy. But pursuing the constant busy-ness left me exhausted, angry, and fear-filled. I feared I was not enough and believed there was not enough of me until I finally crashed. All of us will crash in some form or another until we figure this stuff out, and why is that? Because it is all about the *energy,* the energy that is everywhere and in everything.

Now it's time to hone in on just how the empath actually takes on the energy of other people, places, and things. Each empath, especially if they are a sensitive or psychic-sensitive, takes on the energies in a different manner. The following chapters will go into detail of the mechanics of how energy transfers, further revealing what the empath might encounter along the way.

Chapter Six

Physical and Emotional Empathing

When I teach energy classes, I often share a story of a mundane fast-food drive-through experience I had years ago while on my way to get my computer fixed. Like many days, I was out running errands and decided to pull into a drive-through to grab a bite to eat on the fly. After placing my order, I eased up to the window and came face-to-face with the young man who was serving my order. When taking money and delivering my food, he was disengaged and somewhat flippant. During the transaction, I did my best to engage, but he was not having it and I drove away feeling deflated by the exchange. When I checked my bag at a stoplight, I discovered he had not given me the sauce I had asked for, which quickly switched my feelings of deflation to anger.

As I drove on, I hit every red light possible only to scream in a road-rage style out my window to anyone thwarting my path. My irritation grew as I made my way into the computer store where I found myself verbally tearing down the young man who was doing his best to assist me with my computer struggles, until the light bulb went on in my head and I apologized.

After sharing this story, I typically ask my class "So what really happened here?"

First, it's clear I chose to take the energy from the young man at the drive-through, which then began a domino effect that played out all the way through my appointment at the computer store. But what is more hidden in the scenario is why I chose to take on his energy in the first place. If we remember back to the discussion of beliefs in Part Two, his flippant attitude toward me triggered a buried *belief* within me that I was not worth respecting enough for someone to engage in conversation during a simple transaction. This belief was then reinforced again when I opened the bag and realized I was not worthy of receiving my full order—that he didn't listen to my request, much less give me what I asked for. Silly, right? Well not so much, because we all bury triggers within our emotional field that play out constantly in similar scenarios.

For me, this moment unknowingly ignited a buried subconscious narrative that ran through my personal matrix to reveal a deeply hidden old belief that I did not deserve respect and that I could not be heard. Now, in my conscious mind of course I felt like I deserve respect, and believed I was just ticked off, but the truth is most of us run deeply hidden programming with messages that we are not good enough and we house this messaging somewhere within our body and cell structure. That day my subconscious found that shard of the disrespect and not-heard program without me even knowing it happened. Instead of using the skill of discernment, my ignorant self chose to keep that energy transference going throughout my day, from drivers in vehicles whizzing alongside me all the way to that confused young clerk in the computer store.

But ultimately why I teach this simple story is the ripple effect of energy transference we create through our emotional and physical fields. As soon as I allowed my emotional and physical fields to fully respond to the triggered belief, each person I encountered after that had the opportunity to ignite their own hidden programs of disrespect. And if they allowed my energy to create a similar response in their fields, then they would keep passing the football, so to speak, to those they engaged with throughout their day, whether a stranger, partner, child or pet. Small exchanges and interactions between us humans can have big ripples.

Think of the numerous scenarios that play out for the physical and emotional empath in the world as we engage with co-workers, employees, bosses, or strangers in public on any given day. We find ourselves beginning our day holding a positive, balanced personal field and then instantly we have the rug pulled out from under us because of a simple encounter with someone or something we perceive as negative. It's as easy as engaging in a heated, egoic discussion with a friend or family member or participating in a staff meeting where manipulative individuals suck the energy from the less powerful participants in the room.

Taking on the energy of another or losing yours can happen with or without your knowledge or consent. When that negative controller energy robs the empath of their field, the empath finds themselves deflated and working on an empty tank of self-worth fuel. This results in exhaustion because their ego has taken a beating, and then they often flip that negativity onto another such as a partner, child or even a pet to tap into the other's fuel source to fill their tank once again, either knowingly or unknowingly. This is how the game of energy transference keeps moving from one person to another as our auric fields keep intermingling and the fear-based fuel keeps moving between us through cords and tentacles which further destroys our protective auric tanks throughout the day. This is how we all end up with no genuine gas—sick, tired, and exhausted.

Another piece to these energy exchanges is a level of codependent behavior. Often the empath is drawn into another's energy field by use of guilt, drama, a want to be needed or a craving for attention. If and when they find themselves overcommitted and feeling victimized or enslaved to another, they will then give their individual power away without personal boundaries until they themselves become depleted. Alternatively, they can also begin to give with an agenda to get something back, meaning mind-based giving instead of giving unconditionally to empower the other. No matter the intentional or unintentional motive, we humans play these energy transference games more often than we think when one small negative energy encounter sets off that domino effect that continues throughout your day affecting one person, then another. Let's take a closer look at both physical and emotional empathing to build awareness of how these scenarios show up and have influence in our day-to-day interactions.

Physical Empathing

As we discussed, physical empathing happens when we take on the physical symptoms of other people during an exchange of energy. As a healing practitioner and hospice volunteer, I see this kind of empathing occur most often when people take on the role of the caregiver for a sick or dying person. Over time in their caregiving role, they often find themselves manifesting the same or similar symptoms due to empathing the energy of the vigil situation. I would be curious to know just how many doctors or nurses end up becoming dis-eased or dying from the same illnesses they treat their patients for, especially when it comes to cancer which holds such enormous quotients of fear for everyone involved. It's important for us energetic beings to understand how caregiving, nursing or doctoring can be hazardous if we do not understand how to protect our auric boundaries.

In my first book, *An Energy Healer's Book of Dying*, I consistently reference how caregivers need to come first in terms of keeping their own energy field strong and healthy, whether they are caring for an ill patient or holding vigil for a loved one who is dying. Only then does the caregiver have capacity to maintain a strong auric boundary and assist in a beneficial and loving way. It is likely that each and every one of us will be in some caregiving role during our lives. Often these situations can occur suddenly, and you might find yourself in a burnout situation rather quickly—especially if you are a sensitive empath and have an underlying core belief of fueling self-worth and ego by helping others.

I have many clients whose parents are in some stage of dementia or Alzheimer's and who are filling their day running to appointments, getting groceries and checking on medicine dosages. When much of our own worth is tied into being "the one" who is in control of another's situation, it can become a tricky playing field in terms of energy. This style of empathing can also show up in our parenting efforts when we constantly worry about our kids or in our jobs when we take on the stress of our employees, clients or bosses. Performing any of these duties with a fear-based fuel of *I have to, I have no choice, I am the only one that can do this the right way, there is no one else*, will eventually create a resentment-filled subconscious narrative that will open us to further stress and health issues while doing the tasks at hand for the other. Conversely, if those same duties are performed in a self-love fuel, the caregiver will instead be working in an energy field of *I get to* and *I choose to*, all while holding a different auric field. These are distinctly two different states of mind, one being positive and the other negative. It all comes down to how you manage your energy.

Emotional Empathing

While physical empathing takes on the physical ailments of another, emotional empathing is more about taking on the basic emotions of the other person, place or thing. Basic emotions we humans tend to empath include things like sadness, happiness, fear, anger, surprise, and disgust.

While often these emotions can pass through our energetic field in a short amount of time, we can also hang onto and store these emotions in our field and make them our own. This is especially the case for those we are closely connected to and who we share many experiences with throughout our lives. I have many emotional empath clients who struggle specifically with family-related issues that end up affecting not only their emotions but their behaviors. One client in particular was dealing with a lot of concerns surrounding an elderly parent who was struggling with health issues. My client was one of several siblings and yet it seemed the health and wellness affairs of her mother landed solely on her shoulders along with a good amount of judgment and backlash from her family on the decisions she made about their mother's care. This took quite an emotional toll on my client and her family's behavior escalated over several years until the mother ended up in hospice which only added to the pressure of family infighting. During highly stressed times many empaths will find themselves taking on the emotional anger, sadness or even physical pain of those involved, especially that of the one dying in hospice. This is an add-on to the already stressful emotions being felt in dealing with siblings, family and more. The family emotional rollercoaster continued through her mother's funeral and beyond the final estate decisions.

Beyond family scenarios, the same holds true for work-related issues and even casual or close friend circles. Most often the emotions and judgments being tossed about in typical scenarios are not usually done in a malicious way but show up because people express their feelings in different ways and remember, any negative surface emotion is always anchored in some level of masked fear. In the case of my client, her old beliefs of being "the one" continually kicked into high gear only adding to her exhaustion levels. She pushed herself to be the one to take on the caregiver role, the family planner role, the estate role, etc., completely depleting her own energetic field, eroding her self-care and ending up depressed and fatigued.

Overall, taking on other's emotions can be harmful for the empath because eventually it will manifest into symptoms of imbalance and disease. For example, holding another's unhappiness in our fields can lead to anxiety, stress, depression and more. In the example of my client, it was her knowledge of energy that ignited her awareness of just how toxic this family pattern had become. She decided to do her own work to release the belief of "being the one" and allowed siblings to assist more in the processes surrounding her mother's overall journey. If she would have not been able to manage and release the emotional energies she had taken on from her entire family, these energies could have resulted in her own physical body dis-easing much like her mother's had.

This energy stuff can be really difficult because no one teaches us about energy exchange when we're growing up. Most of us never even have access to this information throughout our adulthood unless we find a book like this. We have no idea how our beliefs drive our actions. We have no idea of the energetic arenas we are playing in. We have no idea that this ability to take on energy is very real indeed. Well, I am here to tell you, it is. Energy is everywhere. And it is not just our interactions with people that can exchange and transfer energy, it happens when we come in contact with any container of Source consciousness, at any moment of the day and night not only through people but also places and spaces, and land and nature itself.

Chapter Seven

Empathing Places, Land, and Nature

Years ago, I remember traveling to Paris for work back in my corporate days. While I was there, I took in a few tourist sites including the Bastille. I'll be the first to admit my knowledge of European history is close to zero and I had no clue what the Bastille was. For anyone like me who is unfamiliar with the Bastille, it was a fortress built in the 1300s in Paris that played an important role as a state prison throughout the French Revolution during a time where beheadings, hangings, and other human atrocities were the norm.

Arriving at the Bastille, I was not aware of its history and had simply made the stop because it was listed as a tourist site. While sitting in the lobby waiting for the tour I began to feel nauseous and sense odd pains in my head, neck, and shoulders. Throughout the tour, I found my symptoms move from physical pain and discomfort to strong emotions of terror and fear—beyond what seemed like a normal response to learning the history of the fortress. I almost did not make it through the tour as I found myself completely overwhelmed by these sensations. I felt the fear of the prisoner. I felt the pain of the beheading. I felt the horror of it all. Additionally, I felt a sense of confusion and activity, almost like static on a TV, that I did not know how to identify at the time.

This was years before my transition to becoming an energy practitioner and I was ignorant to the concept of empathing. I could tell something within the space was affecting my physical body somehow but was unaware my body and heart were empathing the pain and fear held as an energetic file within that brick-and-mortar fortress even though hundreds of years had passed. Even more so, I had no idea the static and confusion experienced was due to the additional energies of thousands of tourists creating a soup of holographic energetic signatures active enough for an uneducated empath like me to become completely overwhelmed. History lesson learned. Empath lesson learned.

Through my studies and experiences to become an energy practitioner, I began to more fully understand how places hold energy—and not only the locations or structures themselves but also the objects placed within. As humans making our way through life we are actually walking through many lifetimes and timelines of holographic energy signatures in our homes, neighborhoods, places of work and more. All of these spaces offer the opportunity to empath these energy signatures with or without our awareness or consent. If our human containers or auric fields are weak or torn, we become susceptible to empathing any stuck or negative energies that may still reside within that unseen field. If we do not consciously command our boundary, the energies take that as a consensual "yes" to enter our auric, physical, and emotional space. We hold a conscious command firstly by working in love versus fear, then can utilize our voice as a verbal command of calling out a boundary, we can offer prayer, light a candle or simply good intent in our hearts.

Homes and Buildings

As an empath myself, I have found it is common to experience the energy of a space or building. Most of us have walked into someone's home or visited a historic site, like the Bastille in Paris, and felt a change in our physical sensations or emotions. Maybe we simply feel a presence yet we're not really sure what it is we are feeling. So if we know we can sense the energy of a place, how does that actually happen?

Some studies say that energy is not really made of anything or is only present when it has physical mass, but I tend to disagree at least in terms of the work I do. In my experience, everything is energy. And energy has intelligence and a vibration. Vibration refers to oscillation or the movement of the atoms and particles caused by the energy. Nothing rests or stops; it only changes in frequency. Frequency is the rate at which the collective vibrations and oscillation cycles occur. So basically, everything we see and experience around us is vibrating at one frequency or another, including not just people but animals, plants, furniture, walls, rooms, entire neighborhoods and so on. This is what makes us one. This IS oneness. We are not separate. We are all connected and united.

When we have an experience in a room or a building, shards of our intelligent energy remain as thoughts, feelings, experiences and more. These energy particles continue to holographically vibrate, move, and sometimes capture the experience much like tiny movie clips invisibly swirling about within the space. This is why after a horrible argument you can feel the thickness still permeate the room or why after a violent crime or accident, you can still feel the horror within the location. Other times, actions that have been repeated over and over again can energetically create a loop pattern known as residual energy, meaning the repeated action continues to replay, but now in the form of stuck memory or invisible movie-clip hologram.

There are various ways this stuck energy can find its way into buildings, throughout our homes and just about anywhere we live, work, and play because energy is always moving and changing. Any stuck, loop pattern or residual energy additionally merges with the present energies from human interaction which then combine vibrations to become more of a collective energy field of information and timelines. If we do not have the skill of discernment, our physical and emotional auric bodies can unknowingly empath that trapped energy ultimately affecting our body, mind, or spirit. If we then choose to keep that energy, yet have no ownership to it, eventually our human mental mind will create a scenario in our life to support the feeling.

Remember, we can empath with or without knowing we are taking on the energy of a person, place or thing. Our frequency will clash, adjust to, repel from or take on the energies we encounter and sometimes that means we take home vibration frequencies or intelligent information that does not serve us. This can happen in an instant as an energetic attachment, or it can slowly secretly seep into our field as we engage with these frequencies over time.

In my work I often help clear stuck energy from clients' homes and buildings. Many years back I was asked by a real estate agent to do a clearing on a home that was priced well but was not selling. I knew nothing about their client or the neighborhood before my visit and I had no information about this home that had not moved on the market for several years. The moment I pulled into the driveway I was hit with an overwhelming mix of feelings and emotions. No one lived in the home but psychically I saw a white truck sitting in the driveway with a man who I naturally assumed was the past homeowner.

As I physically approached the empty home and lot, I intuitively knew this man was extremely unhappy with life. I knew his marriage was in shambles. I knew he was sick as well as had a disability. His energetic signature was holographically embedded within the property as a direct path of stuck energy that went from the truck in the driveway to the front door which anchored his apprehension and dread each time his hand hit the door knob. Inside the house, this energy line further revealed he slept in the living room alone, separate from his wife. The second step leading upstairs exposed the searing pain he felt in his left leg from his struggles with an unhealed amputation and outdated prosthetic. On the first floor, I could also sense his wife throwing harsh words his way from the kitchen which only added to the mix of sadness, fear, and anger. When I scanned the upstairs bedroom, I was immediately aware their son was doing a good amount of drugs and hid in his room to avoid the conflicts surrounding him. The backyard energetically revealed a neighbor who was extremely difficult even though there was no one home at the time of my visit.

Remember, this was a completely empty house. And while I may not always be fully accurate with the reason for each and every feeling I experience when clearing a space, what is most important about why I share this story is we have no idea what energies we are walking into and potentially taking on in our daily life. This empty structure of emotion is a perfect example of what residual energies can remain after the people are gone. When we're in this kind of a home or space with a strong energy field, it's often something many of us can feel on some level yet we do not pay attention to the specifics of what we're feeling because no one has trained us to do so.

Since this home had a lot of showings but no offers, it was clear to me many potential buyers could in fact feel these energy fields. Anyone doing a walk through would have felt a sense of dread when reaching the front door, the pain of the second step, and the confusion and anger throughout the home—especially in the kitchen. Even if a buyer could manage the house energies, the hologram of the yard and its confrontational neighbor would be enough to halt any potential purchase. Although those walking through the home may not have been able to articulate these exact feelings about the space, these kinds of energy fields often leave us feeling off or sensing something about the space, like it is just not quite right. After the clearing, I called the realtor and she indeed validated almost every element of this story and I am happy to say the house sold within two weeks following the work done to clear and balance the home.

Land

Just like homes and buildings, the actual land can hold the energy of those who have spent time upon it. We experience stuck energy within the land much like we do within physical structures—through particles and vibrations holding intelligent information, residual movements, and loop patterns experienced across timelines and more. The land can also lock in any trauma that has been experienced on its surface from the beginning of time.

One evening, I was driving along the highway when all at once a wave of sadness washed over me. It felt like driving into a dense wobbly gel or hitting a wiggly wall, and then moving quickly through it as I could feel the frequency suddenly get lighter again. It felt super strange. Luckily, I was on my way to teach a class on psychic skills, so I was already in a state of heightened awareness. Had I not had my intuitive antenna on, I most likely would not even have noticed the odd density change I experienced.

As I continued to drive, I asked for clarity on the sadness and density until I cognitively received the message that there had been a deadly car accident at the intersection I had just passed through where a young woman lost her life. From my perspective as an energy intuitive, that sudden death event left a shard of her energetic signature stuck at the site, along with the sadness, fear, and unrest caused by the accident. I then thought of the number of people driving through that busy intersection each day, unknowingly passing through the energy field of the accident, ultimately taking it home and making it their own in some way. Whether we are sensitive empaths or not, most humans will somehow be affected by that type of stuck sadness and pain. Just imagine how many people may drive through that single path on their way to and from work each day.

When I arrived at the class, I shared this experience only to find that one woman had specifically come to my class that night because she was struggling with the death of her girlfriend a couple of years ago who had been killed in a car accident at that very intersection. Her story validated my assumptions about what I had felt, and I stopped at the intersection on my way home that night to do additional work to help clear the intersection of residual sadness and grief.

Several years ago, I was hired to clear a home in a small town in southern Minnesota. The family had lived in the house for a while but had recently started a massive renovation of the home and called me because they were now experiencing some paranormal activity. Along with the activity, the family was also feeling increased depression, anxiety, and anger, which was causing actual physical sickness in some of the family members. The stress they endured had pushed the parents to the point of potential separation, yet they were all very confused about what had suddenly influenced their health and well-being.

Upon my arrival, I took some time to drive through this small town that stretched along the bed of the Minnesota River. The only thing I knew about this area was that it had been the location of the famous scene in Purple Rain where Prince and his lady-friend, Apollonia, spent the day out riding his motorcycle. Driving through town, it was obviously not in good economic shape as many main street businesses were closed and multiple homes for sale. I knew nothing about the actual history of this town yet I sensed a lot had happened here which wasn't made clear until I started working on the family's home.

When I arrived at my client's house on the main street of town, I immediately psychically tapped into the space to see what I could sense. Oftentimes when a brick-and-mortar building goes into a renovation the energy held within the space and the land it sits upon and around it becomes activated. This sudden jolt in activity can cause a confusing and imbalanced mix of energy fields. In these scenarios, my job is to find out what exactly got activated and what information is coming through the residual energy.

After a little time in the space, I sensed a flood had ravaged a large part of the town many years back. I also felt there was a fire at another time that had also affected much of the town. The flood and the fire would have explained much of the turmoil experienced by the family living in the energetic space, however, there was more. After being in the space for some time, I experienced a past-timeline scene that at first was very confusing.

It initially felt like a horrific parade of sadness, pain, and fear continually moving past the home. Then, after sitting with these feelings, I psychically saw a scene of indigenous Americans of all ages including many children, that were bound together and herded along the street as an angry mob of white people barraged them with verbal jabs and physical actions. It was heartbreaking, and I knew nothing of what I was seeing in my psychic mind's eye.

When I was done clearing and balancing the house, its inhabitants and surrounding land, I convened with the family and learned one of the children knew lots of history about the town. She validated that not only was their town affected by massive flooding of the Minnesota River in 1965 but that there was also a great fire, years back, that took out most of the block adjacent to their home. Additionally, she educated me on what was known as Minnesota's *Trail of Tears* when on November 7, 1862 during the immediate aftermath of the US–Dakota War, the United States Government force-marched approximately 1,700 indigenous people, the vast majority being women, children, and elders—for six days up to an internment camp at Fort Snelling where they experienced horrific treatment at the hands of citizen-soldiers and mobs along the way. This scurrilous scene marched right down the main street of this town, directly in front of my client's home, while the people were so confused and scared because they didn't know where they were going and what was happening. They were forced to walk all the way to Fort Snelling only to be placed into a concentration camp where their keepers abused them physically and mentally, imprisoned them and subjected them to a campaign calculated to make them stop being Dakota.

The particular home I was hired to energetically clear held within it all of this disgusting history along with all of the emotions attached to each timeline trauma including the flood and the fire. Years of this stuck energy was released through the construction process and now permeated not only the brick and mortar of this house but the divine human container or physical bodies of the people living with it, ultimately affecting their mental and emotional fields and creating actual sickness along the way. The entire town still held all of the sadness, fear, and grief from that traumatic event that likely not only affected the family that hired me but so many others in the town.

Ironically this home was not the first I was hired to clear in this town. Afterwards, I received three more calls to clear homes within that same year all from different clients who amazingly did not even know each other. When I drove to the second client's home for their clearing, I noticed that there were seven homes for sale all on the same block. When I finished my work, I asked the homeowner if there was a public park with a bluff or higher ground that overlooked the town and she gave me directions to just that, a public park on a bluff overlooking not just the town but the Minnesota River as well.

I spent some time there working on the entire hologram of the town to release and remove all that no longer served the land in terms of the sadness that had historically transpired there over many years past. I do this work much like a kaleidoscope where I move all the energies all at once, like a holographic puzzle of sorts. Land carries such powerful information and yet we are not aware of what this can do to not only our homes, businesses, and buildings but also our bodies, minds, and spirits. I personally make an effort to consistently clear my own home and any space I work in by either burning sage, lighting a candle, using rocks and more. Some of these details are suggested in the Appendix for your consideration.

Not that I am in any way taking credit for an economic shift of an entire town, but I do know that energy does indeed change matter. At the very least, it was fun to see that the street with so many houses for sale had only one sign remaining the next time I returned, which ironically was the house I had been hired to clear. At this point the home had been cleared of the residual energies but held the client's emotional ties of not truly wanting to sell the home and that was what was prohibiting this from moving on the market. After some deep emotional discussion with my client and cutting cords of feelings from her past and uncertainty of her future, her home sold within a month of the clearing.

Natural Elements

The natural elements of water, earth, wind, and fire all hold primal and energetic connections for us human beings. Many of us feel an intuitive connection to certain elements of nature. We find these elements can fill us up with energy, spark our sense of wonder and make us feel united with something larger than ourselves. For example, I have many clients who are instinctively drawn to water. They love the oceans, the fish and coral, and the mammals found within. Their souls soar when they are near the rapid movement of streams and rivers or witness the ebb and flow of the tides. They yearn to sit along the shore of a freshwater lake or on an ocean beach like a mermaid while the water splashes against the rocks and the sun shines upon their bodies.

Then there are those who align energetically with the earth element. They hunger for the experience of sitting on top of the mountain, hiking over rocky passes, or simply lying on the earth as their soul-fuel source. Those drawn to the earth element may love to navigate deep within the forest, moving among trees of all varieties, walking through the ferns, shrubs, and mosses. They can be in tune with that spider-web feeling found in the woods, a sense of all things being connected and the sensation of being watched by something beyond our worlds. They intuitively gather rocks of all shapes and sizes, oftentimes displaying them about their homes.

Those connected to the element of air become energized through something as giddy as hanging out the car window while flying down the highway or drawing in a deep, cool breath on the ledge of a mountainside. Air energy is all about a thirst for movement, the thrill of a fast motorcycle, soaring down a hill on a skateboard, or standing on the bow of the boat roaring across the water with arms stretched outward for flight. Those who connect with air also have an awareness of the look and sound of the wind as it races across the skies to create artistic cloud patterns, or dances and sings through the leaves and branches of the trees.

The element of fire draws in those who find mystery in the roaring flame of a bonfire or who crave the hot sun as it hits the body's human skin on a warm day. Oftentimes they can actually invoke scrying by looking deeply into the fire to find messaging in the smoke and flame or feel a subtle connection to an ancient knowing. Fire also aligns to those whose eyes are intuitively pulled upward toward the cosmic sky in the deep dark night filled with stars, planets, and the Milky Way, all while experiencing a heart tug of being called home to the universes outside of ours.

I intuitively have been drawn to the energy of air and fire since childhood and find they are a strong source of fuel for me each day. If there is a storm, especially when combined with strong winds and lightning, you will find me standing outside much like a scene from a Marvel comic filling my body and spirit with the powerful sensations these wonderful elements offer in terms of frequency and vibration. I feel like a superhero plugged into a charger station and believe each of us can find the element that makes us rise up like a superhero and fuels our joy and power.

I remember a night years ago when my kids were still quite small. The night skies were dancing with heat lightning and the winds were whipping like crazy and I grabbed my robe and slippers to go outside in the dark to get my superhero fuel-fill. While standing quietly outside in the dark, I coughed and immediately heard a voice emerge from the darkness . . . "Mom?" Here was one of my children standing outside in the other part of our yard enjoying the ominous energy of the electrically powerful night—doing the exact same thing I was. I can honestly say I was proud of my odd parenting skills that night!

When aligned to the natural elements of earth, water, air, and fire and all they have to offer in the way of consciousness fuel, our heart opens and our soul fills and yet this can also be a vulnerable place for the empath. These spaces and places hold holographic energy information that acts much like a library of experiences and feelings that the empath is susceptible to taking on physically as well as emotionally. For example, while the water empath is initially drawn to a body of water to refuel, they often end up taking on and sometimes even taking home any embodied negative emotion stored within the water, ultimately empathing pain, sadness or information held within the water itself. The empath can intuitively take on the pain of the water's pollution or grief over the loss of its plant and animal life through human abuse within their own divine human vehicle and can end up depressed or physically nauseous, headachy and even ill, struggling for breath. The air empath can internalize the incredibly scrambled frequencies churning throughout our airspace due to artificial frequencies from cell phone tower vibrations and other man-made signals, finding themselves experiencing confusion, vertigo, headaches, body aches, and more.

While immersed in an element, some empaths ignite memories of past lives and unknowingly trigger a sense of Armageddon from timelines in another space or place. This is common for most water empaths who hold fear-based memories of past lives or human experiences that run in their subconscious mind-matrix from ancient civilizations wherein the memory of trauma, loss of life, and a narrative of "not safe" drives their mental and emotional state into a place of dis-ease and sometimes disease. The empathic ability of remembering knowledge and experiences from other time–space continuums are skills of the empath, yet if we do not have proper aware-ness, it can be a dangerous connection when our divine human vehicle evokes fear that is disconnected from our current life experience which leaves us feeling confused and depleted.

For example, if I resonate to the frequency of water, I may find myself feeling sad or overwhelmed with no apparent reason why, and yet if I continue throughout my day without discerning this feeling of sadness, my mind will take action and make the feeling my own by creating or finding something in my life to be sad about. This becomes a dangerous path because I have now misdirected energy that was not mine to own in the first place. Additionally, I have projected the misinterpreted feeling onto something or someone that does not deserve it and if that person chooses to make it their own as well, the ripple effect continues.

The sensation of an energy disconnect feels kind of a flat and far away feeling, like you cannot get your head or hands around it. The first step I take when sensing this sort of sadness or disconnect is to go inward to assess if this is truly mine or if it seems to be coming from something external. Once I determine the feeling is not mine, I then can choose to investigate further into where the sadness came from and whose it is. If we are an empathic person who loves the water, it is important to be open to the idea that I might be empathing the information that the water itself is sad or fear-filled. Possibly it is sad about being polluted and dirty or sad about losing its inhabitants, its coral, and its reefs. It is important to ask questions and trust any answers that come forward even though this may feel silly or as if you are making up answers. Remember, there is nothing silly about embracing the idea that the water is sad because the planet and the forces of nature that make Her up are all bodies of consciousness.

The more you practice discerning, the more natural it becomes to live with sentient awareness of what you are experiencing in your physical, mental, and emotional fields. Once the feeling is clarified and discerned, I no longer have a need to make the water's sadness my own. This puts me in the collective observer role where I can then hold empathy for the sadness and work to heal that sadness on behalf of the collective water energies in any way I choose which can include prayer on behalf of the water and its inhabitants that are suffering from pollution and human ignorance. Or I can choose to participate in outside physical efforts to make change in our water ecosystems. The skill of discernment can significantly redirect the way the empath navigates collective energies not only in nature but in human interaction as well.

Plants and Animals

It is natural for human beings to feel a connection to the plants and animals surrounding us because they are another form of sentient life and use their own consciousness containers to navigate this experience. I live in a neighborhood where the streets are lined with old homes whose yards are filled with lovely 100-year-old trees. A couple years back, a neighbor across the street sold her house and lot to a developer. This particular lot was filled with trees, including that one perfect maple that gifted the entire neighborhood each fall as it turned blazing orange. The size of its stature and magnificence of its color took your breath away.

To the horror of many of us on the block, the developer chopped down over thirty-eight trees clearing the entire lot including our neighborhood's beloved maple. While the chain saws roared throughout the weeks, I could feel the pain and angst of the actual trees screaming out from the lot. The sadness and fear was palpable. It affected not only myself but also my family as well as my clients as they walked up my driveway for their session instinctually clutching their hearts and feeling the pain of the trees dying. It was so incredibly powerful and sad.

About halfway through the clearing, both my daughter and I snuck over to the lot in the dark of the night to do some healing on the trees to release the sadness that permeated the entire block and our homes. We performed a ceremony on the barren land and remaining stumps. We also worked with the trees that were not yet cut, and I told them they were more than welcome to transport their energy and their information through the root system to be saved and stored within my trees across the street. A good visual for the intention of this work is much like using a flash drive on your computer to transfer files to another computer and location for storage. We then cut all negative energy cords attached and released any fear lingering within the land.

This story may sound funny to some, but I believe everything has consciousness and energy and even a tree can emit fear and sadness when its life is threatened. That is why the ancient culture always asked permission from the land and the plant and animal kingdom before taking from it. However, our current culture of human beings has created modern beliefs around the use of our natural world that has led to disconnection from the plant and animal kingdoms. In many cultures, we have adopted a view that separates ourselves from the plant and animal world, leading to our domination over and exploitation of these life forms. We have lost the knowledge and respect of nature as we destroy it for our own selfish gains without realizing the detriment we have done to the energy fields left behind that will affect our body, mind, and spirit whether we know it or not.

Those who empath the plant and animal kingdoms are at substantial risk today as we continue to perform the mass production and slaughter of animals for food products as well as clearing land at an absurd rate, destroying the infrastructure of plant life and habitat for the animals. I am not here to stand on any soapbox for or against eating meat products, but what I do know is regardless of your choice, the agony of this kingdom is felt by not just the empath but by all humans. We were not meant to ingest such tainted food products that are embedded with chemicals as well as the fear and terror of how the actual animal was harvested for a product that is then sold and we ultimately eat. I know many of my animal-empath clients are not able to even look at meat that has been processed through means of mass production because they can actually feel and embody the fear attached to the horrific treatment the animal experiences in harvest and processing. The human body is not meant to ingest such fear, much less chemicals. That is why we are finding each generation moving toward plant-based diets, yet sadly we treat our vegetable kingdom much the same.

So, if you do choose to eat meat, which by the way I still do to a small extent, please consider clearing the terror from the energy prior to eating— this is a form of prayer. Simply intend that what you are taking in is only for your highest and best good. And for those who are finding their tastes changing in what they yearn to consume, please follow your highest guidance without any judgment on yourself or others as we will all be evolving in this area in the years ahead.

Other animal lovers empath the pain of loss during a massive event, such as forest fires, that wipes out a multitude of inhabitants in our forests or have deadly impacts on the patterns of migratory birds or other species. Empaths who additionally connect with the water element or find themselves living near the ocean can actually feel and know what the fish, the coral, the mammals, especially the dolphins and whales, feel and know about the loss of habitat, over-pollution, and other abuses we humans impose upon our water systems. Others experience the pain of domesticated animals who are abused, neglected or bred in inhospitable conditions, triggered when watching TV ads soliciting money for animal charities.

Although it is imperative to our species that we feel a connection to and empathy for the animal and plant kingdoms, we must be careful not to empath and hold the immense pain and sadness that leads to our own depression and physical dis-ease.

I have a client who is a huge animal lover who owns and boards horses. She hired me to spend time at her home and barn to check in on one of her favorite horses who was showing signs of deep depression because he had just lost his horse partner and friend of many years. He was not eating, and his owner had great concern for not only his health but his mental wellness. Now of course it is common, as well as healthy, for a human to grieve the loss of a dear pet and we get to allow ourselves the time and space to move through and beyond that loss in any way we choose. It is also common for a pet to grieve the loss of a companion, but when the pet is not eating it is time to intervene on behalf of the animal's wellness. Additionally, my client was not eating or sleeping well because she herself was not only grieving the loss of one horse but empathing the sadness of the remaining horse, not to mention empathing the residual energy held within the barn and within the land.

When I arrived for the client work, I met the horse in need of energy work and then made my way through into the corral and adjacent pasture only to immediately psychically become aware of the exact spot where the partner horse died. The land still held the energy of its death, plus the repeated emotional grief energy signatures of the remaining horse and my client which created a loop pattern each time either of them came upon this site. Each visit they made added to the layers of sadness and feelings energetically stuck within the land. That is why I personally disagree with roadside memorials for tragic car accidents because the energy of the memorial only further anchors the negative energy surrounding that particular space and land continually offering imbalanced energy to others as they drive by. In the case of this client I did a full holographic healing on the horse who died, its remaining partner, and its owner. This cleaned and cleared the area and following my visit her beloved horse began to eat normally again.

After reading this chapter you may be thinking to yourself, *Oh my goodness, there is just too much! There is no escape from the energies and how do I make it through a day if so much is going on!* It is important to put into perspective that yes, these energies are indeed everywhere but most typical people are not even aware they exist. They can navigate a normal day and many things they encounter will not even necessarily affect them, but there are also those times when something may trigger something in our energetic field. The reason I wrote this book is not to overwhelm or put fear into anyone but to shed light on the idea that there may be a reason beyond your current awareness for some of the things that may be affecting your health and wellness. Most human bodies are not highly attuned to a large amount of what might be stored in the land, spaces, and places and that's OK, yet there are those that do feel more, experience more and sense more. They are the Psychic Empath.

Client Story
The Great Hinckley Fire

I was hired to clear a church where the present-day pastor was being affected by numerous spirits milling about that would turn on lights, move items, cast shadows, and bother unknowing congregants as they expressed their confused discomfort about certain spaces within the church's walls. The pastor also lived in a home on the same land and was himself experiencing paranormal activity but also physical symptoms of breathing issues, nausea, and headaches. When I entered the sanctuary, I was overwhelmed at the number of ghosts that were stuffed into specific pews starting and ending with a couple rows in the back over by the organ. When I pointed it out to the pastor he validated that his congregants never filled those particular pews even if they were uncomfortably packed into the front ones. When I began to psychically tap in and clear the space I noticed that more and more ghosts arrived, standing in a line that seemed endless. There were so many that I decided to open a portal to allow a mass amount of them to cross over together and that drew in even more entities to come forward and cross which also included animals and even plants and trees. This struck me as a bit odd as I had never really experienced animals in mass much less the plant kingdom looking to cross over. I then noticed that there was an actual pile of ghosts in the back corner with what I realized was an old-time parson stretched over them in a protective manner screaming in a chaotic way. At first, I thought he might be a negative entity but quickly surmised that he was actually using his human body to shield a group of people from something, only to finally realize what I was dealing with.

I live in Minnesota and in the year 1894 our state experienced a horrible tragedy known as the Hinkley Fires that took out millions of acres of land, thousands of plant and animal life, and hundreds of human casualties. The acres this tragedy devastated was so large that it spanned from Duluth into our neighboring state of Wisconsin. When I opened that portal to move the initial ghosts through, it invited hundreds more along with miles of distraught and confused entities, spirits, elementals, animals, and plants all trapped in time and space due to this horrible fire. They were all choosing to cross over en masse and the sadness of it balanced the beauty of it as I watched so many different embodiments move back to Source.

It was quite obvious that the church itself was built upon a volatile fire pathway, plus, also gave credence to why so many in that area, including the pastor, suffered from breathing problems as the energy signature still held such massive amounts of smoke and destruction which ultimately still could affect human lung function even today. The pastor is an empath, and the lord knows how many of his congregation are as well, and these stuck energies will take a beating on us as unseen dis-ease creeps into our meat bodies and continues to alter our realities.

Most of us will never know what the building, land, or space we inhabit held before us in terms of an energetic signature. I have been so fortunate as a psychic healer to have had actual experiences that validate that this unseen field is very real and hard at work no matter how much time has lapsed.

Chapter Eight

Psychic Empathing

My personal belief is that we are all born psychic, and it is a birthright of being human. Just like we are all born with the ability to sing, some of us choose only to sing in the shower or car while others have an innate giftedness that creates a great artist. In the same way, we all have psychic abilities. Almost all of us can get better with practice while some inherently and intuitively excel at their gifts. I find that much of our psychic awareness and abilities depends upon how we were raised and the belief systems we are taught at a very young age which often determines our ability to embrace and then maintain and enhance our psychic gifts or shut them down. I cannot tell you how many clients tell me stories of how they were psychically connected as a young child and now they have forgotten how because someone along the way told them that they were silly, stupid, or making things up. Additionally, children are often taught that psychic practices are evil and not to be played around with, often due to religious belief systems or fear of what seems unknown. Usually by the age of six or so, if we have not had an environment that embraces this idea, our psychic gifts shut down until we choose, if we choose, to retrain ourselves and reactivate those skills and gifts.

Being psychic is the ability to divert the conscious mind and focus on the subconscious, to tap into the universe and sense, see, hear and know messages from multiple planes of reality. Some psychic skills deal more with feelings and senses and some with the intellect and knowing, and we use our chakras to connect to this ongoing flow of energetic information. One way to think about it is we all have our basic senses yet when we practice our psychic abilities, we are seeking to enhance our senses in ways that allow us to perceive energetic information on more subtle levels. Several types of these extrasensory skills include:

- Clairsentience—the heightened ability to feel (sacral chakra).
- Clairvoyance—the heightened ability to see with outside or inner vision (third eye chakra).
- Clairaudience—the heightened ability to hear (throat and third eye chakras).
- Clairalience—the heightened ability of smell (throat and third eye chakras).
- Clairgustance—the heightened ability of taste (throat chakra).
- Claircognizance—the heightened ability of knowing (third eye and crown chakras).

Oftentimes those with psychic abilities or who have practiced these extra-sensory skills find they are stronger in one of these gifts or combine multiple abilities while garnering the information. I have all of the above abilities on some level with claircognizance being my strongest gift. As a child, I fully remember third eye vision, telepathic communication, and out-of-body experiences were a normal part of my existence. When I found out that others did not necessarily see, hear or know what I was experiencing, I allowed my gifts to recede only to have them reignite in my thirties.

Just like any psychic, medium or clairvoyant, the psychic empath will either knowingly or not, align to the information using their chakras and auric fields, but there is a vast difference between a psychic empath who is aware of their gifts and those who are not. If they are ignorant to their gifts, they will also be uneducated in the skill set of discernment, most likely not having any idea the information they are channeling can affect them physically, emotionally, mentally or spiritually.

As we are discovering, energy is everywhere—from objects to people and places, to forces of nature, to timelines of past, present and even future. And when using psychic or extrasensory gifts, we are seeking to discern and align to the information of the vibration. The psychic empath will certainly share many of the experiences covered in previous chapters from sensing energies in buildings or land to physically embodying emotions or symptoms of others. However, they will often experience these sensations on a heightened level and if trained, can become well aware of garnering and working with the information coming through.

Unfortunately, I have found many psychic empaths are not aware, educated or trained making them extremely vulnerable to their surroundings including the things they touch and objects in their presence. It is these clients that come to my office with the most severe empath symptoms, yet they often have the greatest ability to turn their empathic tendencies into true gifts that enhance their life with practice over time.

Psychometrics—Empathing Objects

Psychometrics is the ability to psychically receive feelings, energy, and impressions from objects, photographs, or other inanimate things like a ring or a book. This can be dangerous for the empath who likes to shop at antique stores and flea markets or hang onto family heirlooms like jewelry and photographs. Many years back while up north at our cabin, my husband found a knickknack he brought home from the county fair flea market. It was an old wooden prayer wheel that looked a lot like an abacus, complete with numerous spinning dowels. He was so excited with his find and proudly hung it outside the entrance to his basement office in our home. Each time he walked past it, he touched the trinket with his hands, spinning the dowels, and putting intention into his day.

Over a very short period of time, I witnessed a very distinct change in my husband's emotional behavior as he became withdrawn and depressed for no apparent reason I could identify. His actual physical body also seemed to be losing life-force energy as he slipped further into a depressive state of being. Our second son had a bedroom in that same basement adjacent to my husband's office and incredibly he was showing much of the same signs and symptoms. None of us gave thought to the timing of the prayer wheel entering home and as the next couple of weeks passed, the negative symptoms progressed for them both.

Completely stumped about what might be occurring, I reached out to a psychic friend to lament about the changes in both my husband and son. She intuitively tapped into the situation to immediately ask me what kind of "wheel" was in our home. At first, I had no idea what she was referring to and then it hit me, the prayer wheel! I quickly calculated the math on the weeks since its purchase only to realize the direct correlation in the timing between its arrival and my family's odd shift in mood. She claimed this piece of "art" definitely had some negative energy attached to it and recommended I remove it immediately from our home. I will admit it took some effort to convince my husband because he had become quite fond of his wheel but in the end he acquiesced. We removed the wheel and within about a week both my husband and son's emotional and physical states changed dramatically.

Another client of mine had a similar encounter with a Ouija board. She had received a print from an artist who used an old Ouija board to transport the art. After removing and hanging her print, she tucked the Ouija board behind her fish tank, out of sight, out of mind. Amazingly soon after, the fish in her tank started dying and as she kept replacing them, she gave no thought to the Ouija board behind the tank until I shared my prayer wheel story with her. She then immediately went home and carefully discarded the Ouija board and found herself with a healthy fish tank once again.

Negative energy stored in items will disperse through not just by direct physical touch but simply by being in close proximity to them for ongoing periods of time. When removing negative items such as the ones described above, it is important to not simply toss them in the trash or burn them or bury them. This can activate and exaggerate their energies. I do not claim to be an expert on removal, but the way I do it is to intentionally put a seal of protection and prayer around the object and then release it. After some effort of protection is placed around the object, then it is safe to discard it in the trash or it can be re-gifted with the intention that the new owner receives it with the highest and best good attached. I did my prayer bubble around the flea market wheel and then set it on the side of my curb only to find it gone the next day. My Ouija board client did much the same thing, bubbled the board in prayer and set it in the trash area in her apartment complex. It is all about letting the item go with a release of good intention versus burning it in fear or burying it in the earth.

I personally have an aversion to playing with Ouija boards and while everyone gets to make their own choices, I will share that I have worked with several people who have had long-term difficulties after engaging with them. For me the potential danger comes from the uncertainties of working within the group energy and not being able to necessarily control what comes in and out from any portals that potentially open from invoking spirit energies. In the case of a Ouija board the transference of energies are coming from so many different perspectives driven by multiple belief systems all intertwined making it almost impossible to walk away from such an encounter without taking some semblance of transference home with you.

This transference of energy through objects does not only happen with items you live with in your home. I have witnessed an attendee at one of my paranormal events touch an old typewriter and instantly get sick. One client who owns a recycled lumber company even hired me to come to their store to see if I could get any information on where some particular wood originally was sourced from. When working to enhance my own skill set of psychometrics, I asked a co-worker once if I could do a read on a piece of jewelry that she was wearing only to find I hit the nail on the head, as they say, on all the information I received. I personally have an innate ability to read photographs and can get huge amounts of information from whether the person is alive or deceased. This psychometric skill is easily trainable in my opinion and should be taken on as fun and light play in the beginning to allow your confidence to grow but remember there might also be dangerous items if you are not aware of the power items can hold, new or old.

Perceptive and Precog Empathing

One client came to see me years ago because she was being haunted each night in a dream space. She did not have an awareness of why these hauntings were occurring, and they began to physically exhaust her throughout the day because she was not getting enough sleep and had constant mental fatigue from the ongoing experience. During her first session, we were able to understand she was a precog empath, meaning she was able to feel disruptions in energy on a large scale before a crisis or natural disaster would take place. For many, this ability takes the form of feeling a sense of foreboding or unexplainable dread. For my client, these feelings presented in much stronger manifestations during her dream state.

After more sessions, she was able to take ownership for her own energy work and training to help her heal from these experiences and control her skills of precognition. During her self-training, she has discerned she is one who "holds prayer." What that means is that her body is called upon before a crisis or natural disaster and, now that she is trained, she knows her job is to simply hold space without attachment to the outcome. It took her years of energy work and opening up to her gift to accept that she first had this gift, and second, understand she had a choice to either do something with it or consciously ignore it. Because she chose to learn and practice managing her skill it no longer takes a toll on her physically or emotionally. Now she is able to discern what is and is not hers and can choose to pray for assistance for those affected by the oncoming natural disaster as well as the post-experience for healing.

I have several more clients who fall into the category of perceptive empathing or having precognition, and it can sometimes feel like a curse when you experience fear of something you have been shown, heard or know that has not yet happened. It can be scary for the empath who is not educated on what is happening to them and it can be dangerous if the person lacks awareness because they may take on the energy of impending doom or fear and make it their own. I too have this pre-cognitive ability and years ago I would find myself struggling with a sense of responsibility attached to this kind of knowing but I did not know what to do about the information. This often left me feeling helpless or laden with guilt. One of the most important understandings for the perceptive empath is to not take on the responsibility of anything that comes to you in terms of feeling like you are able to change the outcome or even have the right to do so. When we allow spirit and Source to be in charge, we can instead learn to hold that prayer space to allow for the energies to play out as planned from a higher place or realm. Our job is to be the observer and to hold prayer space with empathy to smooth out the energetic movement of the energy and cut any and all cords to it.

Empathing Past Lives

Over the past several years past-life regression has become more main-stream and popular as a technique for those who are curious to learn what their past lives may have entailed. However, as a practitioner I know this can be a slippery slope to navigate.

I once had a client come to see me because she was experiencing extreme physical pain on the back side of her upper left shoulder, out of the blue. As we were chatting, she revealed earlier in the week she had gone to see someone who worked with past-life retrievals. During that experience, she had been regressed and shown a life where her incarnation had been stabbed in the back and died in battle from a sword wound on the upper left shoulder, much like the physical pain she was struggling with presently.

In my client work, I have come across a multitude of past-life experiences during personal healing sessions. What I find is often my client is holding onto an energetic file of the past life, causing them stress or physical ailments in this lifetime. I consider these clients to be past-life empaths, who have the tendency to take on energy of what happened in the past, whether it's through their relationships, their home, land, objects or their own past lives. If trained, it can become a fascinating skill where we can feel or know storylines from lives long past. When untrained, the experience can be tricky.

What happened to my client was that the past-life regressionist allowed her to activate too much of the other life's file, hence she completely empathed the old physical pain as her own. The energy of her past file merged with her current file, resulting with her sitting in my office suffering from a holographic sword that had killed another version of her soul in a completely different timeline. When we intentionally open ourselves up to these memories during a past-life regression without knowing how to manage them, associated energies and information can also ignite challenging feelings of Armageddon, death, and doom. It can even bring forward mental and physical symptoms, ailments, and dis-ease into the body. As crazy as this may sound, finding these overlapping holograms in people's energy fields is actually a common experience in my line of work.

Many years ago, I did one of the most intriguing healing sessions related to a past-life release with a young man who was friends with one of my kids during their college days. He was very handsome yet had self-confidence issues due to the fact that his eyes would tick and rapidly blink especially when under stress. One of the stressors in his life, in addition to college, was the relationship with his parents but because he was a sensitive empath his stress played out in his body through ticking his eyes. Needless to say, self-confidence is already hard enough during college, so we decided to see if a healing session would reveal any information about his eyes and maybe release anything that no longer served him.

Deep into his client session I kept getting strong visuals of a giant rope, then the rope was knotted, then the vision finally revealed the huge rope ran along the side of an enormous old ship. My psychic holographic movie-reel went on to show me the tragedy of one of the world's most legendary events, the sinking of the unsinkable Titanic. The past-life information that came forward for my client showed he had been one of the top-tier naval men in charge. He was not the captain but something more like a third officer in command who was stationed on the bow as the fire was blazing along with mayhem and terror. It was disturbing to watch even as an observer of this past-life movie.

The naval officer who was my client in another life kept closing his eyes to the horrendous scene before him. Then opened them. Then closed them. Faster, then faster. The open-and-close motion continued as the pain and the agony increased because there was nothing they could do but maintain their post. As an officer he was helpless. He knew the ending was hopeless and not something his eyes wanted to witness. Another scene of the movie showed me an affluent woman who did survive this tragedy, and the naval man was fully aware of her and her status as she was herded into a lifeboat designated for the wealthy. She seemed to exude a stately and entitled air about her even in the midst of disaster, and I got a strong message that this woman was his mother in this current life, yet they did not seem to have any sort of relationship in this early timeline.

During this part of a healing session, I do not have any conversation with my clients. For the actual healing work, my client lies on a massage table in the center of the room, and I sit on a couch behind them or sometimes move around the room if I am feeling drawn to be in a certain space. After the healing work is done, I release any energies brought in during the session and then I collaborate with my client to share what we each experienced. It is always a personal choice for my client to share their experience with me. Some share a lot. Some share only parts of their experience. Some share nothing at all. Since it is their personal session to own, it is not necessary for the healing to be effective. It simply can offer additional learning or can be fun when we find our experiences line up.

The first thing I asked this client following his session was if he liked the ocean and his answer was quite interesting; he said yes, but it also scares him. He shared how he's always had a huge fear of drowning, especially in very deep and cold water and how he feared not being able to see the bottom of the water because depth scared him. I asked him if he had any thoughts or feelings either way about the story of the Titanic. This totally surprised him (and me) as he shared that he always did hold somewhat of a curiosity around that historical event and boats in general intrigued him. When I revealed everything I found in this past-life release, he could feel just how much this made sense to his body as a possible truth. It is important to pay attention to our physical body anytime we are doing this kind of work because it will have a physical or emotional "ah-ha moment" when these past lives are revealed.

What was even more fascinating about this case was how his eye ticks changed. I remember my son was having a party at that same time in our home for his college buddies and when this client and I returned from my healing room following the session we joined the gathering. My son pulled me aside and shared that he was astounded that his friend's eyes were totally normal, not ticking or rapidly moving in any way and at that time, I don't think my client was even aware of it. His eyes held this healing for a good amount of time and yet when he spent time with his parents, the tick returned from empathing the auric fields of the mother. At that time, he was still learning how to navigate his auric fields, but since then this client has gained a tremendous amount of knowledge and skills to understand his empathing and maintain his boundaries. He continues to enjoy balanced eyes as a true testimony for allowing the healing experience and continuing to do the ongoing work of maintaining his energetic boundaries.

I understand for many humans the concept of a past life is difficult enough to embrace, much less the idea that a past life can physically and emotionally affect our current one. I am well aware of just how crazy this can sound. But after having the honor of performing so many healing sessions, I have witnessed first-hand not only the past-life stories, but also the complete change in behavior or the release of pain following the session. Watching my clients actually heal as a result of the information has made me a true believer. I hope sharing these stories can offer you the same opportunity to open your mind and heart to the miracle of energy.

To explain this phenomenon of past-life energy transference, I often draw a simple diagram of a stick figure for my clients. The stick figure represents my client in their current life. Next, I put a wide circle around the entire body to represent the auric bubble which is the safety net for the empath—keeping anything out of the field of energy that does not serve the person. From the middle of the stick person's chest, I draw a line upward well above the head and circle and connect it to a rudimentary-style sunshine representing that person's soul. Each ray streaming outward from the sun signifies an individual incarnation of another lifetime. This drawing characterizes how a person (stick figure) is always connected to their soul (sunshine above them) by an energetic cord (line connecting heart to sun). When a person is still alive, the energetic cord is attached to the body but at the moment of their death this cord retracts and becomes a single ray storing that incarnation's information.

The information on every life that has ended is individually stored within its own unique sunshine-ray tentacle. If and when we find ourselves empathing a past-life experience one of those past-life rays from the soul (sunshine above the body) has somehow penetrated our auric field (circle around the stick figure). When that past-life tentacle or ray punctures the auric bubble, the information of the two files becomes distorted or merged. If we are not strong in our boundaries, we can then empathically take on pieces and parts of that past life and partially or fully integrate them into our current body and spirit—like my clients experienced.

I always recommend to my clients who are interested in practicing past-life regression to set the intention of viewing their past-life information as a "read only" file, not fully interacting with the energy of the lifetime and its contents but more so observing them. By activating that past life as a "read only" we can draw information from the individual ray or tentacle into the center of the soul (sun) where it can next move downward through the attached cord to our heart center. Moving the energetic information this way allows us to observe the information with full awareness and prevents the energy from interpenetrating or getting stuck within our fields. When finished reading the file, it is important to cut all cords attached to the process and intend that the information moves back the way it initially came through up the cord, through the soul and stored back inside the individualized ray. This keeps all the energy clean and files undisturbed.

As someone who works with energies in multiple planes of existence, I can tell you these realms often get confused signals, not just in the individual bubbles of our own lives, but within the collective realms as well where timelines can interpenetrate and cause a multitude of paranormal experiences and out-of-body experiences.

The more you get used to living with empath and psychic abilities, the more you then can decide if you want to take your gifts to the next level of more professional awareness integrating it into your everyday life and world of work.

Chapter Nine

Professional Psychic Empathing

Even though being psychic is a birthright, it does not mean that every person will embrace the idea of having and using their heightened sensory gifts and abilities. The professional psychic empath has most likely opened their heart and mind and eventually their body to be able to perform whatever form of psychic tasks they choose to with mindful intention. Many times, the journey of a professional psychic leads the person through many twists and turns along the pathway of connecting to things beyond our 3D world. Sometimes it almost makes me chuckle when people exclaim how lucky I am that I can do this, or see that, or hear guidance and so on. It is not luck. I work hard at my gifts. The work takes endurance and tenacity. It takes practice. It takes patience. And gratitude. I view the entire world of energy as my workplace and have for many years now and I continue to hone my skills each step of the way throughout my day as a human and as a professional. Each thing I encounter can be a lesson if I choose to see it that way. Yes being psychic is a gift but it is also a learned skill set of being present that takes time and fortitude especially if you have chosen as I have, to make this world of energy a profession.

As mentioned earlier, many people are born with a heightened sense of awareness and yet others need years of training. I fall somewhere in the middle. The way that I have professionally trained myself over the years has changed as I find different ways of connecting to spirit and my inner guidance. Sometimes the information comes easily and other times it takes work. I also seek out new and diverse ways to connect to receive answers and information. Some ways of connecting have been with me since the beginning.

Telepathy

As a child and young adult, I suffered from an odd and unclear yearning to go home. Not in a physical sense because I was very happy here on Earth, but I had an inner knowing of things beyond our planet. It wasn't until my adult life that I learned I am what is known as a telepath and quantum energy worker which finally gave me a frame of reference for many things that happened throughout my childhood.

Between six and seven years old I vividly remember having night time telepathic conversations with three giant floating heads that hovered across my dormer ceiling. They looked very alien and skull-like yet I never felt fear when they came to visit. The head in the middle faced forward and emitted a greenish hue while the other two situated on either side in a peripheral manner were white. The middle head spoke to me through telepathy and thought but the side-heads never looked at me or communicated yet I was aware they were fully involved in the telepathic conversation. All of this seemed quite normal to me at the time because at six years old I knew no different and some years later when I saw the movie The Wizard of Oz, the intimidating green-skull version of the wizard seemed oddly familiar.

Our conversations were sometimes just chatty and other times were directly meant to reassure me I was safe. This message of safety was important because on other nights, a barrage of different alien heads came to visit, and I innately and intuitively knew they were not my friends. Whenever these heads arrived my tiny body was riddled with terror, and I would hide deeply under my bed covers snuggled close to my sister for fear of being taken away. They would morph in and out like a creepy lava lamp of skulls, eyeballs, mouths and more, all creating a horror show that I instinctively knew was not safe and yet my three friendly skulls always assured me that I was being watched over and taken care of. All of this conversation was telepathic—it just came directly into my head much like a verbal conversation would come into your ears. Telepathy for me was very simple. It was just an immediate download of knowing.

My continued messages of safety became even more important as I neared age seven and became very ill with a blood disease that doctors were never able to diagnose. As my parents struggled to find medical answers to my illness, weekly doctor visits and hospital blood tests became part of my normal routine. I missed a lot of second grade because I was not able to attend classes since no one knew if my unknown condition was a threat to the other children. Even at my own Catholic First Communication cele-bration, I was quarantined in the back of the church, separated from the rest of the kids, feeling isolated and alone with pasty skin as white as my lacy communion dress.

At first, they thought it might be a virus. Then possibly mononucleosis. Then leukemia, yet my symptoms were odd and never quite matched any diagnosis. One symptom I clearly remember was numerous squishy bumps that floated just beneath my skin on each side of my neck. These were never scary, but more, a fun pastime to poke at and move about while sitting in the hospital waiting for blood draws. No one knew how many nights I would sit all alone at the top of the stairs hearing my parents talk in their room on the first floor supporting each other's fears while crying about the possibility of losing me to this disease that no one could diagnose. Yet when I went back to my room, the heads would appear and telepathically reassure me I was safe.

I encountered similar reactions from the hospital staff who surrounded me while doing blood-draws several times each week. While my physical body sat in the room with the nurse drawing my blood, my higher-essence would float right out of my small body to see and hear the staff in the hallway outside, conversing about how sad it was that this little girl was probably going to die. I wondered who they were talking about just as I realized they meant me. It was all quite confusing as I had such opposing messaging—the 3D world telling me I was probably going to die and my floating aliens visiting me each night telepathically telling me I was safe. I chose to believe the aliens.

Our conversations became deeper at night during my illness. I asked what was happening to me and they told me they were working on my blood. They also told me that the scary aliens were trying to prevent this work but would not succeed so I had nothing to fear. So, I was content. I was a very happy, healthy yet super-sick kid for almost a year. Then one day, "poof" everything simply disappeared. The doctors were stunned. They had no answers. My blood was back to normal and my squishy neck bumps were gone and so were my floating heads. I became a "normal" kid . . . at least for a while.

I stuffed much of these childhood experiences away as I moved into my young adult life. Though it may not be floating alien heads, I do believe many of us have psychic experiences in childhood that illuminate our innate gifts—I see this with my clients all the time. When I started learning about energy healing as an adult, I revisited my experience with the heads and my illness. Some years ago when working with a powerful crystal skull I distinctly heard the voice of my childhood green alien reach out and reconnect with me telepathically. It was a beautiful homecoming for me, and I continue to work with him to this day telepathically for healing and guidance. These heads taught me I am both a telepath and a quantum energy worker. A telepath typically receives information as a thought transfer from one body or being to another. Like I shared in my story, I also have been able to go out of my body since a very young age. A quantum energy worker traverses multiple timelines and space continuums to get information using psychic skills. Since owning these abilities, I have had numerous experiences on and off planet where I additionally get information outside of being in my own body. Again, I empath this information in my own divine human vehicle to do this work and combine it with cognitive knowing. The way this works is partially as an observer where my Suzanne body stays put much like we do when we dream, and my astral body projects into the astral realm to have an experience, yet I take the energy and the information back through my being for this style of work. Every element of these psychic gifts utilizes my empath body and as always the professional level of my skill set of discernment is critical in order to keep me protected but also clear as a channel for myself and for my clients. As I traverse thoughts, space, and information that may or may not be fully mine, it is extremely important for me to be aware of not only my surroundings, who I am channeling, and where I am going, but to be sure I come back into my own personal vehicle safely and free from any attachments.

Mediumship and Paranormal Empathing

The skill set of mediumship is all about the ability to sense, hear, and feel the energies of spirits or ghosts including the ability to sometimes channel them as well. In my professional practice I see people of all ages and have come across several children who have the gifts of mediumship. Because they typically come from homes that cannot help them make sense of their paranormal experiences, these children will often empath what they are encountering unbeknownst to anyone. Their experiences usually affect them in a sleep state and can cause quite a personality change due to the fear they take on. This does not only hold true for children. I have also worked with many adult clients who feel they have this gift but have no context to validate it. They simply think they are going crazy and keep it to themselves until they end up in my office. The reality is that we all may be taking on energies that surround us daily without even knowing.

Several years ago, I got a call from a client concerned about an elevated level of paranormal activity in their home affecting the entire family. The adult daughter most bothered by all the peculiar experiences was highly empathic and the rest of the family were quite sensitive as well. This turned out to be one of the most bizarre paranormal cases I ever had the chance to work with in terms of merging holograms and overlapping timelines. Unsettling activity played out as finding things moved throughout the home that were originally displayed within a locked buffet cupboard, toys haphazardly scattered about the floor that were formerly shelved neatly in the basement and actual dirt in the middle of the rec room that simply appeared out of nowhere.

As I began the investigation portion of the home clearing, I moved into the basement and energetically encountered what I presumed to be the ghost of a gentleman that had once lived in this space still busy puttering away in his workshop. Now, encountering a ghost is nothing new for me in this line of work, and it is common for that ghost to be living and working in what he knows as his workshop even though that no longer exists in our 3D world. It is much like the energy of this man exists in a holographic overlay atop the current home, where he sees and experiences a workshop; we see and experience a laundry room. Again, the ghost lives in the hologram of the energy of the home they know and love during their timeline even though a remodel or new home upon the same land exists. In normal situations I would simply cross the ghost and move on, but this was not the case. As I began to settle in further to psychically clear the space and cross the old man, I began to realize he was not a ghost at all. He was actually very much alive and present in his holographic home that was a completely different dwelling than the brick and mortar building I was currently standing in. He was not dead, or a ghost. At first this was extremely puzzling to me and somewhat concerning as I had never encountered this before, and it took me some time to unravel the mystery of what was actually going on here.

I am well aware that we live in multidimensional layers of reality but up until this point, I had never experienced standing in two distinctive realities at the same time. When I meditate, I can perceive and even traverse multi-realities, but this was an entirely new idea to experience while fully awake and present. The deeper I got into this work, I was psychically shown a town from the late 1800s complete with homes (including the gentleman's), a church in the center of town and a well for water where the townsfolk socially gathered. I was also shown the woman who had hired me to clear her current home, but this was her in a past-life 1800s incarnation residing in another timeline living in a house about one block over from her own. I admit this all did feel a bit crazy, but the visuals and information were amazingly clear.

Unfortunately, sometimes past timelines also offer up some disturbing information and this was one of those cases as it showed me how the parson from the 1800s-timeline church was not a good man; abusive to not only the women in town but also the children. This information may have been why a higher source of energy brought me to this home for a greater capacity to heal many that were affected from this devastating person within the past. I really have no logical explanation of how these two timelines holographically got intertwined but I do know that the children from the 1800s were entranced with the 21st Century toys as they tugged them off the shelving in the basement and scattered them across the floor, all experienced in overlapped wrinkles of time. I also know that the mud pile where the children played appeared in the current home's rec room thanks to that same gaggle of young feisty boys having fun playing in the dirt by the well in the center of town. During the healing work I could see these two twisted holograms much like a strip of licorice, intertwined into one, where somehow experiences crossed over that made no sense to my logical brain. It is especially important to point out that the interchanges were not those of ghosts—as these were both actual human experiences happening in simultaneous timelines running consecutively. This is not a paranormal ghost experience as no one on either side was dead. They were all alive but running in separate dimensions of existence and planes of reality yet somehow, they had the ability to interface. That is why this encounter was so incredibly unique yet unsettling to get my head around. My job here was to undo the holographic licorice strip and put each individualized timeline back into its own reality plane of existence and close any portals or energetic doorways that allowed for the wrinkle in time to exist. Much like I train my clients to stay in their own energetic bubble, it was important to put each timeline into their own individualized bubble container, holographically separate from each other.

When I met up with the homeowner after the holographic work, I admit I was just a bit hesitant to offer my findings as multiple timelines was already a difficult concept for me to comprehend, much less get this client and her family to open to the idea. I was astounded to hear some of the feedback which included the owner admitting that years back she was obsessively drawn to purchase a home and live in the area for a reason beyond anything that made sense to her. She also shared with me that she fixated on a house only a block or so away and had no idea why and she found herself driving by it often. Her husband was abused as a child by a man in religious authority and was just beginning to come to terms with getting some help to heal. And there was what she termed a "yucky neighbor" in a home across the way that for reasons unknown to her she did not like even though she did not really know him well. His house sat upon the spot where the holographic church was. The mud pile where the kids played was exactly where the mud ended up in their rec room and one time it appeared on white sheets out to dry in her backyard, much like it would if unruly little boys were hard at play while someone was busy hanging out their laundry. Like I said, this was one of the craziest spaces and land clearings I ever encountered but after the work was done, nothing in their home moved again, nor did mud appear, and her empathic daughter's anxiety lessened dramatically.

We never really know what we are walking into because we are not told nor trained to believe that there are multiple energies hard at work around us; some we can see and others we cannot. This type of energy signature is incredibly threatening for the empath as they can take on multiple frequencies and vibrations which in turn can affect emotion, physical health and well-being. We build houses upon spaces that may hold suffering and pain. We erect buildings that we work in for hours a day that may have originally housed horrific stories of trauma and abuse. Our children play in parks or learn in schools that may have been the site of a deadly fire that took hundreds of lives. We just never really know.

Personally, I believe true mediumship should be a mentored or trained skill. The sensitive psychic empath who is not taught how to protect their own field, body, and mind can be attacked by many different nefarious energies along their journey and can find themselves getting very sick and mentally unstable. That is not to say that there are not beautiful and loving benevolent energies there to assist, but the bigger you get in your energy field, the bigger the playground gets to shut you down or highjack your mind and body. Remember earlier in the book I told the story of the psychic medium that negatively corded herself to me long distance and taunted me for months mentally and emotionally because she was angry and wanted revenge. Well, it turns out that karma found its way to her for all of the negative things she not only did to me but to so many others and this particular person herself was shut down with disease affecting every part of her body and mind. Integrity is key when working with energies from all sides of the veil and beyond. And as always, so is the skill set of discernment.

Psychic Empath Healing

The true trained empath, regardless of what traits they have, is really a high-level energy receiver and when someone gets to this point, they better know they are an empath and make sure to have a diligent practice protocol to stay safe and protected. They may also have the capability to direct healing energy. The life's work of many sensitive psychic empaths is best suited to the healing professions and this day and age that can include so many different modalities from reiki to hands on healing, to healing touch, to massage, to healing and hospice, to cranial sacral and more. Many empaths are also drawn to more traditional methods of working with healing and energy and find careers in healthcare, counseling, childcare, gardening, caring for animals, or even transformation or renovation of places. Regardless of the style of work the sensitive psychic empath does for work in a healing way, it is imperative that he or she determines some sort of daily routine for self-care, wellness, protection, and alignment so as to not take home their work in any manner.

Chapter Ten

Collective Empathing

Sadly, horrific acts of violence sometimes can be a good learning tool to teach how collective energy works and the 2001 terrorist attacks of 9/11 make a great case study to examine how individual humans experience energy directly or as a shared collective memory. Most of us have logged into our cellular memory banks where we were, what we were doing and how we felt as the violence unfolded before our eyes on international television and additional media outlets not just in real time but for weeks and months to follow. If we personally did not experience the event, we most-likely garnered the energy of the information through storytelling, videos, photos, articles and more. Life-altering events such as this will create an energetic imprint in each individual as well as hold an energetic imprint in the collective.

I personally remember distinct details of that day as I am sure many of us do. At that time, I was a corporate executive running an event in Portland responsible for not only hundreds of show attendees but staff on-site, staff back home, and staff traveling abroad, not to mention my worry and concern for my own spouse, children, family, and friends. The terror of such an event instantaneously fractures our sense of safety and incites dread and panic which is only exacerbated by the unknown.

Each individual human being embodies experiences through their personal matrix or consciousness container. Our immediate sense of safety, worth, and well-being will react according to the narrative running within our unique system. This narrative is then fed additional information from outside sources that will infuse or diffuse the level of energy attached from those we are in contact with, the news sources we are glued to and the others we are worried or concerned about. Three different energetic fields of energy immediately impact us; from our individual field to the collective field of who we are directly experiencing the event with (either in person or from afar), to that of the overall collective experience happening. Energy will project as fear-based thoughts, emotions, and feelings which begin to create a sort of grid weaving tentacles or cords of energy which will continue to be fed or fueled by what we are choosing to think, feel, and sense as individuals, groups or as a collective. Fear based energy, especially when it is attacking core issues such as safety, worth, and well-being, moves at an extreme rate creating more of the same as like-finds-like energies come together strengthening the messaging. This is how hive-mind-based panic ensues at a rapid pace.

If we examine the actual site or sites of the 9/11 attack, we realize just how much energetic imprint happens not only to the actual buildings, land, and surrounding area, but within those experiencing or witnessing the trauma. This overwhelming energy signature will be forever imprinted in the actual place, area, building, land and more until something or someone works to change that vibration. This is why so many places and spaces across our globe affect our human bodies with or without us knowing as the physical site of the original horror still holds that blueprint of trauma even if there is no longer any building, site or physical presence of any kind. This is also why it is important to do the work to clear the energy of any space, land, or building that holds trauma by healing it with prayer, love, and oftentimes a memorial of some sort as this effort will reset the vibrational frequency and reprogram the blueprint offering love verses fear messaging. Again, clearing space can be as simple as burning sage, lighting a candle, drumming, singing, offering prayer, or holding loving intention in your heart. Imagining, seeing, hearing, and feeling what you would like the healed-space to be when cleared is a great way to reset the energy.

We hold information of thoughts, feelings, and emotions energetically within our meat and bone bodies just like the land or space does. Our cells remember. Our fascia remembers. Our bones and muscles remember. We also hold information and experiences within our brain and mind as memory and emotion. Depending on how we as individuals deal with a crisis, this information either causes dis-ease within our system or we choose to let it go. Unfortunately, most of us do not know that stuck energy is detrimental to not only our body but our mind and spirit, so we hang onto it which only adds to the collective field.

Every person holds their own individual container of consciousness which when combined or blended creates and embraces what is known as the collective field. Our world is a reflection of our consciousness which in turn also perceives the world. When we revisit the 9/11 story, as we live the experience by hours, days, weeks, and even months the energy continues to fill all fields with additional soundbites and visuals of on-going fear. Next, the energy of like-finds-like continues to expand filling the collective container with the same fear-based narrative. Another layer of negative messaging additionally forms from the vibrational frequencies of on-going media replaying the visuals over and over again instigating trigger effects. Layer after layer continues to fill the collective container with negative messaging. This layered effect overpowers our human mind and body leaving us feeling anxious and eventually depressed—overwhelmed by the messaging. Finally, this programming becomes so imprinted and eventually implanted that we can be triggered months and even years later just by seeing a visual of the original event reigniting all fear, feeling and emotion. What is even more scary about the media is how they can insert deeper programming by use of deliberate trigger words, photos or phrases in their coverage that anchors in our minds and hearts designed to keep us in panic mode especially if we are a sensitive empath.

Work can be done to free the individual field of fear-based programming to clear old trauma which will ultimately offer freedom, health, and wellness to the human body and mind. Clearing the collective is a bit trickier as this is much like a machine that is continually fed by anyone and anything at every moment. And remember, the collective field is a prime frequency for additional programming efforts from various factions and agendas wanting to keep the general public in a state of unknowing or fear-based messaging. For example, if the media reports a narrative that tips the scales of the collective narrative, my personal container may or may not be affected. How does this work? Let us say a potential terrorism story is presented in real time, it can be skewed to trigger old 9/11 fear programming by use of words, tone or visuals that can then affect what I may individually hold, or we all collectively hold. This is again why it is important for each of us to decide just how much personal energy work is needed to keep our individualized containers clean and clear of fear-based messaging. As each individual holds a cleaner and clearer vibration, the collective also shifts accordingly. Additionally, there are many lightworkers that perform energetic clearing efforts within the collective field and multidimensional timelines on behalf of all as part of their work of service to others.

I actually happen to be one of this type of lightworkers that has for many years worked on the actual 9/11 grid in the collective consciousness field. How I do this is by energetically inserting different endings into the 9/11 blueprint with alternate scenes playing out in peace and love. One holographic visual might be the planes missed the buildings and all passengers were taken to safety. Another may be the plot was thwarted prior to take off. Another may be the idea to commit this crime was never a reality in the first place and so on. With clear intention on behalf of the good for all I then holographically insert this into the grids as alternate scripts. The reason a lightworker will do this type of prayer-filled energetic work is to adjust the information and frequencies found within the collective-story grid or collective consciousness container. Why this is important is because energy works in that like-finds-like manner and if we are all continually filling the collective container with more fear of potential terrorism, this is what will be found and brought into reality; whereas if the overall container holds different information, that potential does not align as easily. And if the overall container holds much more in the way of a love-based narrative or blueprint, this is what is brought into reality. The Law of Attraction can be our friend, or not. We are creating what we want as well as creating what we do not want. The best way to navigate all of this is to be fully aware of how you feel inside of your own personal container of consciousness and truth.

In my client work, I see many people who experience a general sense of unease. They feel as if something is wrong but cannot identify the source of their feelings. They may describe it as a sense of foreboding or of possible danger somewhere out there, yet they have trouble connecting any dots to make sense of the feeling. Often, I find they are empathing collective energy on a subtle level without awareness, and over time it has grown into a more full-blown feeling, which is why they come looking for assistance. Understanding the concept of the collective field and knowing that it is vulnerable to programming, as are we, is helpful in examining foreboding or danger feelings or those that just don't make sense. We can learn to determine if we are encountering a real threat or if it was somehow triggered in the collective field. This can happen by me and others simply watching a news story for example that again may trigger old programming and then I ignite that inner narrative and it begins to run inside my mind and body unbeknownst to me.

This type of client experience is not unique as most of us humans walk throughout our days with untrained minds that can only sense direct physical attributes of our 3D world (what we can see, touch, hear), but energetically we are a multidimensional consciousness all connected as one. Multidimensional existence is a challenging concept to understand. But as we grow in awareness of our own individual energy field, we also begin to become aware of the multiple levels of sentience (feeling), which together form into the entire collective consciousness identity.

As we improve our capacity to distinguish the collective consciousness layers that exist as interconnected to the self, we understand that there is much more than just the individual self. There is a collective participation as we saw in the 9/11 case-example above. Together we create a oneness with our reality, not just with other humans but with all things. Imagine who we could be if we all remembered our connection to all other living things, to our planet, to its inhabitants from an insect to a vast mountain range to the Milky Way galaxy. We are all one in humanity in this lifetime and all lifetimes. This is what is held in the collective consciousness realm, and it is important to remember it is us who are creating and filling this repository of knowledge through our experiences, thoughts and feelings each moment of our day. While it may be impossible for us humans to fully experience and grasp the full sense of our multidimensional existence during this lifetime, the collective consciousness container is our personal and collective responsibility as a humanity.

Empathing Collective Humanity

We give energy form in the world as our human vehicle expresses our mental concepts, emotional sensations or physical actions. Minute by minute we bring energy into matter by giving it some form of expression and, depending on the strength behind the intention of mind and emotion, we are either unconsciously or consciously collaborating and co-creating with many forces that exist within and around us. Through generated thoughts and actions taken, every person on this planet is co-creating what we perceive as our current reality.

Our individual frequencies then harmonize to create a larger collective consciousness body made up of every other body of Source, which is constantly shifting in vibration between love-based frequencies and fear-based frequencies. Tragic events created or experienced by humanity such as war, pandemic, or destruction, can greatly impact the collective vibration and swing it to a lower, fear-based resonance. We as individuals then transfer the fear-based vibration into our individual energy system even if we ourselves may not be experiencing that war, that pandemic, or that destruction in real-time. As empaths, not only do we feel these energy frequencies of fear, but we also internalize these frequencies and make the fear our own through collective energy transference.

When explaining collective consciousness to my clients and students, I often refer to the Internet as a visible example. Technologies such as social media platforms show us how collective energy transference works in real time. Through these platforms, we are constantly sharing our thoughts and vibrations into the collective consciousness through millions of posts each day. Additionally, we are searching and scrolling through the posts of others, reposting and resharing to amplify specific messaging in the process. With media outlets, politicians, corporations, and artificial intelligence participating in the conversation, humanity's systems of control also use these feeds to spread their programs and/or agendas into the collective. We individuals then pick up and share these messages ourselves with our own intent and vibration, often with little thought to the truth of the original message, creating a massive network of messaging. Through these platforms, like finds like which ultimately adds more energy to specific messages and vibrations, yet the message continues to change and distort much like a bad childhood game of telephone.

Whether or not we share our thoughts or intentions through online communication channels, we as sentient beings of consciousness are designed to constantly contribute frequencies to the collective and we do this each moment of our day whether we know it or not. Whatever vibrational frequencies we create or hold within our individual consciousness containers adds to the larger network of energy.

Additionally, it is important to remember that all embodiments of Source energy also add to the collective, not just human ones. That means that the energy, good or bad, of any and all embodiments can add to the mix which can include but are not limited to things like: the forces of nature and the planet, elementals, trees, rocks, plants, the animals, earth, water, skies and its inhabitants, any ghost and spirit energies, the planets, stars, moons and suns, and the entire multidimensional existence and beyond. When things are affecting these embodiments of Source, it also can affect us. As humans, we experience these frequencies constantly on a subconscious level which will then change the collective field of humanity consciousness affecting each individual in a positive or negative manner. Depending on our own belief systems and frequencies, we can find ourselves being triggered by seemingly small interactions or experiences simply by living within the vibration of this larger energy field. Over time, if we do not properly discern or manage our own energy system, it can begin to creep into our own field as a sense of foreboding, as stated earlier, but eventually, we take on these frequencies as our own which can lead to dis-ease in our physical, mental, emotional, and spiritual bodies. The imbalance will begin to formulate as symptoms that if left unattended will only manifest further as dis-ease and disease.

In working with clients, I often notice empaths show one of three key symptoms from taking on collective humanity energies without discernment or awareness. The symptoms are overcharged, depressed, and disconnected as described below.

Overcharged

When I meet a client that is on overdrive, their field is typically overcharged akin to the feeling of holding your finger in an electrical socket while standing in a puddle. There is too much in the way of an electrical current churning through the body unplugging its ability to magnetically ground into the earth. This can cause the body to feel buzzy, or like you are too amped up, experience physical disorientation, dizziness, and imbalance or simply have had way too much caffeine. Oftentimes they will experience a dense humming or high pitch ringing or popping in the ears or head which sometimes blurs vision slightly or causes eyes to jump or twitch. This can affect the mental field in the way of anxious thoughts replaying or rumination. Usually, this type of client fills their day with as many "to do" lists as possible keeping them from slowing down enough to notice the imbalance or address the overcharged frequencies pushing their mind and body. They fear alone or down-time and normally will not allow the body to release by means of meditation or quiet time.

Depressed

Unaddressed issues and imbalanced energy can lead to depressed senses and sensations which can be experienced as a deep inner sadness or loss or feeling lonely with no desire to be with others. This leads to isolation which only increases the disimpassioned; no desire to do anything, numbness and loss of motivation. Residing on the opposite end of the overcharged spectrum, this type of client suffers from various severe energy drains resulting in them feeling as if they can't actually get out of bed nor have any desire to complete tasks. A sense of hopelessness abounds and controls their day as the ups and downs can come in waves depending on the news of the day or events that happen to them or around them.

Disconnected

The feelings of disconnection can affect a loss of ego, or personal identity, feeling disassociated or fragmented and reveal itself as apathy, not caring about anything or anyone with a lack of concern or commitment. This type of client is often seen by others as aloof and not reliable because they will oftentimes have a great desire to flee groups, crowds or noisy situations. Inside they often feel as if others can't actually see them or really hear them because the outside reaction projects a feeling; they are no longer speaking the English language to others. They can experience more clumsiness, lose balance or bump into things due to a lack of coordination. This can also include moments of memory loss of "what was I just coming in here to do?" also known as brain fog or scattered thinking.

Signals of imbalance that turn into physical, emotional or mental symptoms are invitations to heal yet most of us do not see it that way. We humans see symptoms as something wrong with us and we will do anything to ignore it or make it go away. Most of us do not grow up in an environment that speaks to personal and collective responsibility in terms of energy for ourselves and for others around us. If we made our way through life using all our senses, we might be able to see how we are all in this reality as a unified consciousness that is not only affecting one another but is responsible for each other. We can offer and receive positive healing frequencies from this collective container as well as send out and align to negative detrimental ones.

It is imperative to remember that while we are not only influenced by the collective fields, we are intimately involved in creating and maintaining it as each of us contributes through every thought, word, and action we take and therefore have a responsibility to manage how we express our own energy. Oftentimes we are quick to blame others or humanity itself for our state of mind or our current difficult situations. While other people and things outside of us can certainly affect us and our situation, it is us that oversees our reality. It is us that are responsible and accountable for our individual perspective which includes the integrity of any thought, action, and feeling projected into the collective container. We are not typically adept at practices to properly work through and release our own fear, anxiety, and stress, so we subconsciously end up releasing these energies into the collective which then contributes to the whole, affecting other sentient beings. And maybe even more importantly, no one tells us humans how vital it is to also create the quiet time to purposefully send out our joy and love, thought, action, and feeling into this collective container to share on behalf of the whole of humanity with the intention of like finding like.

In addition to the human contribution of thoughts, actions, and feelings that are constantly moving into and through this collective container, the field also embodies vast amounts of information, frequencies, and vibrations that are deliberately programmed then placed into this field from outside sources. When we remember that we are indeed existing within a holographic universe and again view our reality more like living inside of a supercomputer or within the Internet, we can imagine just how many phantom viruses we may encounter that will hack our system both individually and collectively. Some of the outside sources that influence the way we think, feel, and act are institutional systems or structures that are purposefully designed with controller agendas that can either blatantly or secretly affect our lives. Most of these systems are designed to disempower the individual human and convert humanity, resulting in us giving our power to money, medicine, media, and outside controller factions to hold us hostage to fear-based thinking and actions. Remember if we view our holographic world as programmable grid systems, it is easy for us to see how these types of organizations can structure programmed messaging into this collective field. Once placed within the collective container, each of us consciously or unconsciously either individually supports and increases this messaging or helps to modify it or delete it all together. The agenda behind this style of planned messaging will always be designed to directly attack our most vulnerable beliefs surrounding our sense of safety and self-worth.

This is not actually as Sci-Fi movie-ish as it may sound when we observe how planned and programmed messaging is happening around and within us every moment of our day utilizing conduits of mass media, local news, social media, print outlets and more. Any purposeful programmed messaging then becomes daily conversation that then virally spreads through additional layers of these same systems and seeps into our natural daily thoughts, conversation, and eventually actions. The controller factions within our government, medical, education, religious, legal, financial, and especially media systems are currently being challenged right now as many individuals are reclaiming their truth and giving power to their actions which is resulting in these systems crumbling in various ways right in front of our eyes and this offers us additional opportunities to train our bodies to discern what is and is not a program, so we can choose to live in love versus fear. This training called "discernment" is critical for the empath and is explained in detail in the chapters to come. It is important to individually challenge our personal core beliefs and programming played out by use of our true empathy and feeling centers because only then are we safe to challenge the overall programs of the bigger picture and not fall prey to additional enslavement of fear mind-control-victim-messaging especially from media and social media. We each get to choose what resonates for us as individuals which in due course affects what we hold as truth for collective humanity.

As we have learned, we are all part of this collective field whether we choose to be aware of it or not. When we choose to step into our birthright of free will and become present and participatory in awareness of our thoughts, feelings, and actions, we embrace a new level of responsibility of service to self and service to others through deleting victim programming and healing our own personal individual core beliefs first, rather than hiding, blaming others, stuffing or ignoring feelings. *Becoming present and aware comes from taking the time to go within, to become quiet, to honor our ability to feel our truths.*

Increasing sentience intensifies our individual perceived connection to the whole and continually develops our self-awareness. As we begin to take on more responsibility to discern what is and is not our truth within ourselves, we gain more skill at also discerning what is or is not truth within the collective. When we recognize this is part of our human responsibility, we can also choose to see that part of that responsibility is intentionally creating and offering joy and increasing love-vibrations to reclaim our human birthright of empathy for self and others. This is the work we are here to do as human vehicles of Source energy—continuing to raise vibration through personal spiritual work to gain and embody personal truths that shape our collective consciousness.

Empathing Collective Earth Energies

Let us for a moment envision you living out your daily experiences in your brick-and-mortar home over the time space of, say, a calendar year. You encounter physical, emotional, and mental interactions with family, friends, and possibly strangers that will have left energetic imprints within you but also within the blueprint or energetic space of your home. This may include things like the joy felt during a family celebration or holiday. It could also include an uncontrolled outburst of anger or a monumental fight. You may have suffered financial strain or underwent physical ailments that captured fear and anxiety keeping you awake at night. Someone may have gone through a breakup or the loss of another. Possibly a new member of the family arrived in a delightful way generating great waves of excitement and happy events. Your home may have been invaded by a burglar or suffered a fire. Each timeline incident has added to the energetic container that you call your home in either a positive or negative manner. Most often energies have a way of simply dispersing or moving along, but other times they get stuck and become part of the holographic infrastructure we reside within each day, without us even realizing it.

Planet Earth is also our home. When we came into this incarnation, we chose Gaia or Mother Earth as our planetary residence. She is another embodiment of Source energy and while the planet is not made of meat and bone *per se,* she still holds her own collective frequency or vibration just like we do and works similarly in terms of holding her own consciousness experiences throughout all time and space. Just like the home example referenced above, if the planet experiences joy or terror, it has the capacity to hold this stuck cell memory just like our bodies or our homes can, and this can directly affect our human vehicle through energetic transference or imprinting. If our home example has us envision a year's-worth of experiences playing out within our home, times that by eons of experiences spread across and within the planet, and begin to imagine what we may or may not encounter in the way of holographic energetic memories and transference thereof. Just like how we can give and take energy from human to human, we can do the same human to planet or planet to human; from wars to natural disasters, to blooming fields of wildflowers and awe-filled sunsets.

Again, much like us, our planet has an energetic beating heart, a frequency or vibrational tone that influences our heart and body. It is a scientific electromagnetic pulse that runs through her that impacts us and unbeknownst to most, alters not only our body but our minds and spirits as well.

Scientists believe the Earth's core is a giant electromagnet, sending out energy and creating its own unique magnetic field. Though the Earth's field is relatively weak compared to other energy fields (such as the Sun), the Earth constantly radiates electric currents due to moving magma surrounding the solid inner core. This giant magnet creates a magnetic field surrounding the planet which extends thousands of miles into space. The magnetic field carries charged particles along currents that interact with the currents of charged particles coming from our Sun. All of these electric and magnetic fields play within the holographic grids and consciousness containers of our reality affecting our body, mind, and spirit.

One aspect of the Earth's energy field that I believe affects the human body, mind, and spirit is an extremely low frequency (ELF) wave surrounding the planet called the Schumann Resonance. The Schumann Resonance phenomenon is a standing wave of energy resonating from the Earth, sometimes referred to as the heartbeat of the planet. The Schumann Resonance resonates at a low, dense frequency of 7.83 Hertz, yet can experience massive changes or spikes in frequency.

These spikes have greatly accelerated in resonance over the past ten years and as these energies shift and change, our human body takes a hit. For the unaware or uneducated sensitive empath, these dramatic energy swings can be confusing and sometimes dangerous. In April of 2020, Gaia's Schumann Resonance frequency responded with waves of higher frequency that reached a peak of 76 HZ at one point and continued to fluctuate upwards raising rhythms of our planet's "heartbeat" into higher frequencies. The Earth is vibrating higher and faster and her body is constantly changing just like us and if we are out of sync with the Schumann Resonance our own body will exhibit signs of dis-ease or discomfort that are both physical and emotional from body aches, to heart palpitations, anxiety, insomnia, depression, and suppressed immune systems.

Conversely, if we are in alignment with the resonance and in sync with the frequencies the human body is able to self-heal and increase its life-force energy overall. The human whole-body fundamental resonant frequency was supposed to be around 5 Hz (hertz), however in recent years this is dramatically changing and is all over the place on the scales. The great electromagnetic waves are not present all the time but have to experience a change in fluctuation in order to be observed and it is important to know when this happens because our physical and emotional bodies feel it.

Those who study the Schumann Resonance claim fluctuations are not caused by anything internal to the Earth, its crust or its core, but more so related to electrical activity in the atmosphere, particularly during times of intense lightning activity of solar and sunspot activity which by the way is dramatically increasing as well and again, we feel it. Solar flares and sunspot activity also create great havoc for the empath as sudden explosions of energy caused by tangling, crossing or reorganizing of magnetic field lines near sunspots will again affect the holographic grid patterns. The surface of the Sun is filled with hectic activity emitting electrically charged gases that generate areas of powerful magnetic forces. Psychological effects from these flares are much like those of the Schumann Resonance for the empath and while typically short lived can still create demanding symptoms like headaches, heart palpitations, mood swings, and generally just feeling yucky. It can also affect our mental state of mind with chaotic or confused thinking, erratic behavior, overall anxiety, and panic attacks as individuals as well as a collective.

It is critical for the empath to educate themselves on this type of activity and learn to discern Schumann Resonance, solar flares and sunspots to see if they are affecting the body, mind, and spirit. I know it is the cosmic solar activity that throws me totally off whereas it is the Schumann that can dramatically affect some of my friends and family so I make it a practice to check the Schuman levels online plus use the NASA site to monitor solar activity so that I am up to date on the activity surrounding me. I personally align with the collective energies off-planet and find myself affected by the cosmos especially when there is a lot of astrological activity. From solar flares to sunspots to planetary alignments or a combination thereof, I make sure I am aware of what is happening "out there" the moment I feel anxious, or if I find myself feeling like I have my finger in the electrical socket while standing in a puddle. These are some of those energetic overcharged symptoms described earlier that can begin as calling cards and end up as physical difficulties. My head can hurt, pound or zing. I get dizzy. I am forgetful. I am crabby and anxious. All of these things are not necessarily mine and if I am diligent in looking on say the NASA site to see what's up, I can work with the symptoms instead of pushing them onto another or fear I am dying of something undiagnosed.

As we're understanding, there is energy all around us as life takes place on multiple planes of reality. If we are consciously aware and in sync with the frequencies and vibrations of our surroundings, we can choose to allow them to affect us or not. But if we are not aware, we still may be affected especially if we are an unskilled empath. Believe it or not, the Earth behaves much like an enormous electric circuitry system that runs life-force, chi or prana through grid patterns and templates much like our human body does. Just like us, Gaia or Mother Earth is a consciousness container, a unique vehicle of Source. Our human vehicle connects to Source consciousness by use of not only our chakra system but also energy lines or pathways known as meridians that run within our body acting as internal communicators. In addition to having chakras, our planet vehicle of consciousness also has meridians known as ley lines plus grids and templates all designed to link with our human consciousness vehicle creating a grounding sense of connection, safety, and worth. Our Earth works with a set of three grids of sorts, that encompass our planet and each separate grid has its own job or function depending on its frequency and dimensional aspects. Together these intricately related grid templates surround our planet and affect human life.

The first grid located just below the surface of the planet has to do with its magnetics which are in constant flux and are affected by the human race. It is known as a "communication" grid. The planet hears and experiences our vibration and we hear and experience Hers. When the planet changes and shifts we are all affected by this communication action. This grid is accessible to anyone and anything on this planet but most humans will not be tuned into it unless they have activated their ability to do so at the level of a general empath connection. The way I activated my ability to connect with this grid was to play, to practice, and to play some more, especially with nature. To walk the land, to find and feel subtle nuances, to play with pendulums and dowsing rods to see if I could recognize any vibration change or frequency differences. The more I played, the more I opened. There really is no right or wrong way to learn this but I feel the more light-hearted the approach, the better it works.

Because it is basically formed of crystal the next grid is all about "remembrance" in terms of information and experiences and this is also in constant flux as both humankind and the planet are recalibrating and evolving into a higher crystalline vibration right now at this time in our history. Sensitive empaths that are more aligned to accessing both individually and collectively are able to tap into this layer as well as the magnetic communication grid below it. This crystalline grid keeps a balance of harmony within the planet linking it via portals into the universes and beyond, sometimes offering the sensitive empath information from the stars and other dimensions.

The final grid is similar to our bodies which holds within itself an electromagnetic "partnership" that happens when the meridians and pathways are free flowing for consciousness to fuel the body alignments from on-planet to off-planet as a dimensional gateway to our pasts and futures. The Ancients were highly aware of this grid and used it to partner with the wisdom of their ancestors. Again, this will align to the sensitive empath but also the psychic one.

All grids are in constant motion and when they intersect, overlap or get out of sync we can find a myriad of phenomena that the empath is vulnerable to from garnering information to becoming dizzy and sick depending on what they walked over or upon.

Although variations in planetary frequency can be identified with the increases of electric lightning storms or observed solar activity, there are still fluctuations to the Earth's frequencies that we as humans cannot yet explain. From my perspective, this is a sign the planet is changing and evolving to reflect the change in the collective consciousness, which in turn assists us humans to shift our individual consciousness altogether creating the groundwork for our future—the evolution of the human race on this planet. We chose Earth as home to our soul journey and we humans have an individual and a collective role of responsibility to the evolution of this planet as well as to each other.

Quantum Empathing

Although it's not detailed in this book, I want to mention quantum empathing because it is one of my personal empath sensitivities. I have encountered a few clients who have specifically sought me out because they have experienced these energies throughout their life, but struggled to understand what they mean. A quantum energy or light worker is typically a telepath who works extremely far out in the cosmos, which involves adjusting multiple dimensions and timelines. This type of energy empathing is also known as gridwork to those who are trained to navigate the universal blueprints of dimensional reality. This is a pretty unique style of work where the empath consciously uses their own body to "embody the work." It can sometimes affect them not only physically, but also emotionally and mentally until the work they are holding onto is finished.

Our Role in Evolution of the Collective

We gain knowledge about ourselves, knowledge about others, knowledge about our planet, cosmos, and universes by experiencing our personal feel centers stored within our individualized consciousness container that holds our reality. But as we are learning, feeling the collective energies of humanity, the planet and the cosmos can be extremely challenging to manage.

Remember, empathic people can physically experience an area of the Earth that has been filled with conflict, tragedy, and death and can not only feel, but take on the incredible pain and suffering of all of the people, nature kingdoms, and animals involved from a current or even past timeline experience. Even just by walking through it, the untrained empath can take on the suffering as their own. As more and more people awaken to their empathic abilities, they do not necessarily want to feel the pain that has happened to themselves and our planet because it is just that—painful. Becoming depressed or disconnected is oftentimes our instinctual biological response to the collective stress of humanity and the planet. However, training yourself to work with and through the pain is the only path that grants access to gaining truth by using empathy for oneness. Again, quiet time is key for the empath looking to heal via meditation, prayer, and surrendering to guidance. I invite us all to open our eyes to the truth of what has occurred in our pasts in order to know what is, and is not, a truth now. What is real and what is a program running in the collective designed to keep our minds too busy, to keep us moving through life like a zombie unable to connect to our hearts.

Through continually increasing our sentience and incorporating discernment to align to our truths, we can further discern the energetic quality of collective consciousness that we prefer to align with and express through our consciousness body. When experiencing these collective fields, the trained and awakened person moves through life present and connected which then offers them a vantage point to observe and then assist in efforts of service to self and service to others. By monitoring their own container, they can then choose or not, to assist in efforts to rebalance the collective container by intentionally releasing fear-based energy or infusing love-based frequencies or a combination thereof. This ignites empathy and fuels oneness.

Client Story
The 100+ Year Holographic Brothel

Several years ago, I had the pleasure of collaborating with a team on a paranormal investigation in Deadwood, South Dakota. While we were there, we all had one of the most unbelievable experiences of a lifetime. Deadwood, for those that are not aware, has quite a history that offers a plethora of paranormal opportunities for anyone that is open to investigating, especially any empath. During its heyday, this town was known for its volatile nature, which set the stage for murder, abuse, and everything imaginable that for some reason, still chooses to stick around even today. It is filled with ghosts and dark spirits that purposefully choose not to move to the light. It has entities, mostly negative, that roam the streets, buildings, and land and any ignorant empath is prime to be hijacked or jumped at any time. In fact, I personally know of, and have worked on, folks that have had to do energy healings upon returning from this town to clear the attachments they took home from their adventures. Many residents are also aware of the destructive forces hard at work in this town and sometimes seek assistance.

This was the case when I met a woman named Lucy that had lived in Deadwood all her life. She is highly psychic plus a sensitive empath, and when I met her, she was having difficulties holding her boundaries from another that was psychically attacking her and needed some help. I was asked to do a healing session on her, and during our conversation, I came to find out she had spent several of her young years being raised by prostitutes in the brothel just down the block. When she was 3 to 5 years old, her mother had dropped her off and left her there for them to parent. Lucy accepted this as her normal, and after reconnecting with her biological parents, the memories of the brothel faded as she continued to live in the very same town even to the day I met her. Throughout her life, her empath nature took not only a physical toll on her body, but an emotional and mental one as well. The additional torment from the abusive male that was currently taunting her was fully exhausting her and creating illness. The brothel where she was raised for those years was originally active in the late 1800s and was still a viable business until the 1980s. Even though she still lived and worked right in town, she had not stepped foot in that specific building since childhood. Ironically, or not, that brothel was originally located in the exact building our paranormal team had booked to investigate that evening. The building was abandoned and had been for some time. The brothel had been located on the second level of what was now a row of retail businesses and was last used as a spook house for a local event years prior. There was no real furniture except some old, discarded Halloween props strewn about and the spray-painted bare-walled interior was basically destroyed from years of neglect and non-use.

My personal intention as a paranormal psychic is to never have prior knowledge of any space or story of what I am about to investigate so as to not enhance or color the experience I find myself walking into. This was the case when we arrived at the abandoned brothel. Although I am an empath, I have trained diligently over the years as a practitioner to feel and then step back and observe the details of the experience, much like watching a movie. This is exactly what happened that night.

The moment I approached the barren location and walked up the staircase, my holographic experience was a full-blown timeline jump into the past, complete with visuals of what the space looked like in times gone by—from the wallpaper to the carpet to the furniture to the people working within the brothel. It was as if I had stepped into a time machine and it was one of the most unbelievable, yet amazing, experiences of my life as my empath skills were on overdrive. In actuality, there was nothing on the walls, and yet my senses saw and also felt the colors and texture of the flocked wallpaper, my feet felt the cushion of the carpet, and I was drawn into the lobby complete with furniture of years-past, all seen within my psychic mind. I remember knowing that there was a peek-a-boo window that the Madam of the brothel used to approve those requesting entrance, even though that window was nowhere to be found within this devoid building. I distinctly remember seeing a red velvet c-shaped couch in my mind's eye, complete with tufted buttons that adorned the lobby entrance. I was experiencing a full historic holographic tour as I walked the deserted halls of this space still filled with spirit memories and very real energies of the past.

The paranormal team investigation began with a voice-box session, utilizing a device that connects with ghosts or spirits that spits out words that then can be used to validate or communicate with the other side. This is not my personal favorite piece of paranormal equipment, yet I admit it is amazing to use it to cross-reference what I am getting psychically. In this case, it was the names of a couple of the original "Ladies of the Evening" that were residents of the brothel in its very early days. As the investigators asked for their names, what I heard in my head was simultaneously projecting from the voice box and it was remarkable to hear. The team and I went onward to do a room-by-room tour of the entire space. Again, each time we entered a particular abandoned area, it seemed to come alive in psychic vision offering a full-blown holographic experience of not only what the space looked like, but also revealing the essence of those that lived within it. I was able to see and hear the early 1900s timeline clearly, as well as the 1960s timelines in which Lucy was raised when it was an active brothel.

About a quarter of the way through our initial tour of the space, I asked if we could call Lucy to audibly connect with her on the phone to collaborate and endorse some of the things I was seeing and hearing. Fortunately, she was available, and as we entered each room, she was able to retrieve memories and supporting information that validated our findings. It was mind-blowing for us all. The residual energy of each room was so palpable and real, yet here we were standing in a deserted, abandoned space. Detailed stories of each prostitute unfolded as we moved from room to room. It was the residual energy held within that defined the difference between the brothel's top-performer room versus the one housing the newbie in training. It was clear where the Madam lived and worked and where the money was counted and the books were kept. I plainly saw a gentleman that wore a distinctive hat and pinstripe suit that did the books and entered the building from the back side in the night to keep his identity secret from the community during the time period that Lucy was in the building. He also hid money in a secret loose floorboard. This was validated by Lucy as a clear memory from her childhood from the times he would allow her to hang out in the room with him while he worked. We looked on-site for the secret floorboard, hoping there might still be a treasure hidden inside, but sadly had no such luck. I will never forget how nauseous I became as we approached the last room on the front side of the building where I came upon a horrific holographic energy signature of a violent murder of a specific young prostitute. The energy pattern showed her getting choked and stabbed by a patron in the room, then viciously dragged down the hallway through the building and tossed into a back room where the hot water boiler was located, left to die alone. The entire pathway was still embedded energetically within the building even though multiple years had passed. Additionally, there was a room off the back that also made me choke, cry, and double over in pain, where I fully knew men severely beat the prostitutes and performed archaic abortions on pregnant girls. Lucy again validated this information as true events that had occurred during her residency there.

To our amazement, Lucy decided to show up in person later that same evening and met with us on site to personally assist us in our investigation. She had not stepped foot inside that building since she was around five years old, and she was now in her late fifties. I met her at the front door and her wide eyes told the story of how afraid she was to encounter her old memories still buried within the walls of this abandoned building. We took things very slowly, allowing Lucy to turn back the hands of time and embrace the emotions that were spilling out of her mind, heart, and body. It was fascinating to watch as Lucy slowly made her way through each room, once again reiterating the stories we had just previously shared by phone. Room by room, her memories opened much like a lotus flower. It was so beautiful yet, so sad. As a healer, I was extremely aware of making sure Lucy's vulnerability was supported along the way and offered energetic assistance to keep her balanced and safe both emotionally and physically. She validated what we knew as the place where the gentlemen would enter and choose their lady of the night. Lucy remembered the layout of the rooms one by one, complete with furniture, wallpaper, and carpet.

One of the most amazing things I observed was the way Lucy automatically and almost forcefully stopped at a certain point while walking down the hallway. I right then witnessed Lucy completely transform from a fifty-plus year-old woman back into a small child about the age of five that had just hit a boundary that she knew she was not permitted to cross. That portion of the building was where she was not allowed as that tiny five-year-old in residence. It was where serious business took place and no child could enter. We were stunned at how Lucy's adult body still automatically obeyed that strict command. It was fascinating to witness. I did a rebalance of her body's energy field and restructured the energetic signature of the building as well and asked her to see if that felt safe for her to proceed. It did, so we moved onward. She repeated this automatic-stop-pattern in a couple of places throughout the building, especially those that held past horror and memory. I continued to clear both Lucy and the building as we proceeded through the night by releasing sadness, emotion, and cutting cords to memories.

It was like watching pieces of a puzzle coming together as Lucy made her way from room to room, telling us more stories of her memories of times past. When she came upon her own bedroom from when she was that very young girl, she simply melted into the space and remembered and relived the memories of things none of us can even imagine. We all gave her the time and space she so deserved. She laughed. She cried. She remembered the horror of that time. She remembered the love from that time. She healed. We learned.

What I learned most as an energy practitioner was just how vast the experience of holographic energy signatures can be, and how dangerous it is for empaths who are ignorant to the idea or concept of interpenetrating timelines. Think about all we encountered, walked through, and took on during those hours of investigating. We walked through hundreds of years of memories, good, bad, and for sure in this case, horribly ugly. The residual energies that still hold strong within those walls are not things that can be covered up by a new coat of paint or a room filled with new furniture. What the general public is not aware of is that we are all empaths to some extent, and we will feel residual energies from the past whether we know it or not. Working or living within a building that holds that much pain can only offer pain to those that spend time within it, no matter how pretty its outside shell looks. Let's say, for example, that this space is never cleared of its past horrific energy, and someone comes along and purchases or rents it, and puts in, say, an insurance company within the same walls. The employees will in some manner empath the fear, pain, and angst throughout their days, and ultimately some will most likely become sad, angry, or even sick. This is why it is critical to clear space to ensure it is safe and balanced—to be responsible for our own individual energy fields and honor our health and wellness. And for the empath, to learn to discern and release!

PART THREE

Practicing Discernment

✦

Chapter Eleven

Four Discernment Practices for the Empath

Many clients I work with struggle to make difficult decisions. They are unclear on the best path to take or simply feel overwhelmed and are looking for something outside of themselves for guidance. Some even want me to directly tell them what to do. It is a common human experience to feel stuck when faced with the big and small decisions we encounter in daily life. We are unsure about what is right or wrong. What is best or not. What is true or not. And this sense of feeling confused or stuck is uncomfortable, which is why we look to others or something outside ourselves to provide a quick and easy answer.

When clients show up in my office looking for guidance, I first tell them there is not an actual right or wrong answer. There just is a choice, and with any choice comes consequences attached. Some consequences are good, and some are not so good. And each choice has its own mix of consequences. When making decisions, it is us who oversees not only our free will choice but also our version of truths. It is up to us to evaluate the choices and consequences against our version of truth through the practice of discernment. The skill of discernment can give us clarity, and this is what I invite my clients to bring into their life—a way to go "in" for the answers instead of searching outward.

Discernment is the ability to obtain sharp perceptions or to judge well. It is the process of making careful distinctions in our thinking about our truth to then guide our actions. For the empath, we become intertwined with other energy fields, creating more complications for discerning and making decisions. Learning how to go within to discern our own energies

173

and protect our energy fields as a routine practice secures our personal energy fuel and provides a truth barometer to navigate daily life. When we become adept at recognizing our own level of truth frequency, we immediately know when it is challenged, threatened or hijacked by outside forces. When you acquire the skill of discernment, you will be able to limit any effects of empathing or taking on another's energy that may not serve your highest good. So how do we get in touch with our truth frequencies?

As we've learned, our divine physical bodies are containers we've chosen to navigate life on this planet. They are also the perfect tool for tapping into our truth frequencies. However, I find clients often have great difficulty with this concept and grow frustrated. We humans have been taught many beliefs about our bodies and, as a result, most of us do not have a healthy relationship with our physical meat and bones. When we're asked to be still and feel our bodies for truth and information, we grow frustrated because we are disconnected, which triggers old tapes of failure and shame.

Discernment is all about restoring our connection with our bodies. Trusting it to get the information. Moving beyond any fear of failure. Commanding guidance. So, what does it mean to trust your body? And how do we even entertain this idea if we are already fighting internally to have a healthy and loving relationship with it, much less listen to it and allow it to guide us? I encourage my clients to open to the idea of having conversation with their bodies through quiet time. To just be still with your body without any expectations or conditions attached. Then, just ask it what you want to know and trust the immediate overall response.

During healing sessions, I use a simple discernment exercise to help clients begin to see what it feels like to trust their body. First, I ask them to relax back into their chair and take a few deep breaths. Then I have them place their hands on their heart chakra located in the middle of their chest. I inform them I am going to quickly go through a series of questions, and I want them to tap into their body vibration and pull the answer immediately from within their body instead of taking the time to make it up in their head. By this time, I have already asked what brought them to the session and will weave their questions in and out of a series of random questions I ask. I intentionally formulate multiple versions of their question to see if their immediate response finds its way forward more than once. Additionally, I watch the body's response to the answers—how easily it answers, how confident the response flows, and how relaxed it is during the interchange.

Most humans do not really listen to their body. We listen to our heads instead, the egoic mind that houses the mental field of programmed beliefs—we think-feel versus feel-feel. But each time I do this exercise, I find it amazing just how much our own human container already knows if we would just listen to it and honor what it says. And what's more amazing is that when my clients give themselves permission to be still and turn off the mind, it isn't very hard for them to identify what their body is telling them. Through my work I have found four core practices for using our bodies as our tool for discernment that I use each day, in some form, in my client work.

Asking "Is This Mine?"

As you can probably already tell, I use the phrase "Is this mine?" constantly throughout my client work. This phrase is a reminder for my clients to question their own body and identify whose energy or messaging they are currently encountering or carrying. The practice is as simple as that— taking a moment to sit back as the observer and ask yourself "Is this mine?" Sometimes clients find that they can indeed claim ownership to the energy and in other instances they cannot.

In many cases we think we are dealing with something in our own lives, yet outside energies will actually be influencing our field through cords to people, places, and things that drives the messaging or triggers old beliefs— as we have discussed in previous chapters. Other times we have simply stepped into a collective field of energy that is much like a hodge-podge soup of vibrational frequencies. We often will not know the difference if we truly own the energy, idea, situation or message until we break it down, examine it, and communicate with it. The more we practice this kind of dialog with our bodies, the easier it becomes over time to get a quicker response.

Once you get used to working with your body to find out if you own the energy of a situation, you can take the practice a step further. If you do own it, you may choose to investigate deeper to discern if the situation is a result of current beliefs or unresolved issues from your childhood or past. The answers may determine how you choose to work with those beliefs or release them. If you find you do not own the energy, you can continue a line of questioning to get more information of whose energy it really is that is consuming your body, mind, or emotion and why it triggered an attachment to your field.

For the empath, "Is this mine?" is the first step in the discernment process to break down any assaultive energies entering your auric bodies. When we encounter assaultive energies, our mental field begins running on overdrive to try and sort through the confusing messages running through the body–mind matrix. Posing the concept of "Is this mine?" forces a moment of pause. It temporarily stops the mental chatter. And if we have been practicing true dialog with our bodies, in these moments we can decipher programmed messaging from current reality, which in the end offers the empath the choice to either allow the negative energy to remain inside the divine human vehicle or release it fully back to Source. Asking the question trains the divine human body-container to immediately respond before the monkey-mind takes over.

The practice of asking "Is this mine?" naturally flows into further questioning such as "Whose is it?" or "What is it?" Or if it is mine, "Is it mine from my current timeline situation or is it from a past or possibly even a future self?" Or asking, "Is this a collective energy versus an individual one?" Searching for answers to this natural flow of questions is the way to move into the state of truth discernment and energetic healing. If discernment does not occur, most likely our human brain will run these foreign frequencies throughout our body–mind matrix to find anything to attach itself to, to make sense of the confusing messaging we've encountered. For example, if I empathed sadness without knowing it or discerning it, I am unconsciously allowing these frequencies to continue to run within my systems and my mind will find some way to attach this sadness to something or someone to complete the circuitry within my matrix. I will go home and assume I am sad with my partner. I will go to work and have the sense my career is unfulfilled. I will worry excessively for another and so on. This is why it is critical to begin the conversation by asking the question and then to flow into the discernment process to find clarity and set boundaries of what you own and what you do not.

Identifying Boundaries

I work with many clients who are taking on some role of caretaker in their lives, whether it is home raising kids with crazy schedules, responsible for a sick or old parent, assisting someone in a nursing home, or managing affairs for someone who is dying. Determining and commanding healthy boundaries seems almost impossible for many of them as they give their time and energy to everyone and everything around them leaving nothing for themselves. When we deplete our own fuel tanks we then become ineffective at providing the care and empathy we intended to give all along because of resentment or conditions we hold from the situation. Establishing healthy boundaries for our energy is therefore an important practice in the skill set of discernment and knowing our truths.

The footprint of how life works within the home and context of careers can look and feel different for everyone. Many struggle to raise children while juggling the balls of remote offices, online meetings, and chaotic work schedules combined with the challenges of homeschooling and hybrid programs. Those who go to an office or on-site job then hold guilt or angst of not being home or available enough for the loved ones in their care. Even more chaos is added trying to fit in all the necessary tasks of caregiving from picking up medicines, to visiting the care-facility, to managing bills to holding hospice space for the dying. It seems there is never enough of something. Not enough time. Not enough money. Not enough help. Not enough answers. Not enough of me to go around. This type of client places themselves last yet finds themselves exhausted and resentful. Their body and mind crave help, yet they do not ask for assistance nor take it because it is just easier for them to do it—plus then it will be done right!

Some version of this narrative is so common in most humans today and, as I've shared, I know perfectly well just how easy it is to get sucked into this energy trap. It is difficult to comprehend just how many different places, spaces, and people actually drain our energy. It is not something we really examine each day as we make our way through life helping and doing or simply existing. One of my goals in my work is to help clients become more aware of just how many separate energy drains affect them.

When I work with clients on the practice of establishing boundaries, I use a sandbox metaphor to describe the process. I first ask the client to visualize themselves in the middle of their own personal sandbox surrounded not only by sand but all their favorite toys or items. Then, I go through a series of questions and engage in a dialog to sort through the answers. *Who or what do I allow to play within my sandbox? Are there others standing within its boundary or on the outskirts trying to budge in? Is anyone trying to steal my toys? Are there other people's toys filling up my space? Are the toys I am currently surrounded by ones I still love to play with or are they old, rusted, and not usable? Is there anyone or anything invading my sandbox space, pushing me out fully to take over to claim it as theirs?*

There are no right or wrong answers in this practice. There is no right or wrong way to describe what we mean by our toys or who we allow or don't allow in our space. This is simply an exercise used to practice the process of asking your energy field discernment questions about your boundaries when you encounter something or someone who might not be beneficial to you. By asking who or what has affected my auric field (the boundary of my sandbox) and examining how my energy has been compromised, I can then determine how and why I allowed another to enter my sandbox and take my toys or budge into my space, and take steps to release them.

Not only do all of us deserve to have our own space but it is imperative we know our personal boundaries, especially for the empath. The outline of your sandbox, the intimacy of what your sand feels like, the comfort and joy factor of your toys are all good allegories for the personal border-line that our auric fields energetically offer our bodies. The more intimate we are with our individual frequencies and vibrations held within our auric space, the easier it is to feel what does or does not serve our highest good. Sadly, most of us run willy-nilly throughout each other's sand-boxes stomping about stealing toys and tossing out sand while budging and pushing our concerns, fears, and beliefs upon another. It is time to take back our sandbox because sometimes these interpenetrating fields and timelines can be dangerous in more ways than one.

The sandbox exercise can also assist us in visualizing how through our experiences, each one of us builds a personal matrix of information within our mind that can be considered the sand and toys within our sandbox. We spend our lives trying to piece together some sense of order from what we see and experience. Each bit of information gets incorporated into our personal container or auric field and divine human physical container. We are light beings, consciousness from a creational source having a physical experience that exist in a matrix, hologram or virtual programmed reality that we believe is real because our brains tell us it is. Remember, the empath's sensory perception is heightened, and he or she can experience multiple matrices or holograms beyond the current timeline running and fully take on the energies of that time–space continuum. All of this happens within our energy bodies, chakras, and auric fields which can be monitored by performing a body scan to see where there may be energy stuck or distorted resulting in physical, emotional, mental, and spiritual dis-ease and disease. Before we can become adept at body scanning however, it is a good idea to examine what triggers a physical or emotional response within your unique personal body.

Note: A full body scan is detailed in the Appendix under Meditations.

Noticing Triggers

On any given day, humans experience a range of emotions from feelings of anticipation to excitement, to frustration to disappointment. Typically, these are reactive responses to specific events that can vary based on your current state of mind or the circumstances. A trigger hits us at a deeper level and activates a different energy in the response to the event, which results in a more intense emotional or physical reaction. We can all recount situations where family members, friends, or co-workers have had what seems like a disproportionate response to something we've done or said. This is because in that moment our words or actions found a trigger within their energetic field that launched a series of messages from past situations, experiences or programming.

A typical reactive response to any daily encounter usually is followed by some sort of action while a trigger sparks a whole energetic platform across all fields to direct how we move into action depending on the physical, emotional, mental, and even spiritual programming stored within our personal consciousness container. Stored negative messaging sets the stage for how to proceed as it determines the lens we are viewing the situation through. Amazingly the lens we choose might not even be "seeing" the real-time event but instead "seen through" as an old memory lens. Triggers might include reminders of unwanted memories, words, or actions and can include things like challenged beliefs, being ignored or shut down, betrayal or disapproval, rejection, or exclusion.

Even though I am a professional who counsels others daily on their energy I do not get off the hook for being human. I find myself often challenged with and vulnerable to not only my own triggers but those of my partner, my family, my friends, and just about anyone I encounter. This is why I always call it a practice because the work is never done. What I find fascinating about triggers and our reactions to them is how we can lose the awareness of being present. What I mean is when we trigger energy churning throughout our individual consciousness container, it is searching out validations and connections. During these moments, we lose our connection to our divine human vehicle and experience the situation as almost not present. I witness this often with my own husband and, while I find it fascinating, it is also disturbing. After interacting with him for nearly 40 years, I know when a conflict tosses my husband into his matrix of mayhem because I energetically can see his aura change. It is as if a cellophane sheet forms around him, especially across his eyes, which energetically somehow changes his vision of what is truly happening, to instead, align with what he is cellularly remembering. He aurically changes and shifts as his mental mind is on overdrive to do its best to forge a like-finds-like connection to the current event happening. For example, if I engage in a conflict-based conversation with him, he triggers old father-based memories, and I no longer energetically am conversing with my husband. It indeed is me standing in front of him, yet his matrix hears and sees a version of stored memory engaged in negative-based father communication that overpowers him and shuts him down.

As I mentioned, when we witness friends or loved ones in a triggered state, often that alone can produce a triggered response in us as well. For example, I remember a family gathering where one of my children tossed a flippant comment at another of my kids, which immediately triggered them both. The comment was casual, yet somewhat judgmental of someone he was interested in dating. The response triggered a defense mechanism in them both and immediately that cellophane experience was manifesting right before my eyes as energetically they were no longer present and were individually seeing and hearing their own version of what was happening. I was aurically watching the cords of energy surrounding my two children entangling them in a mess that was not even the initial fight, but more so a heated argument seen through the lens of their own stored beliefs, personalized unresolved issues and memories. The scenario became even more intense as another child jumped into the fight prompted by his own disdain of conflict only to trigger his personal cellophane lens, adding to what was happening. Lo and behold, it got even crazier as additional family members joined in the argument, all seeing it through their own triggered beliefs, from grandmothers to aunts and uncles to cousins and more.

This family energetic scenario was bizarre to witness as an outside observer, and yet I am sure households across the globe engage in this form of negative behavior all the time without realizing it. I also admit I am not always the objective observer in these situations because dealing with our triggers is the most challenging of the discernment practices. In these moments our energy fields become a phantom matrix of beliefs playing out on a stage of old timelines and memories entangled with current timelines and events. Therefore, energetically, many continually find themselves fighting the same fights with the same people time and time again, because it is anchored as old triggers that are subconsciously stored as unresolved memories and experiences. Plus, the current negative encounter will only solidify the messy programming further to be triggered at another time.

So, you might be asking, how do we handle this? By managing the moment—but it is not really all that simple. We cannot avoid or escape every tricky situation or conversation life tosses our way and it is guaranteed we will find ourselves faced with family or friend conflicts. When our body produces an elevated response, it is hard to manage our energy in the moment. So we must begin with awareness. And to become aware of our triggers, we must first understand what it feels like in our body when we encounter one. Usually, when triggered, we experience not only surging emotions but also physical symptoms like a pounding heart, shortness of breath, tightening of the throat, shaking of the body or voice and the sweats. To assist my empath client in discerning their triggers, I ask them to think back throughout their week to identify a person or situation that triggered this kind of whole-body response. Then, I ask a series of questions to identify *what happened in the exchange? What deeper message or belief may have fueled the reaction? Is this belief yours and is it necessary? Is there anything held in your field that may be in need of release?* The amazing thing about this work is we can always go back to a situation and energetically feel the experience as an observer in order to connect and listen to the information within our body.

Over time, as we practice assessing our triggering moments, we become more able to notice and monitor the response in real time and track down the origin of the issue during future interactions. Then, learning to stay present with what is playing out energetically is a second step, meaning we monitor for when the cellophane lens wants to cloud our view of the situation and take a mental step back to re-set. Remember, during a tense conversation, it is always okay to take a moment of pause to check in with yourself. It is sometimes a good idea to also take some actual physical space to readjust and shift because typically any negative encounter draws the auric fields of two or more people engaged in conflict into each other's fields, further igniting energy transference and attack. Physically stepping back or actually leaving the area can assist you in avoiding this overwhelming energy drain, so take a short break emotionally as well as physically until you can redirect. The goal here is not to avoid the conflict or conversation as much as change the frequencies at play from the trigger action and once you feel more in control of your energy you can return to the situation at hand if you choose.

Body Scanning

Most of us go throughout our day not necessarily aware of what our body is encountering in the way of energies surrounding us and interpenetrating us. As we become more aware of the fact that we have an energy field, we can begin to practice asking "Where in my body do I have a blockage?" "Where am I storing a belief?" or "Where do I need to shift a boundary?" Many folks use a body scan as a meditation technique for relaxation and healing, however, this practice can be the empath's best tool for doing a quick (or long) method of establishing what energies they are holding onto and also discern if any stuck or corded energies are theirs, or not.

A scan can be a simple effort done in any place at any time, or it can be a full-blown meditative process or technique, it all depends on what you choose to accomplish and the amount of time and effort you choose to put forth. I will oftentimes do a quick overall scan of my entire body when standing in line at any big-box store checkout to notice anything that does not serve me and I follow that with a simple hand chop motion to remove any energetic cords I may be holding onto from the store, including the people inside and the products on the shelves. This style scan is more about intention than method. It is not to be used to feel bad about yourself or feel broken. It is about information. Knowledge is power and when we know what our body is holding onto and why, then we can do something to change that.

I do not perform a full scan as a meditation. I do this work fully awake, present, and connected to my body, my feel centers, my emotions, and my mental field to engage in a dialog with my divine human vehicle of Source energy. I scan for stuck energies and information by relaxing into a safe, uninterrupted time and space where I can move through my body one chakra at a time. When doing a body scan the goal is to look at each spot for physical energies that feel imbalanced, different, stuck, hot, heavy, buzzing, stiff, cold and more. This goes for inside the body as well as around it. You can also look for any trapped or stored emotional energies like sadness, fear, angst, anger, doom and so on. When tapping into each location you want to create an inner dialog with your divine human vehicle and have as deep a conversation as possible. Some may feel like they are "making up" the answers and that is fine, especially when you begin this practice. The longer and more often you do it the more you will trust your information.

When encountering an imbalanced or stuck energy, the first question you want to ask your personal divine human vehicle is: "Is this mine?" and further, "Is this mine right now, or from my past?" The divine human container may answer with an inner knowing, an ah-ha moment, a physical reaction or sensation or maybe even a psychic hit. If the answer to the question indicates it is not yours, then respond with additional deeper questioning as to whose stuck energy is this or what is this all about? Keep questioning until you find yourself satisfied and sometimes it takes more than one scan session to find your complete answer. Some people do not feel as if they get any answer and that is OK too, just keep up the process, as the more you practice the easier it becomes to listen to your body and feel centers and some day you might just hear or know the answers to your questions after all.

The point of the body scan is to find stuck or heavy density and offer that energy the idea of a personality to converse with, ask questions of and find answers to what you are holding onto. There are no rules, no rights, no wrongs to this process. It is simply finding a way to get a conversational trusting relationship going with your divine human vehicle as well as your energy body.

Remember the body is a map of the chakra system and the auric field templates. Refer to Chapter Four and also the chakra info in the Appendix to further examine what you may or may not be holding onto on behalf of self or others. Each portion of the body holds an individual stream of chi, prana or gas coming from Source to fuel the body in alignment to our higher good and when this is not in balance we find stuck energies and by directly correlating this information to the chakra and auric system, you will easily find partial answers to the questions you ask your body per what the consciousness-gas offers. As you move through the scan and get your information you can also choose to release anything that no longer serves you via your breath and intention.

As a psychic intuitive and a trained empath, what I am looking for during each portion of any body scan I perform on myself, or on clients, is anything that stands out as dense, heavy, busy, chaotic, or energy that is buzzing, pushing, pulsing, and holding temperature differences again both inside and around the body. I also look for feelings and emotions that may reveal themselves such as fear, sadness, anger etc., and each feeling or emotion I encounter I again ask the question on behalf of myself or my client: Is this mine? And if I do not feel as if it is mine or if I cannot fully own it, I question further as to whose it is, where it came from and why I chose to take it on.

Below I am offering a sample of a scan from the perspective of a trained empath and energy practitioner to share common information I come across in my client work. The full Meditative Interactive Body Scan can be found in the Appendix Section under Meditations.

Meditation
Let's Begin . . .

Sit or lie down. Relax and release anything crossed like hands, legs, ankles and take a deep cleansing breath. You can close your eyes or keep them open.

Head and Skull: Beginning with the head and only the head, I scan inside, outside, and around the entire skull. I examine and compare front to back. Side to side.

Next, I move to the outside of the skull or outline of the head. Remember with each body portion I pose the question and have the dialogue of: Is this mine? And if not, I question further.

Throat, Neck, and Shoulders: Here I move down to the neck, scanning the throat both front and back. I also scan both shoulders, comparing right to left and outward into the rotator cuffs. I scan the upper back below the base of the neck into the mid-upper back. I will also scan down both arms, again comparing right to left, including the elbows, wrists, and hands.

Upper Mid-body both Front and Back: In this area I scan the ribs, the lungs, the heart and middle of the chest as I compare right to left, front to back for imbalance as well.

Middle or Trunk of the Body: I scan the organs that hold anger like the kidneys and the liver. I scan the digestive organs and the back side of the body as well as the front.

Belly Area and Lower Back: To scan this area, it is important to do both front and back, side to side. I scan the entire digestive track system and the sex organs, especially on women. I especially take time to scan the back side of the body, lower back, all the way down to the sciatica on both sides.

The Hips, Hip Flexors, Pelvis, and Lower Trunk of the Body: I will scan for this right/left tug as well as front/back tug of the energies all the way from the hips to the feet and many times will find an enormous difference in how the body holds itself in the way of stability and balance.

Please note there is detailed information for this Body Scan plus a meditation for each body part in the Meditation Appendix, to take this effort even further for healing purposes.

Chapter Twelve

Honoring the Energetic Journey

In the early days of my journey to become an energy practitioner, I was gifted the opportunity of learning many lessons of how important it is to honor the energy from the soul's perspective just as much, if not more than, from the human one. I was still working within the corporate realm when I initially began my energy practice and learning how to balance the two worlds was a bit tricky at first. My reality would bounce from my 3D entrained go, go, go personality during the day or week and then drastically explode into the cosmos through out-of-body experiences in the evenings and on the weekends, doing my best to remember that I had four kids to raise along the way. Juggling these dualistic realities felt a bit bipolar to say the least.

At the very beginning I never really planned on making this journey into a professional practice or business, I was curious more than anything, to learn about this unknown world and then became incredibly thirsty for more information and knowledge as time went on. As I read books, watched videos, listened to others, and finally took some classes, things actually became more confusing as I never really felt as if I fit into any specific box. My 3D mind was still trying to make sense of it all. I looked into numerous modalities such as reiki, Theta, hands-on-healing and more, yet nothing felt like the glass slipper fit that could unleash my unique personal magic I knew was bubbling up inside of me, so I began down a different path. I focused on myself, my own personal body, mind, and spirit and was open to the idea that my own soul may have a purpose for not just being here as a mother, wife, and corporate executive but for remembering why I incarnated in the first place as a human on planet Earth.

Learning to connect to and find guidance from your own Higher Self, your own soul is an intimate dance of spirit and not something any class can actually teach you. It comes from spending time with yourself first before thinking you are going to go out in the world and help others. This was new for me, and it took time and patience to trust the process. I felt unskilled at meditation and could not sit still for seconds much less hours. I was frustrated doing guided reflections as I could never see what the person on the CD was telling me was over the hill or along the path. I was impatient and often felt hopeless in my efforts, but I just kept trying new and different things and did my best to stay out of failure mode.

Over time, I began to trust myself more, telling myself it was okay to not have the answers, and as it turns out it was. Giving myself permission to not have to know everything allowed me to slow down and trust. I began to hear more of my inner guidance. I began to open up to what is known as a download of information from higher source energies. I began to remember things I had always known since childhood and found courage to unlock the hidden vaults of information inside slowly through trial and error. And as I said, I was offered many lessons along the way. One of those lessons was learning this was my own journey.

Initially, I wanted everyone in my current life to ride this wave with me but quickly found that was just not happening. In fact, I distinctly remember how opening to this new world affected my relationships with not just my family and friends but with my co-workers and corporate world. When you begin to paradigm-shift you ignorantly think others are shifting with you and in truth it is almost the opposite effect. When your vibration heightens due to your spiritual work, others notice something is different but cannot necessarily decide what it is, and this can cause unseen friction or angst as the two different energetic realms once again collide. This played out as short fuse tempers, or unsolicited arguments from those around me. I was also finding myself feeling like I had to defend my ideas and actions and because I was not ready for this, it took a lot of patience along the way to realize that the work I was doing at the beginning was all about me, and only me, and I had no right to expect others to be open to it or readily accept it. Nor was it my job to worry about anyone accepting this so-called new version of Suzanne and believe me, that was tough. Especially because

I resonate very much to the cosmos and off-planet frequencies, and I was rapidly remembering all kinds of things that were alien (no pun here either) to many people. The jokes, the jabs, the ridicule from those in my life was a pretty heavy burden in the early days. Many times I felt alone, isolated, and second-guessed myself but through patience combined with tenacity I found my own way. And eventually chose to share my gifts with others, first practicing on accommodating family members and close friends who volunteered to be guinea pigs while I learned more.

As I began to work on more of the volunteers, I experienced a whole new wave of insecurities that sprung from the feeling of being responsible to heal someone. Working with actual people triggered limitations of right and wrong, good and bad as I found myself again second-guessing not just me but the healing work itself. I was terrified I might hurt someone. I was scared to fail. These feelings were all happening because I believed I was performing the healing. When I awakened to the truth that I was simply the practitioner, the one who was holding the space for the process of moving the energy, it became clear the client, combined with their Higher Self, was actually in charge of the healing along with their soul and Source energy. This paradigm shift changed everything for me as a person and as a practitioner resulting in the courage to move toward a professional practice of energy healing but also soul-based teaching to help others embrace and honor ideas of the Higher Self, the soul and soul contracts, and the Akashic Records.

Soul Contracts and the Akashic Records

In the early days of my journey, I encountered many new concepts, like the Higher Self, soul contracts, and Akashic Records. When initially exploring these philosophies, I remember thinking "I have no idea what this even is!" because it was all so incredibly foreign to me. I had no previous exposure to the concepts of energy healing, and my efforts to study these subjects felt like bumbling through books published in different languages. Added to that, was my initial repulsion to these unknown concepts because the unknown invited layers of doubt. Doubt keeps us from opening up because we feel vulnerable to being duped so instead we stay safely locked into our old limitations and beliefs. Plus, these were particularly difficult concepts offering multiple colorful theories that boggled my mind—it was initially uncomfortable to process these colorful theories so vastly different from the limited black and white ones I was used to. Instead, these concepts left so much room for interpretation and individualized perception, which is why esoteric ideas are often labeled as unstable and not safe. When our sense of safety is threatened, we become triggered from within and find ourselves stuck once again in limiting loop patterns of right or wrong, true or not.

Although feeling overwhelmed and doubtful, I chose to push ahead fueled mostly by relentless curiosity and practiced ways to peel back the layers of my proverbial onion skin that still held deep-rooted fear-based thinking. This birthed a new found courage and trust to entertain new possibilities as I began examining and releasing long-standing trigger programs. As I continued to open up to more ideas, it became clear how this soul contract perspective offered an opportunity to take responsibility for not only my current actions but also embrace and relearn what I originally came here to do on the planet as a human incarnation. One of the best ways to move into a place of spiritual awakening is to acquaint yourself with any idea or process that reinstates within you a sense of empowerment. The idea of the soul contract completely piqued my interest because once I could grasp the reason for contracts, I could connect the dots toward how others in my life offered an integral piece to my feeling of empowerment or victimization. When I intentionally paradigm-shifted how I chose to look at life and my interactions with those in it, I began to move into empowerment. When I no longer chose to see others as a persecution tool, I began to intentionally choose to become present in how I created and observed my life. I choose to see soul contracts as a step toward my liberation and freedom. The more I embraced these philosophies the more I shared them during client sessions and teaching presentations.

Nowadays, most of my work with clients revolves around their soul, Higher Self, and Akashic Records as a source of healing. I never claim to have universal truths on any of these subjects, nor will I ever push my ideology onto another as this is all dependent on each individual's belief systems and free will choices. What I do offer is a perspective of a "higher Source reason" for the struggles they may find themselves facing in current times as well as past ones. Let us examine how a client that has struggled for years from childhood trauma and abuse could entertain and utilize the ideology of soul contract to heal and move forward in love. If someone experienced a childhood with an abusive parent for example, from some perspective they signed on for that parent and abuse prior to their incarnation. This is all done from a place where there is no right nor wrong. There only is.

For whatever reason the souls involved chose to play out actions, lessons, and consequences that are vital to their soul's growth on this earth plane and beyond. There is a soul agreement on both sides. One soul decides to incarnate to experience the offering of abuse while the other signs on for receiving the abuse. In between lives this is all done from the vibration of support and love. Obviously when played out in the earth plane the perspective of this looks differently. It is important to remember this may or may not have to do with a karmic return from a previous lifetime experience between the same two souls—played out as a choice to reincarnate from the opposite sides and perspective. Changing places in the second lifetime offers the experience of what the other had felt last time and balances karma. Now anyone that does not study this concept would argue there is no way anyone would sign on for abuse, but I believe differently. Remember this doesn't condone abuse nor bad behavior. It supports the soul's choice. If the soul in between lives signs up to learn about self-love, personal empowerment, and forgiveness, they most definitely would need a scenario and the players involved in their story to support the mission. They would need a person to sign on to play the role of the abuser, to offer the initial curriculum, lessons, and experience of abuse. At the very same time, the other soul in between lives signed on to also learn their own lessons of abusing another for whatever reason they needed to. To learn what it feels like to take from another, to be cruel, to be hated.

The key to this is the next steps. If the abused person moves through life believing they are a victim, living out their days in anger and resentment, feeling they have no power and no voice to be heard or seen, no reason to be loved or hold self-worth, they missed the opportunity they signed on for in the first place. They will never attain what they set out to do which is to find and live out self-love, personal empowerment, forgiveness, and ultimately freedom. Be clear, what is forgiven is not necessarily the person or the horrific action (though that is a choice), what is forgiven is the victimization. What is gained is a voice, empowerment, self-love, self-worth, and love of life itself. And remember there is a co-agreement between the two souls. The one that signed on to be the abuser is also responsible to find atonement, ask for forgiveness, regain self-love, truth, and empowerment.

Abuse of any kind is horrific, but abuse of a child can scar a person for an entire lifetime and beyond. Again, embracing the reasons for abuse from the perspective of a soul's contractual agreement does not at any time condone bad behavior or let the abuser off the hook for the abomination, what it does do is release the victimization of the act within the person that has been abused. This is one of the toughest concepts to open our mind, body, and heart to and yet I have seen numerous clients find a new found sense of empowerment, peace, and forgiveness when this happens. If I was abused as a child, I can easily choose to move through my life victimized with the messaging of "not safe and non-worth" which are the two primal wounds already held within every human DNA structure. If I feed that belief-narrative year after year, I manifest a reality that ensures I will attract many different people and scenarios that will affirm that I am not safe, and I am not good enough or loveable and life becomes unbearable.

Conversely, if I look at the idea that the original soul contract set the stage for a life-lesson of my return to power and self-love, and I see those involved as critical players that take on a role and script for me to learn from, there is an entirely different journey and ending to the story. The forgiveness is not necessarily directed toward the behavior or the person that has committed the crime as much as the forgiveness is given to self in believing in the victimization from what happened because I was not good enough, not strong enough, not heard or seen. Releasing the victimization is what offers freedom. There is a balance for the karma.

Each of us is guided by what is coined as the Higher Self which can be recognized as the voice of the individualized soul or connection to Source energy found within the personal fields or consciousness container composed of current, past and future lifetimes and timelines. As we examined earlier, we are influenced by not just our personal consciousness container but also the collective consciousness container of oneness which stores limitless information in what is known as The Akashic Records or Library. The concept of the Akashic Records has been studied for centuries and most scholars agree it is some sort of record or embodiment of all that is and all that is possible in every form of energy and spirit. From the time our soul incarnates, our energetic body sends information to both our personal and the collective Akashic Records through our Higher Self. But before we dive deeper into this ultimate container of collective consciousness, let us further examine our individual soul and its contracts.

Obviously, we are all aware that humans come from the interaction of a sperm and egg which initiates the creation of the eventual divine human container for our incarnation here on the planet. Additionally, Source consciousness chooses to drop into our human body vehicle to play out our individualized co-creation plan. Therefore, we choose to incarnate in this body for a specific purpose that aligns with our Higher Self or Akashic Record. We choose our parents, our siblings, our families. We even choose our enemies. Each being we choose to accept into our divine plan is a great ally and helper, though they may take on more difficult roles in a single lifetime to play out a variety of experiences in the flesh. Even those who harm us are said to contract with us, and from the higher perspective it is done from love. We choose everything by way of soul contracts with others prior to every incarnation to manifest and embody Earth and its inhabitants as a co-creation to experience on behalf of Source. The divine plan or Akashic Record of the in-coming body holds the details of the soul contract. Each intricate detail of the Record will be stored and housed as an interactive file of energy for how the incoming life-path experience, or *life-emBODYment* will unfold.

Not only do I fully acknowledge that these were initially extremely difficult concepts for me to process, but also admit they are on occasion a challenge to present to my clients especially when it comes to suggesting they may have contractually signed on for an abusive parent from their soul's perspective. Their immediate response is "Oh hell no!" struggling with *"there is no possible way I would have chosen my parent(s) much less agreed to the personal package of abuse that came along with it."* As a practitioner, I stand by my belief that, "Yes you did" but coming from a higher perspective not a 3D one. I one hundred percent can sympathize with the disbelief that instinctually erupts at the notion, but if the client allows me to continue the conversation and the energetic work to dismantle the belief, astounding healing often happens. Below I introduce a "corporate boardroom" example that offers a beautiful visual of how this can happen in the sacred space of in-between lives and in-between incarnations. Remember we are here on the earth plane for only one short incarnation in this lifetime and oftentimes this is a reflection, atonement or a return on actions from lifetimes before.

As I stated prior, this is not an easy subject to open up to and I hold just as much compassion for clients that choose not to embrace soul contract work. Having and presenting theories allow them only to become "accessible" and does not impose them upon anyone or anything as a truth but my goal in authoring this book is to offer novel ideas that might elicit inner knowing or result in something to ponder and result in a healing. I can attest to the fact that utilizing expanded viewpoints has profoundly changed the way I look at my own life in terms of self-responsibility and victimization programming and I am proud to share that I also know multiple clients that have experienced similar triumphs when utilizing these philosophies.

The Soul Contract

Before we are even born, we have chosen our surroundings—distinct details of our life including those who will be the people who influence us. Prior to birth in our human form, there is a certain incubation period not just in the womb but in between incarnations as a time where we determine not only who we will walk with during our journey, but also what path or paths will lead us along the way. We decide details of this incoming agreement through what is known as a soul contract drafted along with other souls to assist us before we are born as a human on this planet. This is a concept you can choose to believe in or not but there are numerous books, stories, and near-death experiences that share this vision and information for the soul and its contractual agreements. So, what exactly is a soul contract? It is an agreement you make first and foremost with your soul as to what you plan on accomplishing in this life's incarnation where lessons are learned and opportunities are offered through our free will choices. Soul contracts are agreements we make with other souls between lives. Before we are even born, these agreements have been carefully drafted with a specific purpose to teach us important lessons we have chosen to learn throughout the incoming incarnation. Any souls we have contracted with can offer deep change, teaching, and opportunity into our lives through unique connections, both positive and negative, while on-planet and beyond.

When explaining this concept to my clients and class attendees, I often used my corporate background as a metaphor as I ask them to imagine calling together your top staff to engage in drafting a marketing plan to launch a new event. Any great team is made up of many integral players that each add to the overall success of the plan. Some players take on the tough jobs while others float behind the scenes only surfacing when needed. Some players work long hard hours while others pop in for a brief meeting or two. As the team huddles together around the executive boardroom table, they anxiously wait for their leader and boss to arrive to present and explain the plan of action they will take part in. You are the boss. You are the CEO, the CFO, the one in charge. You have drafted the goal of the project, outlined the objectives and strategies and are now here to discuss the tactics of how to best implement this action plan and decide the best team players along with their job descriptions to execute your endeavor. You have final say on this team, who is in and who is out, the timeline of the event including all operational details from beginning to end. We all need participants in our journeys whether it is achieving an event plan or designing a planned experience for a spiritual being to move into an earthly incarnation: we cannot do this job alone.

People we have soul contracts with are team players that will come into our lives with purpose and they will be an important and unavoidable part of our unique path. These team players represent those that will assist you in your event/endeavor called "your life." Some will take a bigger role, others not so much, but regardless, you will have some semblance of a contractual agreement for them to assist you in getting your job done and your goals met with the lessons you need to learn along the way. The souls that sit around your own personal boardroom table represent the people that will incarnate alongside you to share in your life as contracted participants. Some will take the difficult jobs, some the easy ones. Everyone we contract with is either our teacher or our student, and sometimes both and remember these are co-contracts; meaning I simultaneously play the role of teacher or student as a participant in their personal life-path journey.

When we gather, in between lives to draft this agreement, it looks similar to that corporate boardroom but more like a spiritual round-table conference to decide the lessons you will learn in the life to come. Instead of employees, those assisting in drafting your action plan may include what is known as your soul family, soul group or pod. From a universal, spiritual perspective, our soul family is the group that we tend to incarnate with repeatedly and may consist of thousands of individual souls including our guides, angels, parents, siblings, partners, children, friends and yes, even our enemies from multiple lifetimes and timelines.

You can think of this group of souls that continually choose to decide together to be involved in each other's next physical manifestations, each offering something to the other in the way of a lesson or support and sometimes as a karmic return on a past action. Our true intimate soul family includes those we have the biggest contracts with. These people, over many lifetimes, tend to play the roles of our most important individuals . . . even our beloved pets! Sometimes, when you have the uncanny feeling that you have known someone your whole life, even though you've just "met them," this may indicate that they're in some fashion derived from your soul family or have played a role in a past life.

Remember, you give the final approval to soul contract participation knowing every person included in your divine plan is a great ally and helper in the spiritual realm, though they may take more difficult roles in specific lifetimes that play out in a difficult fashion or variety of experiences in the flesh. For example, in our childhood we set the stage of the journey as we begin to embrace patterns of behavior that will establish our lesson plans of primal wounds and belief systems, just so that we can learn to move through the lesson and eventually heal the experience. It is these behaviors led by beliefs that will bring forward the people we have soul contracts with, and they will come in and out of our lives at different times in different ways to teach us about ourselves, who we are and what we are destined to become. Sometimes the soul contract lessons may be to learn the act of forgiveness and in order to align this opportunity, someone may also sign on for a lesson for another to deeply hurt them offering the choice to either forgive and move into love or stay in the victimization of fear. In order to learn to be confident, filled with self-love and self-worth, someone may choose to sign on for lessons where another may abandon them at their worst hour. You may become a caregiver to learn to take care of and love someone unconditionally. We cannot learn the difficult lesson of loss unless someone signs on to leave us, presenting itself as a breakup or a death. Soul contract interactions affect our relationships at deep, profound levels by bringing us awakenings, teaching us love or pain and how to relate with others, giving us healing, and helping us embrace our unique path to find our authentic self.

Our soul's reason for being is not only to fulfill our original divine plan but also to create balance as we strive to seek resolution and revisit our energetic encounters lifetime after lifetime. If we do not learn the lessons we put forth, oftentimes we will choose to reincarnate to take another stab at accomplishing our goal, or if there is a karmic element to an action, we may choose to revisit the situation from the opposite perspective in the next lifetime. Reincarnation is the belief that after death the body may decay but the soul is eternal and will spend a period of time in the spirit worlds and then be reborn, integrating with a fetus to experience life again. The soul travels from lifetime to lifetime gaining more direct experience and understanding of existence through living on the material plane. Our soul, like the legendary phoenix, does indeed rise from the ashes of our former selves to be reborn. Our former lives are like seeds of information for our new incarnation, in other words everything we are today we have been building upon for thousands of years.

When we open up to the concept, or remember, that death does not really exist as we believe, we will know that our opportunity to learn and to grow is never over and that the time to be rewarded or punished for how we lived our lives will never come because life is not a reward and punishment proposition driven by karma. Rather life is a process of continuous and unending growth, expansion, self-expression, self-creation, and self-fulfillment. I am so profoundly grateful for the experiences of working with multitudes of dying patients and channeling my clients' dead loved ones from the other side of the veil to know just how powerful this soul contract work is. Death can then be understood as simply and only a transition—a glorious shifting in the experience of the soul, a change in our level of consciousness, a freedom-giving, pain-releasing, awareness-expanding breakthrough in the eternal process of evolution, yet most of us are not quite there in our beliefs as yet. Instead, we humans tend to hold on to the pain we and others experience; carrying that forward beyond our death and into the next incarnation as part of the next soul's contract resolution. And the wheels of karma just keep turning.

The human being was not designed to endlessly reincarnate, reliving the same karmic encounters over and over throughout multiple lifetimes. The experience of multiple lifetimes gives us an opportunity to learn and restore balance, but it was humanity that created the fear-based karmic mess over the eons of misusing our gift of empathy, replacing it with the egoic act of empathing emotion and carrying the same fear and pain with us through multiple lifetimes; never releasing. This information is critical to the empath as most humans die or return to Source still processing empathed fear, anger, pain, guilt, with the need to heal from the action of taking another's fuel. This is what continues this karmic-based infrastructure of reincarnation ultimately thwarting our path to spiritual enlightenment.

There is a lot to explore when it comes to soul contracts, but the bottom line is most things that you experience in this lifetime and in between are outlined in your soul contracts. Through the process of incarnating on Earth, we are meant to evolve spiritually—to grow in spiritual mastery as we nurture our divine gifts and develop our talents. One of our greatest talents is empathy—having the gift of feeling what another embodiment of Source is feeling while maintaining a respect for energetic boundaries and lessons of the other and ourselves. You are here as a spiritual being in human form on planet Earth to learn, to grow, and to evolve in sometimes positively breathtaking experiences and sometimes pain-filled ones. The major players in your life all signed agreements with you before coming here to support the details of your journey as well as offer you the chance to support their soul's contractual journey.

Now this concept may or may not resonate right now, but sometimes it is important to push beyond old beliefs to gain new perspectives. Expanding ideas of soul contracts and agreements can offer a greater perspective that allows us to trust in divine guidance and divine timing. It allows us to have more compassion for those in our lives and for ourselves. It gives us a chance to accept things that happen with an attitude of inner faith that whatever is happening is happening as it should, when it should and how it should. And ultimately, it allows us to forgive easier. And that's priceless.

The Akashic Record and Library

So how do soul contracts relate to the Akashic Records or Library? The corporate boardroom metaphor showed us an example of how the event action plan notates not only soul-players contracted as team members but also details the strategies, tactics, and timelines needed to execute the agreement of an in-coming life-journey. The particulars found within these elements comprise what is coined as the Akashic Record of the incarnating soul also known as their Book of Life.

Years ago, when I began to study metaphysics and healing, I researched the work of Edgar Cayce a Christian mystic philosopher and intuitive healer who recorded many of the most profound readings and findings on the Akashic Records. His ideas and work still stand the test of time as some of the most detailed information made available on this subject matter. The following is an excerpt from Edgar Cayce's Association for Research and Enlightenment:

The Akashic Records can be equated to the universe's supercomputer system, a reservoir of events, containing every deed, word, feeling, thought, and intent that has ever occurred. Akashic Records are interactive in that they have a tremendous influence upon our everyday lives, our relationships, our feelings and belief systems, and the potential realities we draw toward us.

The Edgar Cayce readings suggest that from a soul standpoint, each of us co-creates our story, our Book of Life. No soul incarnates without a divine plan for the experience ahead. My belief is that we draft our Book of Life's outline in between lives with the support of our guardians and benevolents to determine why we are here on Earth in our current incarnation and identify the lessons we have come to experience, sometimes involving karma.

At this point in our human evolution and collective spiritual mastery, every person's life is still shaped to some extent by karma, including our own karma, the karma of those we have incarnated with in a lifetime, the collective karma of our nation, race, historical ancestors and the karma of the world itself. Each soul that has chosen to individually incarnate has their own book, or energetic file for that particular lifetime which outlines and documents all potentials and chosen life possibilities. No Book of Life is set in stone but instead is interactive and continues to be adjusted by thoughts, deeds, and free will actions as long as the incarnated human is still alive and co-creating. The more we take responsibility to clear negative karma before we physically die, the less we bring the lessons back to the in-between and the quicker we change the overall human reincarnation experience. Eventually we can all choose to erase negative karma for our species and the overall human experience on this planet.

As individual humans we carry our own incarnation's records, which are encoded in our bodies and contain our unique genetic instruction, our inherent code or set of blueprints held within our DNA. The encoded energy remains interactive and continues to be adjusted until our human death when it is then stored for eternity in our soul's Akashic Library Record of that lifetime. When a life is finished the personality of that incarnation is absorbed into the soul and its record is retained, but it becomes a part of a bigger file or record, that of the oversoul which at all times is the sum total of what it has been—all it has thought, all it has experienced, all it has seen, heard, felt through the ages of all incarnations.

I love the Cayce quote: "Life is a purposeful experience, and the place in which a person finds himself is one in which he may use his present abilities, faults, failures, virtues, in fulfilling the purpose for which the soul decided to manifest in the three-dimensional plane." In a sense, each time we choose to incarnate, we are one singular book and, when finished, that unique book is filed away and shelved in our full library, and eventually will be returned to the Hall of Records—the full Akash or Source itself.

Each of our individual incarnations represents just one file or record within the infinite collective memory records throughout time and space. Cayce references an overall central storehouse of all information which includes every incarnation, every individual who has ever lived upon the Earth and most likely beyond. This full and complete storehouse is the Akash or the Hall of Records of all incarnations in time and space. It is an energetic memory comprising the record of the entire consciousness journey over time, so every idea, thought, word, and action is registered in the Akashic Record, plus each universe, galaxy, planet, and being, has its own Akashic Record memory.

I personally feel this main library is what many refer to as God or my preferred description, "Source." For many this may indeed be the energy that they pray to or ask assistance from in church, in their homes or in their hearts, just without a face or "male" personality attached to it. This compilation of collective files, Books or Akashic Records is also interactive as long as any individual life path is still playing out, using the energies of free will and choice in re-editing one individual book's content affecting the collective content. No version of the Akashic Records, Hall of Records or Library is a physical building, but more so a collaboration of energies and information created by and accessed through intention. The idea of infinite metaphorical books in libraries this vast could never exist physically, instead it is recorded energetically in the vibration of the love that makes up everything within Source.

Additionally, there are "places" where these Records and files are initially created and where we do our work to study and grow knowledge in between lives and incarnations to determine the path of our next existence. These places are in other dimensions or planes of reality of learning often described as cities or cathedrals with pillars made of crystalline substance that glow in love and light. Near-death-experience accounts often say that between embodiments we are in a heightened state of awareness, one that seems more real than life on Earth. Some belief-systems may see this as Heaven or in-between-lives where it is often recorded that you meet in groups, boards or councils with spiritually advanced Keepers or Beings who have superior knowledge about those crossing over in death. Their role is to assist them in evaluating the life that just passed and make recommendations concerning the next incarnation or the next book you are co-creating.

These Keepers can include guardians, angels, benevolents, and the Masters of the Spiritual Hierarchy who are real and dynamic beings in energetic form with a purpose to provide us with guidance and processes that allow us to open up to our true Self. There are Ascended Masters that are enlightened spiritual beings who lived on Earth, having faced similar challenges confronting us today that are now reunited with Source energy to assist us and serve as the teachers of humankind from the realms of spirit. We have as guides, a multitude of alliances made up of highly spiritual beings from different star systems and multi-universes fulfilling their mission to protect and ensure that we as a species discover and fulfill our genetic plan of true spiritual enlightenment and multidimensional heritage as was originally intended.

We do work in between lives in these energetic Halls. When a soul returns to Source or the Akashic Library or Hall of Records, it becomes aware of itself not only as a part of Source but as a part of its own soul, every other soul, and everything in oneness. It is where the soul energies continue to evolve and ascend through a life review, making any needed amends and atonements, finding restoration and rejuvenation, and returning to a place of truth and wisdom that reflects our true essence with the ultimate goal of healing one's self in order to assist others. This place where the central storehouse of all information resides is a space where healing can happen for individuals as well as the collective; it is where we together co-create our reality—past, present, and future.

So why is this Akashic Library relevant to the empath? Our job as a human form is to live out our Book of Life, all while returning files to the main Hall of Records or Akashic Library. This plane of existence is where we change our realities, and yes, one individual can make the difference within the collective fields. Any time I have psychically seen a client's Akashic Record it visually comes through to me as energetic sacred art, a beautifully vibrant mandala which indeed is a representation of the unconscious self and a form of prayer. Generally speaking, a mandala is a term for any plan, chart or geometric pattern that represents the cosmos metaphysically or symbolically.

Our job is not just to co-create and experience reality here on Earth but also to understand and work the sacred-art-file system of the Akashic Libraries and Hall of Records in all time–space pre-incarnation, during incarnation and post-incarnation. We do this for our own lives. We do this for our planet. We do this for the human race. We do this for the cosmos. We are also here to learn from the information in our own divine plan to make sense of our life and honor others' choices which is extremely helpful to the empath who often wants to make everyone's life easier all while exhausting their own fields. Examining your record along with your soul contracts can also assist you in turning a blind eye to any victim/victimizer programming where one feels like life has handed them the short end of the stick. When I teach the concept of "we choose," I get a lot of push-back in classes and client meetings and hear things like: "Why would I possibly . . . choose to be sick?, be out of work?, live such a lonely existence?, experience abuse of any kind?" and so on. Again, I will say, you did choose. You chose the players you contracted with and determined the course of action to take all from a higher perspective of love and growth as a soul. The idea of a need for atonement or making amends can come from a free will choice that was made during that lifetime to not fulfill the initial contract, but it can also come from a place of finding a higher frequency of love and rising above and beyond the incarnation's initial contract lessons and limitations.

For example, I may be the one that indeed signed on to be the abuser and I can fulfill that contractual agreement without atonement or making amends. I can also move beyond the initial agreement and make the free will effort to search out and find forgiveness for actions through atonement and making amends. This will increase my self-love quotient during that incarnation and bring back a higher level of wisdom in between lives for the soul involved. Once we learn to work with our soul contracts and Akashic Records we may or may not find the reasons why we chose who and what we did during an incarnational experience on the planet or in between lives.

The biggest lesson for the sensitive empath, when it comes to the Akashic Records, is that of honoring another's Book of Life and the lessons found within by learning to stay in our own sandbox of life and stop stealing another's toys, energy, pain, fear and more. The more I realized I was not the healer as much as the practitioner moving the energy, I discovered my role in assisting another and honoring their soul's contract was best done through meaningful prayer and intention. With pure heart-based motivation in sacred and reverent prayer aligned to Source, one may request to access either their own Akashic Record or that within the collective to offer healing to other lifetime identities, histories, ancestral patterns, and related issues that may have imprinted in various lifetimes and incarnations. Even though I believed prayer was never my thing, I have learned to value the practice as an integral part of energy healing and have found ways to make it my own.

Prayer and the Language of Light

I grew up Catholic, went to Catholic grade-school and high-school, attended church most of my life, participated in sacrament classes, all of which have one thing in common: prayer. I was raised to embrace the traditional dictionary meaning of prayer—that of: *noun. A devout petition to God or an object of worship, a spiritual communion with God or an object of worship, as in supplication, thanksgiving, adoration, or confession. The act or practice of praying to God or an object of worship, a formula or sequence of words used in or appointed for praying: the Lord's Prayer.*

As a kid I never liked prayer.

That said, as an adult I feel differently; as my spiritual journey has evolved so has my concept of, and connection to, prayer. I have opened my heart and mind to new perspectives of prayer, and I offer them here as my personal opinion and in no way claim to have a right to tell others to pray, or not to pray or much less how to pray. Prayer is personal. I distinctly remember being in about 4th grade attending church as a part of our class-day. I was kneeling, listening to the priest and the moment he said "Bow your head" mine instinctively jerked upward to the Heavens. I am not claiming to be right or wrong as there are no rules to prayer, but what I knew then and still know now is that our beautifully designed gift from Source, our divine human vehicle knows how to pray in a way that is intrinsically true to each individual and in the case of my 4th-grade self—it certainly was not to bow my head in servitude but to look upward in co-creation. It is the power of our prayerful individuality that allows the oneness of prayer. It directly connects us to higher intelligence or Source.

I attended church for many years and admit I began to use church as a setting to enhance my psychic skill set by scanning the priest's aura while he spoke, as well as the congregation's as a whole, while they droned through rehearsed prayers. This is actually what moved me to eventually leave the church because my sensitive-empath-body sponged the dense vibrational frequencies permeating the sanctuary from disengaged congregants, including myself. For me, church simply did not feel good, especially when I was engulfed in the automated prayer that bounced off the walls. I made efforts to monitor my own self and found my body actually felt anxious when I said certain words and phrases I did not believe in or fully own. To me this meant there was limited heart-felt engagement to my words that I intuitively felt "should be" a magical connection to Source. Now, I believe the frequency of prayer honors the sacral chakra or feel-center, and when the energies are aligned it emits beautiful swirling colors of love and light around anybody engaged in sacred word. But in the church setting, the collective resonance of prayer sounded robotic and flat, and my body wasn't feeling it. That is not to say there weren't many congregants holding a sacred space while in church that indeed emitted a beautiful auric field as they were in attendance of their truth, having every right to be there in that manner.

I was not then, nor am I now, judging anyone else, only myself and my opinion does not criticize or belittle anyone that feels congregational learned prayer, or if a dogmatic setting works for them, it just does not work for me. I much prefer sitting in the beauty of Source in nature at my cabin at this time in my life. This awakening time was when I began to expand my journey of what prayer might energetically look like if I personally owned it.

Over the past several years in searching for my unique truths, I have found that prayer has become a totally different concept for me than was originally introduced through the Catholic Church and by modern-day society. When it comes to energy, the vibrational frequency of our words are a vital piece to the equation of us co-creating and manifesting. The information sent and received through prayer is "supposed to be" accessed with an open heart and based on our intention, the energy will then flow guided by the Higher Self resulting in a channeling of love-based fuel. Additionally, when the intention is driven by a feeling rather than surrendering mentally-based emotions of helplessness asking a higher power for assistance, it becomes a creative collaboration, a sacred dialog with the subtle realms and planes of existence that embody Source energy.

You can imaginatively utilize prayer as a powerful tool to converse your desires to manifest your future using the present moment and the beauty of the gifted divine human container feel-centers, shifting from a powerless or faithful request into a conscious co-creation. Not to sound flippant or disrespectful in any manner, but most humans still pray to a "He," yet I always tell my clients there is no "guy" sitting up there on a cloud with a long beard, robe, and a book. We are taught that "Source is a He" and we use that verbiage consistently in conversation and in prayer. Remember, our words have frequency and vibration behind them and when we tag a gender onto Source, this additionally adds-on the frequency of personality and with personality comes traits, which end up being human and judgmental. This is why many people fear the judgment of death because we gave Source a personality that can be disappointed, angry and, for some, even have the ability to abandon us. Source does not have a personality. Source is not a He. Source is a design intelligence. Source is the I AM presence. Period.

If we reconfigure our ideology of Source and view it as the full Akashic Library, the vast and infinite Hall of Records made up of every embodiment of experience we can then begin to see how we are all Source. We are incarnated and embodied so Source can know itself. Source cannot know itself without us all. Whether we are a tree, a bug, the wind or a human, we are all one. Whether on this planet, or another, in this timeline or past or future, we are all one. We are individuals. We are a collective. Each individual and collective soul is making the choice to continuously reincarnate in unlimited embodiments to experience what we call life. When we choose to remove the separateness of Source we can then begin to take more responsibility for being here. For embodying the experiences.

For honoring the way another chooses to live out their experience. To return the information of each experience back to the Hall of Records in the Akashic Library so that we might heal the past and better create our future. I see this movement of energy and information as prayer. Prayer is our library calling card, our connection to boundless records of informational support, knowledge, wisdom, and enlightenment. The internal action of empowered and intentional prayer transforms on the Akashic level and transforms our creational reality and our futures. So, how do we actually do that? We work with the information we hold within us, in our DNA, in our Akashic Records as a language of light itself.

This language of light is perceivable throughout our world in sounds, colors, movements, vibrations, and geometric shapes that originate from our human thoughts, ideas, words, and feelings. While we may not be aware of it, we are feeling and experiencing this energy each and every moment of our day and if prayer is a vibrational feeling, we are in some sense offering prayer or receiving prayer from Source all the time! Each moment of our existence is a prayer.

If humans took this theory more seriously and realized that prayer is already incorporated into a daily thought process in which one is in constant interactive collaboration with Source, we might pay more attention to what we are or are not communicating. How prayer can correlate to the Akashic Libraries takes the idea of co-creating to another level and empowers each of us as not only individuals but as a collective force. With or without any words, hands folded, knees or heads held in a certain position or any outward physical expression, the energy of prayer activates our birthright of empathy and invites us to feel a clear and powerful feeling sometimes on behalf of self, other times on behalf of others. Through Akashic-based prayer as the intangible language of light, we have the ability to jump time–space continuums and participate in the healing of our bodies, the abundance that comes to our friends and families, heal ancestral pain, and align peace between nations and beyond our galaxy.

When we remember that true empathy creates understanding, an energetic connection, and resonance with the emotions and feelings of someone you interact with resulting in a supportive closeness, we learn to honor the other and the way we pray for changes. When we find out someone we know has cancer we no longer pray for them to "get better," we pray for their highest and best good at this time. Empathy for another is not about you changing them, fixing them, doing it to them or for them. True empathy is giving them love-based energy with no conditions attached and realizing that maybe their Akashic Record was written for them to have a cancer journey at this time, at this age, in conjunction with the family scenario attached and I have no right to alter that course even with my prayers. I *get to* pray for their Higher Self's direction and guidance in accordance with the Book of Life they chose to author between incarnations. I honor their record.

Honoring another's energetic journey keeps us in the energy field of empathy and not one of empathing the other. The importance of allowing one to fulfill their Akashic Record and not derailing it because of our own desires is utmost if we are to spiritually advance both here on Earth and in between lives. I have no right to pray for someone to stop something, start something, do something, change something that may not be in alignment with not only their original plan, but all of the co-contracted plans involved with the incarnation. Our human head and hearts cannot get around the idea that someone would sign on to die at an early age leaving say a household full of children behind, but I will tell you from the spiritual standpoint, they did—and no prayer gets to change or alter that unless the Higher Self is involved in the healing. Sometimes the healing is the dying, just not presented in the container we, from the outside looking in, necessarily would like to experience or witness. I have been blessed to witness this first-hand time and time again not only as an energy healer but as a hospice worker. I have watched families transform as their loved one transmutes back to Source when they take into account their part in the person's soul contract and death experiences.

And remember working with the Akashic Records is not just about pain and fear, it is also about joy and love. The more we return the information of the experiences of true joy in life-situations and relationships, the more the collective consciousness container holds this frequency on behalf of all. Logging and housing multiple story books of sheer joy makes for interesting reading of the Akashic Library that can be utilized in between lives to determine positive lessons in future incarnations. I make the effort to do this as I relish the beauty of nature up north at my cabin, witnessing the eagles flying and the sun setting, sending gratitude for being part of this delightful planet. I send back the immense feeling of love as I watch my grandchild giggle and laugh as she plays with her father knowing the human experience of birth and rebirth is a miracle. I embrace the freedom and vastness of the night sky as I am filled with wonder and awe at how infinite our cosmos must truly be. You too can find countless ways to send joy too, if you choose.

Releasing and Shifting Energy

The Akash is a powerful place with unlimited opportunities for us to send prayer too that can offer change, and the human sentient divine vehicle of a body is the best tool to do that work. When we do the work to allow our true feelings and emotions to be acknowledged, honored, felt, and then released back to Source, we return the information to that main branch of the library and this is an important concept.

Let us say we do find our loved one fighting a battle with cancer, and I feel somewhat helpless to do anything of value other than pray and yet this praying effort feels hopeless because of how fast the cancer is spreading. I feel like my prayers are not heard. I feel like I am failing somehow to help. Instead of praying for the person to get better, I choose to pray for their highest and best at this time and this honors their record. However, there is another step to the prayer-process and that is *truly feeling* the helplessness, the hopelessness, the fear, the anger, and the confusion that you personally are experiencing.

If we ignore or stuff these feelings, or obsess about them, either way we will create dis-ease and potential distress and sickness in our own body along the journey. What better suits the overall situation is giving that feel-based information back to the Akashic Library as part of the prayer. Feeling it, then sending forward what that feel-experience is like for you, what scared feels like, where fear is stored in your divine human vehicle and body, how hopelessness drives your mind insane in the middle of the night. Maybe it feels like you are going to explode or implode as your heart races and your body shudders. Maybe it feels like electrical charges coursing through you, zapping and destroying your system of circuitry and you are frying from the inside out. Maybe you feel like you are fading away into an abyss of darkness because no one can really know, hear or feel what is happening so you continually shrink like Alice in Wonderland until you simply are no longer. Maybe your heart feels like it is truly breaking inside piece by tiny piece and the density of it is so enormous it is like a giant boulder on your chest and you cannot breathe or take air into your lungs and it is suffocating. I know these are not necessarily pleasant words to read, but this is the depth of the feeling that is aching to be released from your divine human vehicle's existence as true feelings that can cause damage.

Whatever your deepest, darkest, most terrifying feelings are, do your best to identify them, embrace them, and release them. Many will argue they do not want to feel that pain again, and I am here to tell you energetically you are feeling that pain each and every moment on a subconscious level. The moment you invite it into your conscious self and do the work to embrace it with self-love is when the magic happens. Feel it, allow it to exist—not denying it or shoving it down—hold it and then release it from your body as information back to the Library. You can move these "feels" or feelings by praying, meditation, breathwork, or even things like running, gardening, a walk or a fire burn; regardless of the way you choose to send it—just send it. Simply being, being present and intentional is partly sending it, but intentionally connecting to the act of sending can assist in making your connection to Source stronger and supports your responsibility for uploading the Akashic Records in a more tangible way as a fully present participant. It is what can fill your soul as well as your soul contract. Why this is critical to the collective oneness of humanity is that the in-between needs the information. The benevolents, the guides, the angelics, the incoming incarnations . . . they all need the information because that is the only way we learn from it and then ultimately change it on behalf of self and others and Source itself. The library book of pain, of fear, of bad decisions is returned back to the Akashic Records where it is stored and made available as Source and wisdom to learn from for the future of our species and our planet.

For eons humans have not learned how to work the Akashic Library information system which ultimately created the mess we are currently in with regard to how we all keep creating cycles of karmic reincarnation which ultimately keeps us stagnant in our overall spiritual growth as a species and a planet. We as humans have not understood how to release our depth of feeling back to Source such as the horror and pain of losing a son to wars filled with carnage and hate, so we keep sending our sons to war. In terms of our feeling centers, we do not send home to Source the human atrocities of abuse, rape, and murder, therefore the cycle continues. We do not send home to Source the isolation and agony of separation, abandonment, and depression so we continue to medicate, hide, and die alone. We never return our books! Maybe think of it more like a 3D version of a library—if there is a great book that reveals a marvelous story filled with joy and wonder or agony and pain—a story that everyone should really read, if no one returns it to the library, the next person and then the next will never have a chance to get their hands on the book much less the vital information inside that might change their lives unless someone returns it after they experience it! It is about sharing the experience. Sharing the information. When I pray it out (or return the book) on behalf of my individual story, that pain-release happens not only for me but is offered to the collective masses that may have endured the same or similar pain. This works much like the universal Law of Attraction where *like finds like*. If I offer release of something on behalf of me, the prayer will be contained within the universal collective consciousness and quite possibly there are infinite numbers of embodiments that are struggling with the same vibrational fears and like energies will find like to assist them and ultimately expand our prayers into oneness. It is as if we all immediately have access to that information in that great book!

To me true prayer is to get the feel-center information back to the place it belongs, which is out of our meat-and-bone-bodies and back to the Akashic Library as a book of experience that everyone and everything can now learn from in between incarnations and through the collective. When the book is back on the Source shelf, we learn from our mistakes as a species, as a planet, as individuals, and as a collective. When this information complete with the empathy-file included is presented at the table of any incoming soul choosing to incarnate, this is how they make educated choices on behalf of self and the whole. If an incoming soul empathically knew the pain rape causes, they would never rape and possibly incarnate with purpose to command system changes. If an incoming soul knew the true essence of the angst of cancer, they may choose to alter their DNA and incarnate as a scientist to eradicate cancer, and so on. This knowledge is how individuals and the collective change and co-create our futures. And know, we do not have to wait for generations for this sharing of information to co-create our realities through new incoming souls as future incarnations. This information when made available through Source, can be a drop-in message to someone in a dream state, knowledge found in meditation, a thought or inspiration to any one at any time. Once the information is returned—it is shareable. The problem is that no one looks at prayer this way nor do we look at our pain this way. Most humans hold their pain, do not share it, die with it, and then reincarnate with it or that pain is vampired or taken by another, usually the empath trying to fix them. And remember the Akashic information is not only about the pain and the fear. Sending back the records of joy, awe, magic, and love is just as important to enhance the experiences of the incoming souls that may choose to embody positive lives and healthy relationships.

The empath who feels so much more than the typical human is a great one to send their experience forward in this manner of prayer. They can feel the fear of polluted and dying oceans including the fish and mammals that are suffering in agony. They can feel the freedom of the wind and the freshness of the rain. When trained the empath can discern and send that information back to Source so the next incarnated generations may create policies to change climate control and clean up our oceans. The empath, aware of fear and chemicals stored in meat harvested from barbaric tactics, can make change through Akashic prayer, educating incoming generations that champion new ways to feed themselves. The empath that embraces a healthy lifestyle can offer the information of wellness and gratitude. We cannot fault incoming souls that incarnate here that are looping in the old recycle programs of times past if we do not ourselves get this information back to the in-between where it can make a real difference and change our future timelines by simply putting the books back on the shelf.

This style of prayer can even change family histories and DNA challenges if we know how to move the energy. Say your family has suffered for generations from a particular DNA-related dysfunction or disease. When we stay out of victim mode and open our hearts to accept the details of our Akashic Record and soul contract, we can shift our attention to releasing fear and sending home the feel-centered emotions plus request genetic healing from past to present to future. This may or may not change the current lifetime experience but will offer the release and healing through all time–space continuums, meaning generations before, during, and after will be offered the chance to release this issue, if they choose, in their next incoming incarnation. This is the way we offer prayer to our past generations as well as our current and future ones with no conditions attached.

Remember, empathy is the truest sense-organ of the divinely incarnated human vehicle, but it cannot properly function through the individual ego—only through the collective unconditional energies which is another description for prayer. Empathy is a gift for garnering information, both positive and negative, that moves as energy via prayer to align to, and harmonize with, every living thing on the planet and throughout the cosmos. This means our prayers not only affect human existence but also the unconditional collective oneness of the forces of nature, the plant and animal kingdom, humanity and even the cosmos filled with stars and planets within multi-universes. We can unconditionally pray on behalf of anyone or anything in any time–space continuum because we are genetically designed *to be one*. When we ponder the mind-boggling idea that our current life is actually positioned as the past-life of our future self, we can see how important this Akashic Library file system is to all timelines.

Chapter Thirteen

Advanced Strategies for Protection and Teaching the Teachers

When I began my spiritual journey there was really no one who helped me find my way. No mentor or teacher. No real supportive resources. So I just stumbled down the unknown energetic path of the infinite pretty much alone. I admit it was scary not having anyone to turn to, to validate that I was not going crazy, that this stuff is real but can also feel desperately lonely and even disturbing. I learned a lot along my personal pathway of hits and misses and grew in skill in spite of myself, but I think we all deserve a little help as teachers and practitioners, which is exactly why I am including this chapter.

Things have changed immensely since my humble beginnings and nowadays there are multitudes of healing modalities of every variety, endless retreats, limitless training courses, and outlets for information and ideas to introduce you to the world of energy. Oh, and by the way, everyone is the expert! This vast variety of opportunity truly does offer something for everyone, unless you happen to be a practitioner yourself. Having spent over 18 years studying the field, I am finding more limited opportunities to upgrade my own skills through formal training or programs. I did not personally set out to position myself as a teacher of teachers, but over time I have noticed my client base grow to include professional healers looking for advice and support to guide their work and improve their skills. I believe we all can benefit from sharing our successes as well as failures as practitioners, and in this section I would like to share just some of the ideas and practices I offer to practitioner clients. If you find that this is not the level of information that applies to you and your journey at this time, you can either decide to skip this section or use it as something to ponder if you choose. Most teachers and practitioners within the healing profession are sensitive empaths as well as psychic intuitives and if you are one who works with clients you may want to consider some of the following steps to maintain clear and healthy boundaries.

Protection

When I began to entertain the idea of working with energy as a professional, people in the field always told me to be sure to learn how to protect myself. This was frustrating because in my ignorance and limited awareness of energy, I thought if I were working in the light everything would be just fine, and I would also be just fine. I quickly discovered I was wrong, and the world of energy is more complex than simply the concept of working in the light. Most practitioners do learn the importance of having some form of protection practice as they grow their skills, but I was initially misguided in the concept of protection overall, thinking it was only about setting protection from evil or negative energies. However, I learned through my work myself that protection is not always about keeping something out as much as keeping something in. It's about maintaining a level of fuel to do the work. Over time I have shifted my view of protection to focus much more on learning to be aware of and intentionally strengthen my auric field. This allows us to not only set our energetic boundaries but also maintain our own fuel. This book is designed to teach the everyday empath, but I've seen how the teacher or professional can benefit from these reminders because most healers are sensitive and psychic empaths themselves. It can be easy to get caught up in our work helping others that we forget the basics of maintaining our own personal health and energy. We cannot teach what we do not do for ourselves. So, if you do not yet have an ongoing practice for setting auric boundaries and protection, I highly suggest you invite the idea into your work. The Ground and Bubble meditation I provide at the end of this book is a great place to start as a daily routine.

Additionally, setting energetic boundaries of protection not only applies to the individual healer or practitioner, but also the space in which they perform their professional services. I teach this concept to many different specialists who work in any capacity of energetic transference, from RN's (registered nurses) and nurses, to massage therapists, to family counselors and abuse therapists and more. As a daily routine, I suggest any professional should begin their day by clearly setting an intention for the energy of their office or business with a secure boundary of east, south, west, north, Father Sky (upward) and Mother Earth (downward), and then surrounding their own individual body. This effort is similar to calling in a Sacred Circle or locking down your workspace. I have opened my professional healing office with this practice every day for over a dozen years. Throughout the day I also intentionally release and reboot this protective boundary for each client and then release it at the end of my day.

Intentionally setting boundaries for the space and for each client ensures no one takes another's discarded energy home along with them, nor do I. By having a specific ritual I follow before and after each client, I offer the best in my integrity to work only as a practitioner-observer—not taking on what is not mine to own nor transferring energy to my client. There is no right or wrong way to do it because it is purely about the intention you set. I also use some specific prayers to align with the Universal energies as a handshake connection to Divine Guidance to further solidify my intention of assistance from my guides and Source. I light candles to set intention in my space. I ring bells and chimes and use singing bowls. I spray scented waters, essences or use essential oils. I cut cords between each client and after my day to ensure my personal container is clear from anything I encountered during the time I was professionally working with the energies. What's most important is you create a practice or ritual that feels authentic to you. Any time I am in a hospice situation, especially when physically in attendance in a nursing home or in a dying person's presence, I make sure to do double duty by not only cutting cords when I leave but also opening my windows in my car for the first several blocks of driving home from the session just to blow out anything that no longer serves me. Again, this is not all about worry or fear or taking on something but more so about honoring and leaving the other's energy in their space. Each person deserves to have their own personal fuel returned to them especially in a healing session and I have no right to cord to another and disrupt that flow. When I return home or leave my healing room for the day, I consistently do body scanning of my own divine human container and energetic field to make sure I am only taking myself home.

The level of protection for the teacher or professional practitioner will likely need to change as their level of skill changes, suggesting that the protocol of protection practices may need to be revisited as your playing field increases. The bigger the energetic field you are working in, the bigger the negative forces that come out to play. I include this not to incite fear as much as to offer a reminder that a hijack is always possible no matter how confident we are in our work. Even the most diligent practitioners are vulnerable to the collective consciousness field and all of its nefarious programs. However, it is important to not do this protection work out of fear. It is all energy and as healers we always have command of our space and our own energetic frequencies if we choose.

In my early days of professional work, I held the belief that anything that no longer served the client, or the space, or whatever I was releasing had to "go" or be removed, or even be contained as something that might not serve as "good" energy. There was even a time when I formally used portals in and out of my professional office space to make sure I was diligent about not allowing anything to cause harm. Through years of practice and gaining confidence in not only myself but in the ways of infinite energy, I have completely changed this practicum. My focus is not necessarily to remove anything as much as "transmute" it. This is a completely different thought process and belief system. I now hold and maintain that dark, or evil or negative energies all have the right to be present, yet I also have the right to work with them or without them in any way I choose. A metaphor here is much like having a neighbor or a co-worker that is not someone I want to be around or spend time with, and I do not have to move from my home or quit my job, I just do not have to engage with them in any manner that does not serve me. The need to banish an energy is based in fear and I have learned to simply rise above that frequency through loving intention and allow whatever is there to exist. At this point in my career I choose to transmute the energies, to first and foremost make the concentrated effort to raise my own vehicle vibration and that of my work so that the negative, heavy dense vibrations cannot even find a place to play with me. This is not ignoring the knowledge that they exist. Instead it is owning the knowledge that I do not have to allow them to influence the space or client I am working with. This is a complete reversal of where my initial beliefs began years ago.

I have purposefully done a tremendous amount of work to change my personal professional perception that dark energy means bad as a belief. Words can be difficult when it comes to our infinite existence. They are limited and can cause ignorance and restraint in the way we embrace and move energy. I have spent endless hours opening to the idea that the I AM presence has to include the dark—it is the Mother-God or the Female-God energy that has been deliberately left out of the picture for eons causing most healers and dogmatic religions to believe and trust they only work in the "light" of God. The use of good and bad, the words light and dark, these are all programmable verbiage that can cause distortion or confusion when we offer healing. It stimulates judgment. Even evil has a reason for being. Not that I need or even want to choose to embrace something that does not serve me—it is the fear behind the removal—the make it go away and destroy it frequency messaging that is not serving us. Be very clear, the more you honor all aspects of energy, the more you are empowered to utilize your free will choice and discernment for true protection. I do not have to fear something as much as honor it exists and then make effective choices followed by actions that align to my highest and best truths. The passion to do anything and everything to heighten my own vibration has been my driving force for the past several years now and has expanded my quantum work at a rapid pace. I feel this is a very personal place to get to and, if this is not where you are at this time of your professional service or career, take anything here that resonates and toss the rest— or toss it all if nothing resonates.

Again, the concept of the egg or bubble of safety can assist in all protection efforts. With intention, you can choose to generate larger and stronger fields around not just your own field but also around your office or home to assist in knowing who or what has entered your sacred space to contribute healing energies or support.

Downloads, Upgrades, and Integration

One of the most important lessons I share with other teachers and practitioners is that of downloads, upgrades, and integration of energies. No one told me about this during the years of my practice, and I make it a priority to share this with anyone who is purposefully doing the work to increase their skill set and gain higher knowledge. We can receive wisdom and sacred knowledge in many different ways from learning, reading, attending classes, and simply gaining empirical evidence and experience by working with clients and ourselves through sessions, quiet time, and meditation.

Sometimes the information comes to us in the form of what is known as a spiritual download or an intuitive experience wherein we gain immediate knowledge and clarity. So what is a spiritual download?

A spiritual download can be experienced in a number of ways, from a knowing that came through as a message in a meditation, to a vision in a dream, to words or ideas that come through journaling or the energy of taking a walk through the woods. Regardless of the packaging, a download is super-fast access to and from the higher realms that offers wisdom you would not otherwise be able to access or even know exists. Some feel it is a direct line to Source or our Higher Self. The messaging can come through your clair-senses—meaning your heightened sense of awareness either audibly, visually, sensing or even just knowing. How does a download feel and how do you know you are having one? The more you are in touch with your own personal frequency and auric energy center, the easier it is to recognize you are experiencing a download—another good reason to learn to bubble!

Oftentimes people feel physical sensations in addition to receiving a message or information. Some feel their body parts tingle in places like their hands, feet, head, or third eye. Others heat up or actually feel like informational energies are pouring frequencies into their crown chakra on top of their head. Emotionally, spiritual downloads can bring in a feeling of joy but also can sometimes overwhelm the body and its senses. Typically, when a download is happening you feel the experience but do not necessarily have access to the information just yet. In fact, sometimes you never actually connect the dots of a download as the wisdom simply integrates into your field as a knowing. On the flip side, sometimes a download nudges you to action with a sense of urgency and you may find yourself compelled to write something down, call someone or do something—and typically inner guidance will assist in the way any end result plays out. I personally do not feel like we get to command a download to happen, but we can help make the occurrence more frequent by setting intention or making the space in our body and in our day to allow and surrender control to the soul or Higher Self to ask for the information. Sometimes it is all about divine timing and sometimes it comes, sometimes it does not. It is about trusting in divine guidance of the process.

The energetic result of a download can also give us what is known as an energetic upgrade, like our vehicle just got an incredible tune-up and it now runs at a higher level of efficiency. Upgrades can seem euphoric at first. Then, sometimes within hours, days or weeks, we often encounter what feels like a disconnect or a flatline sensation in our energy, which is somewhat disorienting. It's as if you just got cut off from all that wonderful new fuel that had been directly poured into you, resulting in exhaustion and confusion.

Moving from a state of euphoria and confidence to disconnection and exhaustion was horribly perplexing for me at the beginning. It felt like I was the star of the benevolent-guide get-together and then all of a sudden no one wanted to hang out or chat. I used to think I did something wrong or pissed off something or someone "up there" who turned off the flow of information. I would say it felt like my guides were all having a party and I was not invited, or I was invited but they were all congregating in the next room, and I was alone listening on the other side of the door—much like the teacher in the old Charlie Brown cartoons that sounded like . . . *waah waah, waah* . . . distorted and muffled. This experience was so frustrating, and I felt like such a failure until the day I was told by inner guidance that this was all about integration of energy.

This is now what I share with the sensitive empath professional: the upgrade we experience from new incoming knowledge needs time to fully integrate into our human body and energetic circuitry, and each auric field additionally needs to fully embed it to retain it. This time of integration can feel much like going backwards because we experience a feeling of coming down from our euphoria. We are tired and depleted while our body works to integrate the new energies. No one explained this to me, but it certainly made sense and has allowed me to feel much better about not believing I was invited to the party! Aligning downloads and integrating upgrades is common work I now perform regularly for many of my professional teacher-clients, as it is often difficult to do this on your own and, if any upgrade or download is not fully integrated, it can cause havoc on the body, mind, and spirit.

Asking Questions, Delegation of Duties

This book has already covered numerous reasons why discernment is important for any empath but for the teacher discernment takes a critical role of knowing how and where you are working with that individual client. Asking yourself questions like: Is the energy we are together working with in the present or attached to a past-life energy? Is there a hitchhiker involved? or, Are we navigating the individual or collective field or a combination thereof? Discernment is not only about learning what playing field you are working in with your client, but as a practitioner it is also our job to eliminate any possibility of energy transference between clients. Similar to how we dust and vacuum our home or office to eliminate clutter and dirt, using discernment skills you can clear out unnecessary energies in your home or office space by cutting the cords and releasing the energy of each session so as not to transfer influence onto anyone or anything that enters the space throughout the day.

In addition to being adept at recognizing your own boundary for discernment, you can learn how to use your own guides as well as those of the clients to assist in the healing and the messages that come through. Intimate knowledge of your own auric fields and your professional space field offers you the ability of immediate awareness when something enters your space to either assist in or thwart the efforts of your client's healing. Throughout years of working in my professional office, I have become highly sensitive to its vibrational frequency and am able to immediately become aware of any presence that enters my space, and this empowers me to make healthy choices for me and my client. I can discern if the assistance is a deceased loved one that may have a message, or a guide that is here to help or an energetic being that is doing the healing work with and through me. It also allows me to be aware of anything that may or may not serve my client's highest and best good and gives me the opportunity to consent to the energy or not.

Another concept I present to my practitioner clients is that we do not and cannot do this healing work alone. The professional is the channel of the healing. Each of us has energetic help available and it is important to invite and accept that help—that is what makes for a strong empathic healer, to know the boundaries of self and when to channel higher assistance. I learned this all on my own and wish I had had a mentor to offer this idea and teach me how to do this. The best way for me to describe this is that I began to delegate much like I did when I was a corporate professional with a full marketing team. I would instinctually ask for help by delegating duties to my guides, angelics, benevolents, and the light itself. I would telepathically multi-task a piece of me to be diligent in maintaining the body scan of the client while I would enlist an angelic to maybe find the auric breaks and repair them. I would go out and check in with the client's soul contract and invite the light people to surround the client on the healing bed to shift the energy block. I would go speak to the Higher Self of the client and ask the benevolent to cut past life cords and repair timelines. My work became a team effort and still is to this day, in fact the bigger my work gets, the bigger my team gets. I also intuitively began to ask more and more questions about where I was working in the body and why I was doing a particular thing at that moment in time. I would command answers. When I tell this to a teacher-client they often repel and say I cannot command Source—and I tell them who you are commanding is you, your higher version of you; again, take what resonates here and toss the rest per your personal beliefs. This clarity is critical for me to align to a level of integrity in my work, or at the very least find that ah-ha feeling within me guaranteeing I am working on behalf of my client's highest and best good. I learned to use my own divine human vehicle of Source as the barometer of truth and trained myself to trust it implicitly and I still do each day as not just a practitioner and teacher but as a human being.

Training the Sensitive Empath Practitioner

So how do I use my own body and how do I teach that skill to other professionals? Personally, I believe it all begins with the mindset that my empath-skills are a gift from Source. Ever since I was young I was a strong sensitive and psychic empath. So if my soul came in this way, I believe it is my responsibility to determine what that means in terms of how I choose to live my life. As an adult, I chose to take ownership of my innate psychic-empath gifts and turn them into professional skills. I know being an empath is different from my birthright of empathy and I work hard at being present at all times as to which skill I am operating within. I constantly nurture the relationship I have with not just my divine vehicle or physical container but more so my energy bodies. I take pride in the years of training I have imposed on myself to be able to trust my intuition and instincts when it comes to knowing and owning my own frequency container intimately. This ongoing work is what turns gifts into skill. This is why and how I can use my vehicle to assist others. And use it only with permission.

If I were to technically teach how I use my empath gifts as a skill in my professional work, I would say that I have a step-by-step process to this work as follows:

1 I settle into myself and intentionally choose to do the work. Choice and intention is what makes a practitioner different from the untrained empath. To set the intention, I first always have permission to enter and work within another's energy field. Second, I am completely aware I am taking the action to merge with another's body and fields. Third, I choose to enter another's field as an observer-practitioner for the specific purpose of assisting my client's Higher Self in their own healing process. This means I take full responsibility for my position and also remain present as the observer to monitor the work as it moves through each stage. I am diligent on behalf of not only my client but myself to make sure the energy is honored and moving in the best possible way for all those involved.

2 I open my body, mind, and spirit to move into an energetic connection with my client. This second step is a bit more of a heart-based opening or healing handshake to begin the process, agreeing to allow my divine human physical vehicle and energy fields to act as a channel for healing. This reminds me that I am not "doing" the healing, as much as I am the professional mediator offering service to self and service to others.

3 I allow myself to holographically merge with not just my client's divine physical vehicle but also their energy fields, their Higher Self and any assistance that steps forward to do the healing. I have no words to actually tell someone how to technically do this. I simply allow it. I open. I merge at the beginning as a kind of overlay of the client then the energy moves into a full immersion. To be clear, at all times I know of the boundary of where Suzanne starts and stops and where the client does as well, even though our fields are temporarily merged.

4 Once merged, I scan my own Suzanne-body and all auric fields to get a baseline of what my client's field holds or experiences in the way of energy blocks, dis-ease, distress, and information. I am always moving between both bodies to clarify what is mine and/or theirs and discern

the differences. This includes in the body, around the body, outside the body and anywhere spirit takes me for the information. During this time I move into a very deep process of scanning that includes emotions, feelings, memories, beliefs, and physical symptoms, wherein I will actually feel my own Suzanne-knee hurting if the client's knee is hurting. My throat will experience a choking feeling if the client has been restricted in their life in offering or sharing their truth and so on.

Once I begin connecting to certain emotions or symptoms, my psychic skills will get additional thoughts, pictures, voices, and clarity of what is happening outside of myself to assist in learning more. This can be extremely vivid for some clients and not as much for others. For example, if I feel our merged throats experiencing energetic clutching in the front, my clair-senses may offer up an actual vision from childhood of a father who shut down their voice. Other times I may find an energetic cord or tentacle of energy running from the closed throat area that wraps around the body connecting to the back side of the right hip. This would indicate anger toward father energies or dis-ease due to belief systems or actions used by a male figure to verbally shut down the client, again validating the reason for the dis-ease. So in essence, I combine the merged body experience with my clair-psychic senses to garner all of the information applicable to understanding the dis-ease held as an energy block.

5 After completing the merged scanning, I pull back my own Suzanne-essence, release my own energy from my client's field and shift my intention upward above the scene to take on more of the observer-role. The energy healing still continues even though the formal scan is complete, and I invite any and all helper-assistance to come into the healing session such as benevolent energies or guides.

6 As the session continues, I tap in and out of the client's body through the entire time the work is happening all the way through the end of the session—using my own personal container to reference the sensations experienced throughout the healing. If my own divine human vehicle senses anything that aligns to what is being healed in that moment for my client, our two holograms merge to *both* receive the healing energies, and this is something that is extremely important

for the advanced healing empath to learn. This in no way takes away from the client's own healing work but sustains the container of the healer allowing them to fill with Source light and love while the work is in progress. This is the reason any seasoned professional will tell you that the work does not exhaust them but invigorates and empowers them. That is the difference between an adept empathic professional and an untrained one. Any professional, especially a sensitive empath, who is not continually filling their tank will burn out through taking the dis-ease of the client into their own field and not also healing themselves along the way.

7   Many times during the session I am off in multiple dimensions or planes of existence to do my client's healing to find the pertinent information needed and during those times I no longer use my body as theirs. At this time I am fully separated energetically and holographically, yet my telepathic mind splits between the two worlds or multiple planes. Additionally, I merge with the client's guides and helpers and often bring my own guides into the session as well. Throughout the entire session I am tapping in and out of these realms mostly using the observer mode once again.

8   At the end of each session, I diligently remove myself fully in every way holographically and energetically to ground the client before they are finished. I physically, emotionally, mentally, and spiritually chop my hand to cut the energies from all four corners, up above and down below as well as fully around my own body. Then I intentionally place the client into the Earth connecting their heart to Gaia's and wait for messaging that the healing is complete. For me this comes in the form of a bird I see that flies into my telepathic vision. Each healer likely has their own personal way of knowing the work is done and mine just happens to be a bird or a flock of them. By now, I am fully disconnected from not just my client but all of the work, the realms of assistance and from the energy in my room.

If my client is not a human but instead a space, building, or area of land, I use a version of the same protocol to receive permission, merge energy fields, and facilitate the scanning and healing process until complete and then end with release.

This style of work may or may not connect with you because not all energy professionals are telepaths, nor do they traverse the quantum fields like I do. As a quantum worker, I move energy using grid patterns, sacred geometries, and off-planet assistance, and this may or may not resonate for you as a practitioner. We all have different skills and gifts. My belief is we all are intricate, unique pieces to a beautiful puzzle, and we each get to do what we like and know what best suits us. Regardless of your style, some of the ideas presented are valid for everyone—mostly the idea of knowing your own personal space separate from your client's, and being diligent in protection and discernment. No style of worker is better, it is just different, but it might be a good idea to examine and own where your talents lie as well as where your weaknesses lie. Embracing a group of diverse skilled professionals as your community for growth and accountability can assist you in keeping yourself healthy, balanced, and in touch with the changes happening in energy each day. Every professional still needs love and support to keep their physical, emotional, mental, and even spiritual body in top shape—I know I do! I value my "Soul-Sisters," my close peers and my professional cohorts more than I can say. They are also all sensitive psychic empaths, and we often do body scans or merge efforts with each other to tap in to help one another out and it is because of them that I am able to do my work and share my gifts with others. Every great student becomes the teacher and then that teacher again becomes the student and so on. That's the way this stuff works best!

Client Story
The Mermaid

During a healing session with a client of mine, who I call a serious mermaid energy, we were given the experience of a visual download or movie of that past-life death and it was fascinating. This particular gal is a long-term client and a very strong healer who completely resonates to the element of water with a heartfelt alignment to the mermaid energies and often uses this vibrational frequency to heal her clients via her hands. She had been experiencing stabbing mid-body pain and was struggling with an onset of an overwhelming sense of fear and sadness that made no sense in her current lifetime, thus the reason for booking a healing session with me. During her time on the healing-table, we both were made privy to some astounding past-life memories where she had incarnated in another time–space continuum as an actual mermaid. My mind's eye still clearly holds the image of her. She was nothing like the Disney version of Little Mermaid's Ariel, but more the fiery fish-like creature found in the Harry Potter movie *Goblet of Fire*. What the download or past-life movie clip showed us both was that while she was swimming freely in the sea, she was instantly made aware of a near-by fishing boat on the hunt. Those upon the boat tracked her, eventually capturing her in their netting: as she violently struggled and thrashed, her tail became lodged in the net's meshwork and there was no way out. The fishermen were taunting and abusive in their attempt to hold her captive. The fear of this memory to escape was so intense and tangible as she felt what it was like to be stalked and eventually snagged in that net. And while terrorized, this mermaid also felt such sadness that humans would treat her kind this way and her heart was broken. Eventually the fishermen plunged a long spear deep into her chest violently killing her. It was a horrific scene filled with revulsion, pain, and terror.

We released the past-life file and healed the current client body, then tried to determine why this particular wound had shown itself. While I admit neither of us were quite sure, we both believe it had a lot to do with the collective healing for past lives of aquatics on all planes of existence quite possibly related to reemerging consciousness of Atlantis and Lemuria. What is important to note in this case is that my client, while being an empath, is a trained one and is diligent in discerning her energies daily. She was completely aware that while this pain was happening to her—it was not *of* her. *To* and *of* are distinctly different and knowing the difference can effectively allow you to move through the pain and ultimately release it.

Conclusion

When I wrote my first book *An Energy Healer's Book of Dying*, I didn't initially set out to actually author a book. I wrote it as a journal to myself so I could document what was happening to my hospice clients as they moved through their journey of death. Those ideas then transformed into educational materials for hospice staff before they ultimately were edited together for publication. This book on empathing has been a very different voyage for me.

After working with thousands of clients that struggle with the challenges of stress, worry, self-worth, and dis-ease, I purposefully set out to create an honest reflection of what I encounter, heal, and teach each day as a professional practitioner. In my practice as well as my daily life I serve multitudes of empaths. Over the past year while writing this book, I would find myself in conversation with clients, friends, and family as I literally burst out loud; *"Oh my, you really need to read my new book!"* because at some level we all empath.

The human body is designed to be empathetic—it is our birthright and assists us with feelings of compassion and love. That said, we are not designed to empath, but we do, and we can safely. After reading this book you hopefully now know there is a difference between having empathy and empathing and have garnered ideas on how to not only identify the qualities of the empath but have identified tangible ideas to help you traverse life in a protected, healthy way. Or possibly this information has opened your eyes to another person in your life who struggles with empathing and has offered you the ability to find patience and understanding around their daily plight.

As I stated earlier in the book, many of my clients see their ability to empath as a badge of honor and others see it as a curse. I do not see it as either. But I do see it as a skill set that is something to be culled, honed, and respected. I see being an empath as a responsibility to oneself first, followed by honoring another's space.

I wrote this book so others may know they too can traverse their day without taking on energies that are not in alignment with their highest and best good, and to learn that the idea of selfish can mean something completely different than most of us were taught.

I wrote this book to shed light on honoring the journey of another and to open our eyes and hearts as to how important it is to not steal energy even under the guise of concern or worry for a loved one or even a stranger.

I wrote this book to share amazing client stories to not just entertain but as a reminder that these energies, good, bad, and sometimes ugly are anywhere and everywhere and we do not have to be afraid, we just want to be educated.

I wrote this book as an extension of my professional practice as a healer and an energy worker to teach and share. My goal in everything I do is to empower others to heal and manage their own energy—to not look to a guru or outside source as their truth. With that in mind, I didn't want this book to just scratch the surface, but to dig deeper into how our human energy system works and provide tangible tactical tools to use in your daily life.

I personally have experienced being an empath as something dangerous, something difficult, something exhausting, but more so I have experienced being an empath as something exciting, something amazing, and something exhilarating.

As a trained professional empath, experiencing these energies has opened my eyes to the magical world of oneness and for that I am eternally grateful. This is what pushes me to stay diligent in my discernment and I continue to be thankful for the ability to connect, or not, to everything that surrounds me daily with complete awareness and presence. I encourage you to do the same—*if you choose!*

Cosmic Hugs!

Appendices

✦

Appendix One

Chakra Balancing Practices

The chakra system distributes the flow of prana or energy throughout your subtle or energetic body and auric fields, which works much like gasoline fueling your divine human physical container or vehicle. The system is made up of seven main chakras running down the spine that interconnect with our nervous system and all other functioning systems within the human body. The meaning of the word chakra is Sanskrit for "wheel of energy." These wheels are energy vortices or fuel destination points that pull in energy from the outside world, drawing it into the human vehicle affecting body, mind, and spirit. These same vortices also move stored energy from within the body back into the outside world using a motion that moves like a funnel or whirlpool—clockwise to spin the energy out of our body into the space around us and counter-clockwise to pull energy from anything within our external world back towards us. This includes energy frequencies from people, places, emotions, feelings, and mental or physical vibrational programming.

In order for the chakras to be healthy, they need to be in balance. However, our chakras are always in flux depending on the energies surrounding us daily. When in balance, each chakra is in its optimum state with each individual wheel or vortex of energy spinning clockwise at a medium pace. When out of balance, chakras can be either under-active or overactive. An underactive chakra spins too slowly to effectively move energy through the system. This is due to a blockage that is preventing the chakra from taking in and distributing energy. When a chakra is overactive, it is distributing too much energy and working in overdrive with a spin factor that is too fast. Chakras are susceptible to drawing in more negativity than is healthy when they are not spinning at an optimum speed or if they are only spinning in a clockwise direction, which continuously draws energy into the system. Both too much fuel or too little fuel creates imbalance to the chakra and affects overall health and wellness.

Each of the seven chakras builds upon one another, meaning when one experiences a blockage or imbalance it affects all the others. These blockages or imbalances within the chakras disrupt the energy flow through the system and can manifest as symptoms in the physical, emotional, mental or spiritual fields, affecting organs, emotions, and thought patterns. Ultimately any unattended blockage or imbalance in your chakra system can show up as stress, anxiety, pain, illness, emotional distress, depression, and conflict causing your body, mind, and spirit to suffer.

We can create the right balance within chakras by making slight shifts in our energy that do not disturb the overall system. Because these vortices are in constant fluctuation, it is a continual process to rebalance our energetic system both inside the body as well as outside it. This is why discernment is such a valuable skill set—to stay present with the divine human physical vehicle and the subtle body shifts toward realignment. This is possible only if we are functioning in a state of conscious awareness and are educated in how to stay present with the divine human container. The higher our personal frequency or vibration, the more love fuel we give out and receive. Conversely, the more fear fuel we are using, the more negativity and density we draw in and give out. In this way, the condition of our chakra system influences our lives on a daily basis. The following information outlines methods for working with each chakra to create and maintain balance throughout your energy system.

The Root Chakra

The energy of the first chakra, known as the root or base chakra, is foundational to the entire system. Its energy extends from the perineum or tailbone and moves outward and downward to connect us to Mother Earth. This energy center also works through our legs and feet much like a root system with minor chakras on the soles of our feet (and hands) to make a rooted connection of the physical body to our planetary body. The fuel or consciousness of this chakra embodies our planetary relationship, our primal self, and our basic sense of survival and worth.

The root chakra is our physical chakra, which relates directly to our divine human vehicle's needs of eating, drinking, sleeping, mobility, and other functions of the physical body. It is our grounded anchor to the earth and influences our primal survival instincts of fight or flight and protecting our physical health. Because it is related to the physical world, our root is also connected to our programmed belief systems relating to material issues such as finances, security, safety, stability, and sense of worth.

We initially upload these beliefs from those we grew up with by watching, listening, and learning their version of safe. We are much like a super-computer that stores and runs these tidbits of information, which we hold within our container of beliefs as we play out each day. The problem is most of the beliefs we run through our computer are someone else's and do not necessarily bring us the safety we need.

Identifying Imbalances in the Root Chakra

The root chakra facilitates the flow of energy within the lower part of the body, including the hips, legs, lower back, and sexual organs (men). Therefore, imbalances in the root chakra can create physical symptoms such as digestive disorders, constipation, hemorrhoids, immunity-related disorders, varicose veins, skeletal problems, osteoporosis, pain in legs and feet, lower back pain, rectal tumors, stress-related ailments, obesity, anorexia, and allergic reactions. If this chakra is blocked, an individual may feel anxious, fearful, insecure, depressed, and frustrated.

Note: A man's sexual organs are located primarily in his first chakra, which is why male sexual energy is usually experienced primarily as physical.

Signs of an underactive root chakra:
- Physical fatigue, lack of stamina
- Disorganized, lack of focus
- Feeling disconnected, floaty or flakey
- Feeling fearful, anxious or restless
- Excess worry about financial insecurity

Signs of an overactive root chakra:
- Anger or irritability
- Rigid boundaries or stubbornness
- Difficulty accepting change
- Materialism or greed
- Impulsiveness or a reactive nature

How to Balance the Root Chakra

When the root chakra is balanced, we have a healthy connection to the earth providing us with a grounded energy of manifestation to make things happen in the material world with a positive balanced energy to succeed.

Practices to connect to Mother Earth:
- Do physical activity and bodywork, yoga, massage (feet too), reiki, Tai Chi, Qi Gong, etc.
- Stay aware and connected to the nature that surrounds you daily.
- Get outside, hug a tree, sit on the grass, walk barefoot, spend time in the woods, do whatever makes your heart sing.
- Plant a garden and play in the dirt, plant your feet in the dirt or sand.
- Keep plants inside your home.
- Study land meridians and energy grid lines.
- Align to the natural elements of earth, air, water, and fire by discovering your favorite elements and working with them. Also work with your weakest fuel element to overcome fears.
- Read and study ancient mysteries of Earth to uncover universal truths within your being and trust your body's inner knowing.

Yoga poses to help balance the root chakra:
- Warrior II
- Standing Forward Fold
- Garland Pose
- Head to Knee Forward Bend
- Easy Pose
- Mountain Pose
- Bridge Pose

Essential oils to help balance the root chakra:
- Patchouli
- Nutmeg
- Vetiver
- Bergamot
- Pine
- Grapefruit
- Myrrh

Stones to help balance the root chakra:
- Bloodstone
- Tiger's Eye
- Hematite
- Fire Agate
- Black Tourmaline

Affirmations to help balance the root chakra:
I feel deeply rooted and connected to Earth
I am grounded, stable, and standing on my own two feet
I love myself
I am worthy
I feel safe and secure
I trust myself
I am connected to my body

Colors of the root chakra to wear or bring into your home: **red, brown,** and **black.**

The Root Auric Field

The first auric layer, called the etheric body, stores and templates the root chakra gas associated with the physical functioning of the body. The field extends from one quarter to two inches beyond the physical body and pulsates about 15–20 cycles per minute. It is the physical body's energy blueprint and looks much like a light blue or gray matrix of light. Its overall shape mirrors the physical body but is composed of web-like energy lines or a sparkling field of light beams similar to the lines on a television screen. It has the same structure as the body including all the anatomical parts and organs, and the physical tissues exist as such only because this vital energy field is behind them, that is, the etheric body field is prior to, not a result of the physical body. Because this energy template creates the blueprint for the actual physical tissue, having an understanding of our energy field is critical to maintaining health and balance in the actual physical body.

The Sacral Chakra

The second energy center, located in the lower abdomen below the navel, is known as the sacral chakra. The sacral chakra is connected to our emotions and relationships and is influenced by core beliefs expressed or repressed during childhood. Motivated by pleasure and joy, the sacral chakra is the driving force for your enjoyment of life and when balanced, it enables you to feel and experience life to its fullness. We were designed to be a feeling race—this is what makes us so unique and is a divine aspect of being human.

As the center of passion, our sacral center also awakens our sensuality, sexuality, and our ability to create and enjoy intimate relationships with flexibility and adaptability. This empowers us to accept change, move forward and transform. Not only does it influence our relationship with others, but it also embodies our relationship to the discovery and exploration of our world.

Working with the sacral chakra can help you develop and cultivate relationships with other humans and other things in life and on our planet. Plus, it awakens all creative expressions and encourages discovery and experimentation with anything that you are truly passionate about, offering well-being and enjoyment of life itself.

Identifying Imbalances in the Sacral Chakra

Located in the lower abdomen, symptoms of imbalance in the sacral chakra can include menstrual pain, inflammation of ovaries and cysts, sexual ailments or fungus, bladder or uterine ailments, digestive problems, ulcers, prostate and testicular problems, impotence, diabetes, hypoglycemia, kidney problems, lower back pain, pain in hip joints, skin problems, sore backside, kidney weakness, constipation, and muscle spasms. From an emotional perspective, energy imbalances in this chakra can manifest as anger, menace, hatred, apathy, blame, guilt, greed, power, control and morality.

Note: A woman's sexual organs are located in her second chakra, which is why female sexual energy is usually experienced primarily as emotional.

Signs of an underactive sacral chakra:
- Fear of joy or pleasure
- Lack of creativity
- Fatigue or lethargy
- Deficiency in desire and passion
- Inauthenticity and insecurity
- Detachment from self and relationships to others

Signs of an overactive sacral chakra:
- Addictive personality
- Aggressive or anxious feelings
- Emotionally overreactive or dramatic
- Excessive emotional attachment and codependency

How to Balance the Sacral Chakra
When the sacral chakra is in proper balance you have the ability to flow with emotions freely and to reach out to others for relationships, which can include romantic and sexual, or not.

Practices to connect with partners, friends and family:
- Approach relationships with respect and foster open communication.
- Listen, twice as much, as talk.
- Be open to honoring different perspectives of truth from others.
- Recognize when the other person is seeking simply comfort and a shoulder to lean on versus advice, fixing or action-based solutions.
- Spend quality time together away from electronic or outside stimulation so you can truly connect to each other's energy fields.
- Consider making food a way to connect, by cooking together, eating together and cleaning up together.
- Balance one-on-one individual time with group gatherings.

- Feel the differences in energy when you are interacting with another when they are sad, lonely, happy, excited, etc.
- Take a step back in group setting and observe the energetic interactions happening within the room.
- Be involved. Be present. Be Open.
- Practice forgiveness and compassion when applicable.
- Offer gratitude and words of love and support to others and to yourself.

The Sacral Chakra also connects to the 2D Plant and Animal Kingdom so here are some tips to further connect to this realm.

Practices to connect with the Mother Earth and the animal kingdom:
- Hug a tree, stare at the clouds or the night skies.
- Concentrate on working with water: sit by the sea or a river, take a bath.
- Discover devic faces in shrubs, flowers, rocks, and trees. Sense the faeries, gnomes, and sprites.
- Vibrations and connections can be so soft and subtle, be aware to connect.
- Feel the differences in energy when you touch or hug trees or plants.
- Take a walk through the woods and see if you notice a sensation like moving through a spider web or being watched.
- Look to find nature's aura, much like heat waves that come off the pavement on a hot day.
- Practice telepathy with animals.
- Try hands-on-healing on animals through placement of hands and intention of healing prayer.

Ideas for creative play:
- Dancing, flow movement.
- Journaling and writing.
- Entertain old and new hobbies that allow you to create.

Yoga practices to help balance the sacral chakra:
- Goddess Pose
- Warrior One Pose
- Frog Pose
- Mountain Pose
- Bridge Pose

- Corpse Pose
- Wide-Legged Forward Bend C

Essential oils to help balance the sacral chakra:
- Neroli
- Spicy Cardamom
- Ylang Ylang
- Sweet Orange
- Sandalwood

Stones to help balance the sacral chakra:
- Citrine
- Carnelian
- Agate
- Orange Calcite
- Tiger's Eye
- Moonstone
- Coral

Affirmations to help balance the sacral chakra:
I am passionate and I have desires
I am open to experiencing new relationships
I am comfortable in my body
I trust balance
I am a creative being

Colors of the sacral chakra to wear or bring into your home: **orange**.

The Sacral Auric Field

The second layer, called the emotional body, stores and templates the sacral chakra gas associated with the emotional aspects of being human. This fluid field is much like a lava lamp of energy colors of the rainbow, from brilliant clear hues to dark muddy tones depending on a specific feeling or emotion. Clear feelings vibrate as bright, pure color and confused energies hold a frequency that is dark and muddy. It extends one to three inches from the body roughly following the same physical outline with a more flowy structure of these colored clouds of fine substance in continual unsolidified motion.

The Solar Plexus Chakra

Located in the upper abdomen two inches above the navel, the third chakra or the solar plexus is the core of your identity. This center houses our deepest connections with the power of our will and self-worth. In addition, it fuels our self-discipline as the source of our personal power and confidence, which embodies our unlimited potential to manifest and enables us to discover who we truly are and blaze the path of our life.

As the center of our identity, the solar plexus is the center of our personality and is responsible for our self-esteem, how we see ourselves and how we present that to others. When balanced, the solar plexus chakra allows our authentic self to shine brightly, overcome fears, be the master of our thoughts, and make conscious choices.

Identifying Imbalances in the Solar Plexus Chakra

The solar plexus chakra influences the organs and parts of the body directly below our sternum, including our stomach, liver, gall bladder, pancreas, and small intestine. Physical symptoms of imbalances can include stomach ailments or ulcers, liver, spleen or gall bladder problems, digestive problems, obesity or anorexia, heartburn, stomachaches, back pain, digestive difficulties, liver problems, diabetes, nervous exhaustion, and food allergies.

When imbalanced, the solar plexus can bring an overall lack of control in life resulting in a potential loss of identity. Additional mental and emotional ailments can include nervous disorders, self-esteem issues, fear of rejection, oversensitivity to criticism, self-image fears, nervousness, and poor memory.

Signs of an underactive solar plexus chakra:
- Lack of Confidence
- Lack of Purpose
- Helplessness
- Indecisive
- Low Self Esteem

Signs of an overactive solar plexus chakra:
- Desire for Control
- Judgmental
- Overly Critical
- Excessively Stubborn
- Angry and Aggressive

How to Balance the Solar Plexus Chakra

When the solar plexus chakra is balanced, you may express cheerfulness, be outgoing, enjoy new challenges and experiences along with a strong sense of personal power and self-respect.

Connect with others in your life, both alive and deceased, to heal past power issues, unresolved relationship problems, disputes or trauma:
- Release judgment in current or past relationships and find forgiveness where appropriate for self and others.
- Be an unconditional observer of humanity by honoring varied perspectives, thoughts, and truths.
- Practice service to others by supporting community, volunteering your time and talent to those in need.
- Spend quiet time in contemplation or prayer to connect with passed loved ones for release, love, and support, allowing the heart to stay open.

Work with your own energy bodies and auric fields:
- Practice calming your mind, incorporate meditation techniques.
- Hone your sensitive empath abilities.
- Practice your psychic skills, telepathy, prayer, etc., to balance out the ego mind programs.
- Try new things to stretch your abilities.
- Spend time in the sun.

Yoga practices to help balance the solar plexus chakra:
- Full Boat Pose
- Reverse Plank Pose
- Sun Salutations and Sun Mudra
- Half Lord of the Fishes Pose

- Firefly Pose
- Bow Pose

Essential oils to help balance the solar plexus chakra:
- Pine
- Eucalyptus
- Juniper Berry
- Vetiver
- Helichrysum
- Grapefruit
- Lemon

Stones to help balance the solar plexus chakra:
- Malachite
- Yellow Calcite
- Citrine
- Topaz
- Tiger's Eye

Affirmations to help balance the solar plexus chakra:
I love and accept my power
I am authentic
My ego is balanced
I am free to choose
I direct my own life
I embrace higher guidance

Colors of the solar plexus chakra to wear or bring into your home: **yellow.**

The Solar Plexus Auric Field

The third auric layer, called the mental body, stores and templates the solar plexus chakra gas associated with our mental life and linear thinking. This field appears as bright yellow light radiating around the entire body, head to toe, and extending three to eight inches beyond the body. Within the field those with psychic sight may sometimes see thoughts, ideas, and even emotions as energy blobs of varying brightness, color, and form.

The Heart Chakra

Located at the center of your chest, the heart center is the fourth chakra and is associated with compassion, endearment, affection, tenderness, and unconditional love. Known as the bridge, this chakra connects the lower three physical chakras to the upper three spiritual chakras acting as a passage between earthly matters and higher aspirations embodying our ability to love unconditionally.

Not only responsible for moving love throughout your life, this healing and unifying chakra activates the ability to recognize that we are all interconnected allowing you to show love to others as well as show love to yourself. Key characteristics include connection, forming deep bonds of unconditional love with everyone and everything, compassionate respect and forgiveness which allows you to understand other people's ideas, thoughts, and boundaries, with the ability to release and let go of past experiences and forgive others.

Identifying Imbalances in the Heart Chakra

The heart chakra influences our circulation, heart, lungs, shoulders, and upper back. Therefore, imbalances or negative characteristics can include coronary illness and heart attack, asthma and breathing disorders, lung cancer, pneumonia, colds, allergies, high or low blood pressure, elevated cholesterol, breast cancer, shoulder pain, backache in rib cage, rheumatism in arms and hands. Mental and emotional symptoms of imbalance can manifest as lack of confidence, hopelessness, despair, hate, envy, fear, jealousy, and passivity.

Signs of an underactive heart chakra:
- Withdrawn, Isolation
- Lacking Empathy
- Unforgiving, Judgmental
- Overly Critical of Yourself and of Others

Signs of an overactive heart chakra:
- Codependent
- Emotional Self-Care Neglect
- Lost Sense of Identity
- Lack of Personal Boundaries, Saying Yes to Your Detriment
- Giving to Others Without Restraint

How to balance the Heart Chakra
When the heart chakra is balanced you may feel compassionate with a desire to nurture others with empathy, be friendly, and be open to the innate good in everyone.

Quiet the Mind:
- Practice breathing techniques.
- Spend time alone.
- Incorporate meditative, calming music into your day.
- Do a silent retreat.

Connect with the mystical to ignite your creativity of this realm:
- Read books, oracle cards or surround yourself with dragons, faeries, unicorns, etc.
- Watch mystical movies like Disney, The Hobbit, Star Wars, Avalon, Sir Arthur, etc.

Perform rituals or attend reenactments:
- Participate in events like the Renaissance Festival, Burning Man, Ceremonies and Rituals.
- Design and perform your own personal rituals.
- Volunteer and spend time giving of yourself to others.

Yoga practices to help balance the heart chakra:
- Half Camel Pose
- Wheel Pose
- Bridge Pose
- Upward Facing Dog Pose
- Reverse Plank Pose
- Bow Pose

Essential oils to help balance the heart chakra:
- Rose or Rosewood
- Palma Rosa
- Lavender
- Sweet Marjoram
- Geranium

Stones to help balance the heart chakra:
- Rose Quartz
- Kunzite
- Green, Watermelon Tourmaline
- Jade
- Green Calcite

Affirmations to help balance the heart chakra:
I am open to giving and receiving love
I love and accept myself
I am grateful for my life and my relationships
It is safe for me to connect lovingly with other beings
Unconditional love resides in my heart

Colors of the heart chakra to wear or bring into your home: **pink** and **green**.

The Heart Auric Field

The fourth auric layer, called the astral body or bridge, stores and templates the heart chakra gas associated with humanity and unconditional love. Here we see the same rainbow colors as the emotional body but this template houses more vivid colors that are usually infused with the rose light of love. Composed of clouds of color more beautiful than those of the emotional body, it extends six inches to one foot from the body.

The Throat Chakra

The fifth center, the throat chakra, is located in the region of the neck and is associated with speaking your authentic voice and owning your truth. The energy of the throat chakra starts in the center of the neck at the level of the throat and expands through the shoulders and even can run down the arms to the hands. The throat chakra is motivated by expression and truth, embodies your true originality and authenticity, and allows you to communicate effectively without conditions attached.

When your throat chakra is balanced, it gives you the ability to be inspired, project your ideas, and align your vision with reality. As the center of communication and creativity, the throat chakra allows you to seek truth and express your version of it all while listening deeply to others, allowing them to own their own truth unconditionally. This chakra is also the source of your personal integrity, which allows you to be honest with yourself and gives you the courage to stand up for what you believe in.

Identifying Imbalances in the Throat Chakra

The throat chakra is connected to the throat, neck, teeth, ears, and thyroid gland. Physical symptoms of an imbalance in the throat chakra can include throat pain, tonsillitis, mouth ulcers, laryngitis, voice problems, gum or tooth problems, swollen glands, thyroid imbalances, fevers, flu, neck or shoulder pain, scoliosis, speech defects, hyperthyroid, skin irritations, ear infections, sore throat, inflammations, and back pain. From an emotional and mental perspective, the throat chakra influences communication, addiction, criticism, faith, decision making. independence, self-expression, sense of security, loyalty, organization, and planning.

Signs of an underactive throat chakra:
- Excess introversion or withdrawal from social situations
- Insecurity
- Feeling the need to walk on eggshells around others
- Fear of speaking up
- Small and timid voice
- Worried about hurting others' feelings

Signs of an overactive throat chakra:
- Gossiping
- Overly critical or condescending
- Arrogance
- Gaslighting
- Using language that is rude or abusive
- Inability to listen

How to Balance the Throat Chakra

When the throat chakra is balanced you may feel comfortable with voicing and sharing your truths, feel centered, be musically or artistically inspired, and may be a good public speaker. A healthy throat chakra allows for creative expression that empowers you to be yourself and share it with the world.

Connect with the Ascended Masters

Most Ascended Masters are spiritually enlightened beings who in past incarnations were ordinary humans, but who have undergone a series of spiritual transformations and now reside in the higher realms. Examples of those believed to be Ascended Masters may include beings such as: Jesus, Buddha, Mother Mary, Kwan Yin, Saint Germaine just to name but a few. Some of my personal favorites are Melchizedek, El Morya, Merlin, Lady Nada, plus I include Archangel Michael in this category.

- Study, do meditation and visualizations.
- Quiet your mind with music or breath techniques.
- Ask for specifics from them while in prayer or meditation. Each Master embodies individual gifts and offerings; study, learn, ask for help.

Practice divination:

- Use oracle or tarot cards. Do a daily card pull or a bigger spread for guidance.
- Practice scrying or reading signs in nature.

Work with sound:

- Do vocal toning.
- Work with all genres of music.
- Drum, bowls, chimes, strings.

Yoga practices to help balance the throat chakra:
- Head Rolls
- Neck Stretches
- Lion's Breath
- Supported Shoulder Stand
- Supported Fish Pose

Essential oils to help balance the throat chakra:
- Lavender
- Lemon
- Vanilla
- Chamomile
- Coriander Seed

Stones to help balance the throat chakra:
- Azurite,
- Lapis Lazuli
- Turquoise
- Aquamarine

Affirmations to help balance the throat chakra:
I am open and honest in my communication
I can allow others to own their truth
I have a right to speak and own my truth
I am heard and validated
I nourish my creativity and self-expression
I know when and how to listen

Colors of the throat chakra to wear or bring into your home: **light blue.**

The Throat Auric Field

The fifth layer, called the etheric template, stores the throat chakra gas associated with divine will and power of the word. This template contains all the forms that exist on the physical plane in a blueprint or template extending about one half to two feet from the body. It looks like a narrow oval shape with clear or transparent lines appearing on a cobalt blue background much like an architect's blueprint for the entire structure of the field, including the chakras, organs, and physical form with limbs all in negative form creating an empty space for the etheric body (or first level) of the aura to exist.

The Third Eye Chakra

Located between the brows, the third eye chakra is the sixth chakra and is responsible for how we perceive reality, much like a link between our mind and the outer world, embodying our ability to see both the inner and outer realms through clear thought and self-reflection. It is often referred to as our psychic chakra; however, all chakras are psychic centers to some extent.

Motivated by knowledge combined with intuition, this chakra symbolizes your connection to wisdom and insight, allowing you to access the inner guidance that comes from a higher source as well as deep within your being. This guidance and sense of knowing enables you to cut through illusion and access your individual truths. Key characteristics include self-reflection, self-examination, and vision based on divine yet logical thinking and creativity.

Identifying Imbalances in the Third Eye Chakra

The third eye chakra is connected to our eyes, face, brain, lymphatic and endocrine systems. When the third eye chakra is unbalanced, physical symptoms can include headaches, migraines, brain tumors, strokes, eyestrain, poor eyesight or blindness, seizures, learning disabilities, sleep disorders, deafness or hearing impairments, colds, and sinus problems. From an emotional and mental perspective, the third eye chakra can affect mental health, discipline, judgment, concept of reality, confusion, pride, arrogance, suspicion, and emotional intelligence.

Signs of an underactive third eye chakra:
- Not Able to Meditate, Quiet the Mind or Self Reflect
- Fearful of the Unknown
- Lack of Concentration

- Lack of Intuition
- Unable to See Past Illusions
- Disconnected From or Disillusioned with the Universe

Signs of an overactive third eye chakra:
- Judgmental, Overly Analytical
- Floaty Feelings, Out of Body, Anxiety
- Mental Fog, Mentally Overwhelmed
- Excessive Daydreaming
- Lack of Clarity in Thoughts
- Spiritually Self-Absorbed

How to Balance the Third Eye Chakra

When the third eye chakra is balanced and open you are moving to a high plane of knowing, see death and dying with a new perspective, are not attached to material things, may experience telepathy, astral travel, and past lives.

Connect with sacred geometry and constellations:
- Meditate and do breath work with sacred geometrics, the Flower of Life, Tree of Life, the Constellation of Sirius, etc.
- Understand how things are connected through pattern and form.
- Study and color mandalas.
- Do puzzles.
- Entertain the Fibonacci sequence in nature and plants.
- Work with appropriate YouTube materials to open the third eye, mandala graphics, hertz.
- Sky-watch in the dark of night.
- Do Full Moon ritual and work.

Connect through the arts and the sciences:
- Do yoga, martial arts, other physical disciplines that bypass the mind and bring the body into alignment.

Yoga practices to help balance the third eye chakra:
- Child's Pose
- Wide-Legged Forward Fold

- Candle Gazing
- Alternate Nostril Breathing

Essential oils to help balance the third eye chakra:
- Sandalwood
- Rosemary
- Chamomile
- Frankincense

Stones to help balance the third eye chakra:
- Amethyst
- Sodalite
- Lapis Lazuli
- Purple Fluorite
- Black Obsidian

Affirmations to help balance the third eye chakra:
I am aligned to my inner guidance
I hold wisdom, knowledge, and intuition
I trust my intuition
I am open to inspiration, bliss, and enlightenment
I am one with the wisdom of the universe

Colors of the third eye chakra to wear or bring into your home: **purple, dark blue,** and **indigo.**

The Third Eye Auric Field

The sixth layer, called the celestial body, stores and templates the Source energy moving through the third eye chakra associated with celestial love. This field extends about two to two and three-quarters feet from the body and appears as beautiful shimmering light composed mostly of pastel colors. Its form is less defined in that it simply appears to be gold-silver light with an opalescent quality, like mother of pearl sequins, that radiates out from the body similar to the glow around a candle, and within this glow are also brighter, stronger beams of light.

The Crown Chakra

The seventh chakra located on top of the head and radiating upward is known as the crown chakra and is said to be the convergence of individual consciousness and our higher state or universal consciousness.

When you have aligned the energy of your seventh chakra, you are able to experience spiritual growth through the physical body, universe and soul connections of oneness allowing access to clarity and enlightened wisdom as this center transcends all limitations. Key characteristics include awareness of unity and enlightenment anchored in the energy of serenity, bliss, and deep peace.

Identifying Imbalances in the Crown Chakra

When we experience imbalance in the crown chakra, physical symptoms can include headaches, epilepsy, multiple sclerosis, weak immune system, right/left brain disorders, coordination problems, and photosensitivity. From an emotional and mental perspective, blockages in the crown chakra can create mystical depression, mental illness, senility, forgetfulness, sleep disorders, and lack of purpose as well as confusion over values and ethics.

Signs of an underactive crown chakra:
- Lack of inspiration
- Spiritual depression
- Greed and materialism
- Mental fog or floaty feelings

Signs of an overactive crown chakra:
- Lack of empathy
- Apathy toward self, others, and the world overall
- Sense of elitism and superiority
- Disconnection from your body and earthly matters
- Mystical depression

How to Balance The Crown Chakra

When the crown chakra is in balance you most likely have attained an ability to open up to the Divine with access to the unconscious and subconscious and multidimensional planes of existence.

Quiet and open the mind:
- Practice breathing techniques.
- Spend time alone.
- Practice astral travel and lucid dreaming.

Connect with the "fabric of reality":
- Physically create mandalas in sand, art.
- Weave, knit or crochet.
- Color.

Connect with sound:
- Use sound as a powerful art; music, high flutes and strings.
- Do toning.
- Incorporate meditative music using singing bowls, both crystal and brass.

Connect with the Andromeda Galaxy and its guardians:
- Use meditation.
- Invoke Archangel Metatron.
- Sky-watch in the dark of night.

Yoga practices to help balance the crown chakra:
- Headstand
- Rabbit Pose
- Corpse Pose
- Silence

Essential oils to help balance the crown chakra:
- Lime
- Spicy Sweet Lavandin
- Neroli
- Vanilla
- Frankincense

Stones to help balance the crown chakra:
- Selenite
- Clear Quartz
- Oregon Opal
- Amethyst
- Diamond

Affirmations to help balance the crown chakra:
I am of Source and align to Source
I honor the divine within me
I listen to the wisdom of my Higher Self and guidance
I am open to ancient wisdom and inner knowing
I am at peace
I live in the present moment

Colors of the crown chakra to wear or bring into your home: **white, purple** or **amethyst.**

The Crown Auric Field

The seventh layer, called the ketheric template, stores the crown chakra gas associated with the higher mind. The outer form is an egg-shaped oval and contains within all the auric bodies and chakras associated with the present incarnation. It is a highly structured template extending two and one-half to three and one-half feet from the body composed of thousands of tiny golden threads of shimmering light creating a golden grid structure that pulsates at an extremely high rate. This is the strongest level of the auric field as it contains within it all other fields and is sometimes known as the auric egg or the bubble.

✦

Appendix Two

Meditations

Our world is evolving at a rapid pace, and nothing is really the same as our old forms of reality crumble and new ones emerge. It is difficult enough traversing this massive change but for the empath it can be debilitating physically and emotionally so it is important to take care of your divine vehicle of Source energy and meditation can be a great tool to do this.

This chapter includes several different meditations that are designed to assist you in your journey. You can do these meditations sitting, lying, or being awake and present to the information. They can be read as text or you may choose to read and then spend time with the information bit by bit, or you may choose to record your own voice reading them and use them in a meditative state of full relaxation, or you may find a different manner in which to work with this information.

Grounding and Bubbling

The Grounding and Bubbling Meditation is designed to offer you a sense of safety for your human meat body. Creating a shield of protection of love and light can also assist you in maintaining your energy, your health, and your happiness. The creation and maintenance of the technique can also assist you in the process of discernment allowing you to determine if you are empathing or stealing another's emotions, feelings or fuel. This skill is critical in maintaining your health, emotionally as well as physically and mentally.

Meditation
The Ground and Bubble Technique

Let's begin.

As we begin, take a deep breath in through the nose and out through the mouth. Close your eyes and embrace the darkness behind them as you settle into a sense of peace. Continue to breathe in and out as you now fully align with your breath.

Begin to imagine and envision your Source essence—whatever your God-package looks like to you. It may be a white light, it may be a symbol, a feeling or simply a knowing sensation. Feel it surround you as an omnipresence, a universal energy. Now with your breath, begin to draw this universal essence into your heart chakra located in the middle of your chest. Breathe it in. Breathe in the omnipresence of Source. Take the time to feel the fuel of creation as it enters your chest and ground it there for a couple of slow, intentional breaths and then anchor it within your heart.

With creative imagination, keep the anchored connection of the energy within your heart and now begin to move it downward through your body along your spine. Allow it to slowly connect with each of your physical chakras; your solar plexus chakra located just below your ribs, your sacral chakra located within the belly and your root chakra located at the base of your spine. Continue to creatively imagine this cord of Source energy moving down your legs to create somewhat of a root system moving into and connecting with the Earth's energy. Now feel this energy planting your legs and body much like the roots of a tree embracing the inner earth, down into the core of the planet then into the heart of Mother Earth. She is much like us. She has a heart deep within her. Using your imagination, you may see this as a crystal, a beautiful glow or an actual heart beating, however it comes to you, simply allow your heart to now connect to hers as this connection firmly unites you with Gaia, Mother Earth. She provides safety for the female maternal energies within your body. Embrace and feel her unconditional love and light as you draw it in with your breath. As you breathe, continue to move this rooted cord of energy back up your legs, back into your body and fully connect and anchor it within your own heart. This magnetic heart to heart connection now fills the lower portion of your physical body, aligning your physical chakras while remaining anchored.

Take a deep cleansing breath. Once again imagine and envision Source energy surrounding you. This time we are going to take that anchored heart energy and move it upward, slowly connecting up and through each of your spiritual chakras: your throat chakra, your third eye chakra located between your eyes and mid-forehead, and eventually your crown chakra located on the top of your head.

As you continue to breathe—move this heart-anchored energy upward beyond the spiritual chakras, upward to fully connect with the Cosmos, the Father Sky energies. This paternal connection is the counterpart to the maternal energies of Mother Earth. He is much like us. He also has a heart deep within him, so once again use your imagination to find this heart, see this heart and connect to this heart of multi-universal electric energy. Feel the upper half of your meat body firmly uniting with Father Sky, as he provides safety of the male energies within our body. Embrace and feel his unconditional love and light as you draw it in with your breath. As you breathe, continue to move this cord of energy back into your body from the top down and fully connect and anchor it within your own heart. This electric heart to heart connection now fills the upper portion of your physical body, aligning your spiritual chakras while remaining anchored.

As you take in a deep cleansing breath, feel how you have connected fully to your Mother Earth female energies as well as your Father Sky male energies, flowing through each and every chakra point along your spine activating in love, light, and protection. Embrace the ebb and flow of these powerful energies as every cell in your system, every organ in your body responds to the radiating light filling your body.

Once again bring your attention to your heart chakra and envision Source energies bursting forth from the center of your chest to surround your entire body with a protective bubble of love and light. A beautiful, sparkling shield of defense against anything that is not for your highest and best good. Feel the cool essence of Source within your bubble. See yourself safe inside of your bubble armor, knowing fully that it is anchored and fueled by both Mother Earth and Father Sky.

You may remain in your grounded bubble as long as you intend, as you now thank any guides, helpers, and Source energy, sending gratitude to all.

So be it.

Cutting Energy Transference Cords

As humans we go throughout our days and lives creating energy connections to others. Sometimes these energy connections do not serve our best good and can be seen much like an umbilical cord that is holding onto another as a strong feeling or imprint between two or more people. Usually this is due to unresolved or imbalanced physical, emotional, mental, spiritual or karmic energy between two or more human bodies, and/or spaces and places which can influence behavior and emotion in a variety of ways until we let go of or remove those cords. It is important to learn to cut all cords and release any energy transference between the connections of people, places, timelines and objects, especially when the interaction is deeply sensitive in nature and may play out as repeated or addictive emotions as an inability to positively move forward in your life.

Meditation
Cord Cutting

Let's begin.

Get comfortable, sit or lie down and begin to concentrate on your breathing pattern. As you continue to feel the rhythm of your breath, relax the toes, the feet, the arches of your feet, the ankles, the calves, the knees, the thighs and hips. Just sink into yourself as you release all the tension you carry in your lower limbs. Bring breath and attention to the hip flexors, the pelvis, the lower spine, just breathe in and out allowing the breath of life to relax the lower portion of your physical body both front and back. This is the home of the root Chakra—the physical chakra that carries all of our beliefs. As you continue to bring life-force energy in with your breath to this lower portion of the body, begin to allow yourself to float back, back, back in time in your life. Go back as far as you possibly can to remember your initial beliefs on any messaging surrounding the idea of "should's" and "have to's."

Try to remember all of the family beliefs, the societal beliefs, the cultural beliefs that may have altered your energy even way back then. Bring to mind any images, thoughts or memories of when you allowed others to suck your energy field dry by either taking your power physically, emotionally, mentally or spiritually. Or possibly you took someone else's power. As you continue to fuel your lower body with deep relaxing breaths, let go of any energy transference you may have experienced because of your beliefs. Release it from the root chakra—the physical chakra. Breathe in and out as you continue to let go. Let go in the feet, the ankles, the calves and thighs, the pelvis, the hips and flexors, and the lower back. Take some deep breaths now and just release by cutting any belief cords that bind you. Use your hands and perform a smooth chop motion around any portion of these lower limbs.

Next bring your awareness and breath into your abdomen area both front and back. This second chakra called the sacral chakra holds your emotions, your passions and desires. It also holds your relationships with others. Breathe deeply into this part of your body as you feel the energy enter and fill your belly. Release anything no longer needed in the intestines, the colon, the reproductive organs, the lower back and sciatica. Begin now to concentrate on any energy transference you encounter in relationships in your life. These include those beliefs of the "should's" and "have to's" surrounding doing things for others. Remember, sometimes we feel we are helping others by doing for them, by holding their energies, by holding their fears, worries, failures, etc. This is not healthy for your second chakra, and it is time to allow yourself to let go. Breathe and see yourself cutting any relationship cords that bind you.

Take some deep breaths and just release by cutting any relationship cords that bind you. Use your hands and perform a smooth chop motion around your belly front or back. By cutting these cords you do not in any way lose the relationship with that person, only the energy of the binding energy transfer that ultimately depletes your individual fuel tank. Breathe deeply into your tummy and lower back area as you allow yourself to be free.

Next move to your third chakra—the solar plexus that houses the mental chakra. This holds the brain chatter and monkey mind, forever processing. This energy transference comes in the form of manipulation and control felt from others and can include guilt, shame, fear, just to name a few. Try to identify your energy transference issues when it comes to this chakra. Who or what ignites a loss of power in your mental field. Is it family, friends, work? What runs on overtime in the dark of the night when you cannot sleep as a mental tape going over and over in your mind. See the cords that are connected to those tapes, those people, those thought patterns. Take some deep breaths now and just release by cutting any egoic cords that bind you. Use your hands and perform a smooth chop motion around your mid-body front and back as you breathe in freedom, serenity, balance into your stomach, your liver, your spleen, your kidneys.

Now bring awareness and breath to the heart chakra—the chakra of unconditional love. Realize all the conditions you put on your love. I love you if you . . . when you . . . Or maybe it is you that feels conditionalized. I'm only loveable if I, when I. Imagine all the times you do things you really do not want to do yet you do these things to make others happy. Think of all the pressure you put on yourself to make others happy. Yet we are not responsible for others' happiness. We can support it or cherish it but not change it. Envision any cords that are connected to those conditional love actions, those people, those thought patterns, those beliefs. Take some deep breaths now and just release by cutting any conditional cords that bind you. Use your hands and perform a smooth chop motion over your chest as you breathe new fresh energy into your heart and fill . . . fill that heart both on the front side of the body as well as the back.

Next we move to the throat chakra—the chakra of truth. We are going to spend some time here on how we all try to make our truth be others' truth. We do anything and everything to make others' truth align to ours because then that means we were right. We fight for ego power with our words all day, every day with so many people, ideas, and actions. As you continue to breathe in and out, bring to mind all those people, situations and energies that challenge your truths and really feel how draining that is to your energy field. Now one by one, just let them go. Breathe them out of your stiff, tight throat and neck including your shoulder where you carry others. Release your upper back into the rotator cuffs and even all down your arms, elbows, wrists, and hands. Breathe out any non-truths. Breathe in truth. Cut all cords of energy transference by using your hand in a chop motion anywhere needed and examine any connecting cords that may come from the throat to another place within your body and chop them as well. Feel the breath of life returning truth to your system. Feel it move completely down your spine, your central nervous system, and back up again, realigning your body to feel your truths.

Take in a deep cleansing breath as you move to your third eye chakra in the middle of your forehead. Your inner sight. Realize all the ways you see and experience energy transference. Think about how you see yourself—how you see others. Breathe out any judgment. Breathe in being the observer of all things. Allowing others to be, with no conditions attached. Breathe in love and light to your eyes, your temples, your face, ears and lower skull. We take in so much inauthentic energy with our physical eyes. What is it that you do not want to see? Is it that homeless person on the roadside? The World News tonight? That person with the perfect body, hair, and clothes that you envy? The horrible parent and child that live in your neighborhood? What is it that you judge or do not want to see in yourself? All of this can create major energy drains for our body, so just breathe out anything and anyone that no longer serves your truth. Cut the cords with a smooth chop motion anywhere you find the energy calling out to you now.

And lastly we move to the crown chakra—the top of the head. This is your Divine Mind spiritual chakra so consider letting go of any conditioned and transferred spiritual concepts and ideas that no longer fit in your life. Let go of unwanted dogma or maybe cultural, family, or even political beliefs that break your spirit. Think of anything or anyone that you allow to banish your magic. It may be a spouse, a child, a parent, sibling, friend or enemy. It may be your job, your duty to something or someone; whatever it is that allows you to deplete your energy bubble, identify it now and with full gratitude and joy let it go. Hand chop any cords attached as you remember you are a human being, not a human doing. As you breathe deeply, feel what it feels like to just be.

And when you feel it is time, begin to bring yourself fully back into your body starting with the top of the head—to the tips of your toes, filling with rose light of love and joy free from all conditional cords.
So be it.

Meditation
Emotional Alignment

Let's begin.

Get comfortable, take a good, deep cleansing breath in and out to get yourself started. Continue to breathe.

As you tune in to the sound of your breath and your heartbeat, notice how the rhythms of your body are beginning to slow down, relax and let go. Give yourself permission to spend this time in a state of deep relaxation letting go of all thoughts, worries or cares that can distract you. Anything that is on your mind simply give it to your guides to caretake of including all thoughts and issues now. Breathe in and out feeling as all your muscles begin to unwind, becoming loose and limp as you go deeper and deeper into a state of beautiful relaxation with your angels.

Feel the presence of your guides and angels surrounding you now as you give release to your muscles, your toes, your heels, your feet, as you continue to breathe into your ankles, unwinding your calves, your knees, your thighs, as you sink deep and deeper into relaxation with every breath, giving yourself permission to let go any tension, exhaling any stress and worry. Inhale feelings of peace and tranquility, knowing it is safe to go on this journey with your guides, to give you the answers and the information you are searching for. As you continue to bring the breath into your legs, your hips, feel your lower back muscles begin to loosen and relax.

Take a breath now into your stomach and mid-body, your chest and ribcage, your upper body, your shoulders, your throat, your arms and entire upper back: now unfold into relaxation. Release the base of your head and the inside of your skull, relax your jaws, your face, your eyes, and even the top of your head. Breathing in and out. In and out.

You are safe and you are in control for the purpose of this healing meditation as you allow your body to completely unwind and receive full assistance from your guides and angels and continue to let go of any energy of your day including all thought patterns embedded in your mind matrix. Let go and give way to your natural state of peaceful relaxation.

Begin to sense the space around you. Breathe with the space as you become aware of the rise and fall of your breath, its coming and going, the sensation, sound, temperature. Breathe down to where the weight of your body rests, below the base of your spine to your root chakra that houses your beliefs. Breathe into your base, your foundation, as you let it soften and gently expand with breath. Allow yourself to go deep into where your beliefs are stored to examine how you feel about "doing for others." Is this a belief you grew up with? Do others always come first and if so, how does that feel? Does it feel genuine or is it more of an "I have to, I should" feeling? What are your beliefs of taking on everyone else's emotions, responsibilities, worries, concerns? Whose beliefs are these? Did they get handed to you and you allowed them to become real? Make a mental note of anything inauthentic. Find any fear, failures, emotions.

When you are ready, allow your awareness to move up to your belly, just below your navel—your sacral chakra of emotional intelligence. Breathe into it, let it gently soften and expand on your breath, as you further examine your true emotions and feelings. How are you programmed here? Determine if you carry pity, sympathy or true empathy. Are you an empath? Examine how you honor others', feelings as well as your own. Are you truly connecting to actual feelings and emotions or are you finding programmed thinking masked as feelings? Make a mental note of anything inauthentic. Find any fear, failures, emotions.

And when you are ready move your awareness up to the soft area below your breastbone—to your solar plexus chakra of personal power. Breathe deeply, allowing your solar plexus to soften and expand on your breath as you examine the truth of your mental body. Are you in a war in your true power center fighting the divine mind versus the instinctual programmed mind? Do you fight your ego self with your Higher Self? Do you fight "have to's" versus "get to's"? Make a mental note of anything inauthentic. Find any fear, failures, emotions.

When you are ready bring your awareness up to the center of your chest to your heart chakra of self-development and unconditional love and the home to your soul matrix. Gently breathe into your heart letting it soften and expand on your breath as you invite in the color green or rose pink, or both, whichever feels right. Bathe your heart center with nourishment, renewal, and healing as your heart takes what it needs. Release anything inauthentic you found along your journey. Say the words "I am greatly loved. I allow myself to give and receive love freely. I am nourished by the power of love." And if you did indeed find programming, allow yourself to release it now, fully and completely with your breath.

In your own time, move up to your neck, housing your throat chakra of self-expression and personal will. Invite truth into your throat center to soften, expand and breathe, clearing, opening, softening the need for control, freeing self-expression and creativity. Allow your throat to take what it needs as you say the words, "I hear and speak my truth. I express myself freely. I allow myself to go with the flow of life."

When you are ready, take your focus up to your forehead between your eyebrows or third eye chakra of wisdom and intuition, gently allowing it to soften, expand, and breathe. Ask your guides and angels to bring clarity, insight and understanding, offering your third eye to take what it needs as you say the words: "Everything is now unfolding as it should."

Moving up to the top of your head to your crown chakra of oneness allows alignment of your spiritual chakras with your physical chakras. Gently invite in a light violet color to softly bathe your crown, balancing, restoring, and harmonizing as you let your crown take what it needs. And say the words, "I am one with the universe. I am one with the whole." Feel the emotion of the words as you bring that soft violet down back through each of the descending chakras, back down through the third eye, the throat, the heart, the solar plexus, the sacral, and anchoring in the root.

Relax into this thought of being one with the whole as you become the observer of your own Higher Self and physical self. Sit back and see if you can find any uncomfortable energy blocks, erratic movements, stuck, dense or blackness anywhere in your body. Go deeper to connect with any density to know, see or feel if there are still any programs that you are now willing to release. Maybe it is an old program from a belief you may have grown up with that no longer resonates with you and your life at this time. Or a program of collective consciousness that you resist. Or even possibly a program of fear of a past life that no longer serves you. Sit back and observe to gain knowledge from it now allowing yourself to move forward in your spiritual development of self. And if you find yourself encountering old energies that no longer feel of use simply envision hitting the "delete button" to move it fully back to Source and thank it for leaving. Take some time to scan yourself and observe.

When you are ready, come back to yourself as a whole, back to the ebb and flow of your breath, back to your center; breathe into your core and again, say the words within your mind and heart: "I am whole and connected to my soul. I am perfect just as I am." Allow the energy of the words to bathe your body, mind, emotions, and spirit. Feel the emotions, then own them.

In your own time become aware of the air on the surface of your body; the sounds around you, near and in the distance, and connect to the support beneath you. Notice how you feel.

Now, hold yourself with loving kindness, for the beautiful, unique being that you are.

So be it.

Humans Create Their Story

We all have a story we create for ourselves and then tell or show others. It is the inner narrative that tells us and others who we are, what we do and includes the masks we wear for each role we play in the story, all fueled by significant life experiences and events. Some elements of our story are found within our actual DNA but most are given to us by others usually in childhood and continue to develop over time to drive our path in life according to what our lineage and soul history offer as life lessons.

Meditation
Examine Your Story

Let's begin.

Take in a deep breath and relax. During this meditative time, sit with the narrative of your life story and do your best to feel if this script is truly yours at this time in life.

Let's now go deeper as you breathe in and out. Again, in and out as you continue to relax and feel your breath move throughout your body. Go deep into the darkness of a recessed mind and allow yourself to go back in time, back through the years of your physical life. Breathe and float back, back, back to your earliest memory. It may be five or six years old, maybe younger. Give yourself some time to just go deep into your memory bank of childhood.

Settle into whatever time period you have gone back to and try to get a clear picture, a feeling, a smell, a sound, a touch, a message. See if you can get a sense of your life story from this time of your early existence. Examine who were the people in your life that helped write the script of your story. What characters did they play? What did this story feel like? What was the script? Did the script feel programmed or forced? What masks did you choose to wear or be forced to wear?

Sit with this memory for a bit and fully observe the story of your life at this young age and with a deep and cleansing breath, release anything that no longer serves you.

Now affirm: *All is well in my world. Everything is working out for my highest good. I am safe! We are a family of humanity and the planet is our home. Life supports me in every possible way.*

Take some deep breaths and move forward through time to your grade school and middle school years and again find a memory of this time in your life. Try to get a clear picture, a feeling, a smell, a sound, a touch, a message. See if you can get a sense of what it felt like to be the story of your life at this age, and because you are older now, does love feel different? Does your life story feel as if you are fully creating it, owning it, fully believing in it or does your story feel like it is someone else's and it is somehow forced upon you, or expected of you?

Once again, examine who were the people in your life that helped write the script of your story and what characters they played. What does this story feel like? What was the script? Did it feel programmed or authentic? What masks did you choose to wear or be forced to wear?

Sit with this memory for a bit and fully observe the story of your grade school and middle school life and release anything that no longer serves you.

Now affirm: *That past is over. I am beautiful and everybody loves me. Everyone I encounter today has my best interests at heart. I am healthy, whole, and complete.*

Take some deep breaths and continue your life timeline moving into high school, college, and young adult age. As you try to get a clear picture, a feeling, a smell, a sound, a touch, a message, see if you can get a sense of your life story at this time. You have gained some independence by now, so does the script you are living reflect your own truths in regard to friends, family, school- and work-mates? Are you following a culturally accepted script and wearing the masks to fit when it comes to relationships and lovers and enemies? Are you doing what you are supposed to or doing because you truly choose to? Are you simply being versus doing? How does the script of your life feel at this time, in high school, college, and young adult age when you look back at it now, is it genuine or forced? And who were the people in your life that helped write the script of your story then; what characters did they play and do any scripts feel programmed? Sit with this memory for a bit and fully observe the story of your life at this young adult age and release anything that no longer serves you.

Now affirm: *I am at home in my body. Wellness is the natural state of my body. I am in perfect health. I trust my intuition. I trust my physical body and my relationships. I am willing to listen to that still, small voice within. I am willing to ask for help when I need it.*

Moving forward even further through time, breathe deeply into your mid-adult life to get a clear picture, a feeling, a smell, a sound, a touch, a message; see if you can get a sense of your life script. What are the scripted beliefs around career, family, relationships, children, money, doing, not doing, fear, love? Who are the people in your life now pushing or supporting the scripts in your stories? Are the scripts programmed or genuine? Are you still wearing masks and have the masks multiplied or are you no longer needing them? Sit with this thought for a bit and fully observe the story of your adult life and release anything that no longer serves you.

Now affirm: *I forgive myself for not being perfect. I honor who I am. I do not have to prove myself to anyone. I come from the loving space of my heart and I know that love opens all doors.*

As each of us moves onward through our individual lives, we can change our story if we choose to and we can, together, create a different future for humanity and our planet.

If you were to tell your story to another person right now—would you find yourself telling it differently?

Take some time to allow this timeline to merge and flow into a lifetime of full Source energy letting go of anything inauthentic. Breathe out release. Release might include energies like forgiveness, judgment, jealousy. Now breathe in energies like compassion, joy, and magic. As you slowly allow yourself to fully come back into your body, feel your re-scripted story, the authentic one that follows your own true heart.

So be it.

Body Scan and Loving Your Body

Most humans are not in love with their physical manifestation or divine vehicle they have been gifted from Source energy and this causes many to disconnect from the love fuel needed to stay healthy and balanced. Each of our individual body parts carry significant information that communicates what is needed (or not) in terms of wellness. A loving body scan is a great way to connect to the divineness of your human vehicle and listen to what it wants and needs. Most of us go throughout our day not necessarily aware of what our body is encountering in the way of energies surrounding us and interpenetrating us. A technique of a body scan can be the empath's best tool for doing a quick (or long) method of establishing what energies they are holding onto and also discern if any stuck or corded energies are theirs, or not.

Meditative/Interactive
Full Body Scan

Sit or lie down with this information at hand. Relax and release anything crossed like hands, legs, ankles and take a deep cleansing breath. As you move through the content, take your time with each section. As you read each description follow that with a personal scan of your own body to see if you find similar or different information. Sit with what you get for each section for whatever time feels right.

This exercise can be done as often as you choose. Let's begin.

Head and Skull

This houses the crown chakra and the third eye chakra that relates to our higher connection to Source and our psychic skills of intuition. Beginning with the head and only the head, I scan inside, outside and around the entire skull. I examine and compare front to back.

Side to side. Inside the head I am looking for anything imbalanced, stuck or dense including scanning the eyes, inner ears, jaws, and throughout the entire skull and whatever is held within the head is usually "mine." Next I move to the outside of the skull or outline of the head where the energy is usually "not mine." What I am looking for here is anything that stands out as a busy feeling or sensation residing outside the skull itself. Energy that is buzzing, pushing or pulsing while surrounding the head indicates programming information and belief-messaging that comes from outside of you—from your childhood, society, controller programs and more. Remember with each body portion I pose the question and have the dialogue of: Is this mine? And if not, I question further.

As a healing practitioner, I see many clients that hold density in the crown chakra on top of the head, shut down tight, like a cork stuck in a bottle indicating trouble receiving Source energy. This does not mean that you are not connected to Source, but that there may be some dogmatic or family structures blocking full access to this fuel. I find dis-ease and confusion in the third eye especially in the temples, the forehead and around the head pressing like a band. I also see a lot of people holding stuck energy in their actual eyes and the sockets that support them indicating that they are not wanting to see something in life or have been programmed out of their psychic skills. Most clients hold some density in their jaws combined with clenching or grinding of the teeth and mouth indicating not speaking truth, holding back or not even knowing their truths. And the biggest area of stuck energy for most everyone sits at the base of the skull on the back side which stores our overall programming, indicating others still tell me what to think, feel, and do. Additionally, I look for any tentacle or corded energies anchored in the head area that then attach to other portions of the body and I follow those lines to see what additional chakra is being affected. Lastly, I look to see how connected the client is to the electric-male-Source energy of the universal cosmos. Depending on where they are in their personal spiritual journey, this may need to be cleared, reconnected or upgraded to optimize this connection to that fuel center.

Throat, Neck, and Shoulders

This houses the throat chakra, holding our communications and truth. Here I move down to the neck, scanning the throat both front and back. I also scan both shoulders, comparing right to left and outward into the rotator cuffs. I scan the upper back below the base of the neck into the mid-upper back. I will also scan down both arms, again comparing right to left, including the elbows, wrists, and hands.

As a healing practitioner, I consistently find clients holding density in this area of the body especially the throat and upper back. Stuck energy held in the front of the throat feels like you cannot swallow, like you have something stuck in your throat similar to a big lump and this indicates not speaking your truth. This can mean that you are fearful to speak up or you walk on eggshells in terms of your voice, or you spew anger which is not your true essence. This neck area can also hold density on the back side indicating that the client cannot receive true messaging from others beyond self and do not trust that there is not a condition attached to that messaging. Another form of stuck energy manifests around the neck much like an energetic hand clutching or choking the life out of the throat which indicates verbal and sometimes also physical abuse. Many that hold any essence of shame will also have an energetic drop-angle to the neck where the head hangs forward putting a lot of pressure to the back side of the neck. The more shame held within, the further the head energetically droops and the neck bends forward.

The upper back area is a major indicator of an empath wherein they carry what feels like an energetic backpack affecting the upper body and rotator cuffs where the energetic bands of the backpack lie. The empath carries everyone's stuff in this energetic backpack from people to worries to things they cannot control and the more they take on others' stuff the heavier the pack gets. It is critical to question who and what is stored in the backpack and release what does not serve you. Stuck energies in the arms, elbows, wrists, and hands often represent someone that is egoistically driving through life in fear—like hands and arms glued to the steering wheel while fighting the concept of the guidance from cruise-control.

Upper Mid-Body Both Front and Back

This houses the heart chakra related to unconditional love. In this area I scan the ribs, the lungs, the heart and middle of the chest as I compare right to left, front to back for imbalance as well. The front side of our chakras reveal how we give out our energies to others whereas the back side shows how well (or not) we receive energies from others. I look for any protective energy shields surrounding the heart and chest area both front and back. In this portion of the body I also look for what we would call an etheric or energy band that shows up much like a bra that is too tight, putting an energy squeeze on and around the body directly below the breast area. I also scan to see how the energy is flowing through the esophagus to find indications of dis-ease in moving the breath fully through from the throat to the diaphragm. I look for stuck or trapped emotion in all portions of the body but especially here in the heart center.

As a healing practitioner, I find the heart center to be an extremely vulnerable area for almost every client as it seems to easily hold emotion, grief, and pain from an incredibly early age and onward. For anyone that has been hurt the scan will reveal some sort of energetic shield that keeps others out of this weak area, however that does not benefit the person because it thwarts the flow of love. If this shield is dense in the front of the body the person has difficulty giving out love and if found on the back side it indicates fear of receiving love with conditions attached, plus lots of folks carry the shield on both sides. This center is also where I will find much in the way of trapped or stored emotional hurt, fear, sadness, and lots of abandonment or failure issues. The etheric energy band mentioned above that squeezes the mid-body indicates someone that struggles to integrate their physical self with their spiritual self, not in a dogmatic way necessarily but more about how they consciously flip a switch in their intention. It is much like—right now I am going to be busy and doing, then I consciously flip to now I am going to meditate and go with the flow. The integrated person does not flip the switch as these two separate energy signatures have already unconsciously become one. The empath struggles a lot here as their belief system tells them to do, do, do for others oftentimes putting themselves at the bottom of the list where the hidden energies can store feelings of resentment resulting in victimization, unfulfillment, and self-love issues. Lots of clients here begin to manifest blood and immune system issues as well as heart-related difficulties plus lung dis-ease/disease in this part of the body.

Middle or Trunk of the Body

This houses the solar plexus chakra that relates to our will, power, and mental field. This definitely is a center that the empath struggles with because it relates directly to the monkey mind of doing and the mental chatter that goes along with that much like the proverbial hamster on the wheel. If I have a list-maker client, I look closely at the way they hold their entire energetic body overall plus track any cord that connects this chakra to another as a tentacle of energy. I scan the organs that hold anger like the kidneys and the liver. I scan the digestive organs and the back side of the body as well as the front.

As a healing practitioner, this is a portion of the body I scan closely with any client that struggles with self-worth issues and physical symptoms. I look to see if there is any overall "C"-shaped pattern to how the entire body holds itself as this will reveal just how far back the internal negative programming of the client is anchored; the tighter the C-shape, the older the destructive messaging. I have clients that struggle with self-worth issues from the messaging they received *in utero* and in this kind of case the scan feels like their mid-body has almost been forcefully punched inward and is now energetically stuck in the C-shape. This creates a mental narrative that is typically carried into adulthood if this center is not cleared of the negative messaging offered while in the womb. This can then create tentacles or corded energy that attaches to corresponding chakras to create further dis-ease, like the throat (indicating truth of being heard, or not) or the hips (indicating beliefs from parents).

Belly Area and Lower Back

This houses the sacral chakra that relates to our feelings, passions, desires, and our relationship to others. This particular chakra is one that the empath will oftentimes shut down and not fully connect to even though they feel that they may be an emotional person. Being emotional and knowing your true emotion are two different things. The empath will drive a lot of the emotion through the mental matrix in the solar plexus we just reviewed versus owning their true pain. To scan this area, it is important to do both front and back, side to side. I scan the entire digestive track system and the sex organs, especially on women. I especially take time to scan the back side of the body, lower back all the way down to the sciatica on both sides. This portion of the body is another place that will hold a lot of trapped emotions, feelings and memories so be aware of what might reveal itself while moving through this area.

As a healing practitioner, I believe this is one of the more critical centers to do work in because we humans are so trained to think-feel versus feel-feel and are masters at ignoring or stuffing our true emotions. No matter what sex we are, the right side of the body holds our male energies and the left our female ones and this comes into play for this chakra and the next in deciphering what we are holding on to in terms of dis-ease. Anger, especially in this chakra, shows up on the back side of the body and in this area it is most often stored in the lower back and sciatica. If the anger is held against a male relationship or person it will show up on the back, right side, and conversely if it is a female we are struggling with, it will show up on the left side. The level of the anger directly correlates to the level of the pain stored. Some clients actually store their unresolved issues in energetic boxes and stack them in the back of their belly's energetic closet assuming they have walked away from the unsettled issue, person or situation but this never works. These stored boxes continually steal fuel not only emotionally but also physically in this portion of the body ultimately ending in some type of dis-ease or disease. Another way unresolved distress shows up in this area is that individual hurts throughout years energetically bundle together much like grapes on a vine. This holds like a goopy cluster on the applicable female or male side of the belly as unresolved small hurts that have multiplied throughout our lives. This can be something as trivial as my third-grade girlfriend making fun of my dress and then my eleventh-grade buddy mocking me in gym class, and so on. These seemingly inconsequential events are emotionally stored away to then become an underlying belief system of non-trust. In the case where the client has goopy grape cluster density on the left side of the belly this indicates they hold a hidden non-trust of women overall, formed as the cluster of emotional energy that ultimately creates dis-ease and disease, and any male dis-ease will show up on the right-hand side of the belly as a cluster. The sensitive empath can fall prey to this style of energy hoarding especially when coupled with being a victim or having psychic vampiring drive their life. This sacral center is one that every human may want to spend time with—in terms of asking the questions of: is this mine, and if not whose is it and why am I holding it?

The Hips, Hip Flexors, Pelvis, and Lower Trunk of the Body

This houses the root chakra, the foundation of our belief systems, fight or flight mechanics and our sense of worth and feelings of safety. This is again an area where we want to scan all sides of the body but pay attention more so to the right/left tug. I will scan for this right/left tug as well as any front/back energies that may also tug from the hips to the feet. Many times I will find an enormous difference in how the body holds itself in the way of stability and balance. If I find a dis-ease on one side I can often find an overcompensation element on the other side of the body which will eventually create harm. This is also an area that I will scan for in the way of any tentacles or cords from or to other portions of the body to learn what is affecting what as a combined message.

As a healing practitioner, I find that this portion of the body is off in every single client I see, myself included. No matter how diligent we are, this will always be affected by the beliefs we hold and the way we choose to (or not) change them as we age. To remind you, the right side will hold the beliefs and messaging offered from the male–father and the left side will hold those of the female–mother. Now this never is a blame situation as no matter what a father or mother said, did or did not do, it is us that creates the belief about ourselves according to what we choose to validate as our truth in conjunction to the experience with that parent. Anger toward that belief will pull the body backward especially in the pelvis and hip flexor. If the hip pushes forward it is because that parental belief pushes at us, and we push ourselves to align to it or we push ourselves to directly align against it—either way it shows up energetically as a push forward. Most clients have one hip going one way and the other doing the opposite, never making a balanced foundation or secure energetic base to our human body. I sometimes see a twisting motion to a leg and the energy looks like a piece of licorice which indicates the client is still confused about the messaging and programming of the particular parent. Blocked knees often indicate the unresolved messaging of not being needed and the unstable legs are all about not being able to stand up for oneself. A disconnect in the energy of the feet and ankles are all about instability and not being rooted or grounded in feeling safe, most often in terms of material things and money. One of the things I look for energetically is if the client is grounded into the maternal Mother Earth energies with this lower trunk of their body. Most people are not even aware of the term or concept of grounding, so if this is you I highly suggest you consider doing the Grounding and Bubbling Meditation technique also offered earlier in the Meditation Chapter. This particular portion of the body scan is probably one of the most critical spots to ask that barrage of "Is this mine?" questioning and further examine just where the messaging of stuck energies came from as belief systems handed down from others. Remember this foundational chakra retains that primal wound of separation of Source, the fight or flight and the safety and self-worth programs which are all critical to how the entire structure of the chakras above are either balanced or not.

A body scan can also include a peek at or examination of the auric bubble or the templates. Generally, I scan the body as detailed above and intentionally reboot the entire auric egg or bubble with the intention of anchoring both to the magnetic Mother Earth energies below and the electric Father Sky energies above.

And So It Is.

Meditation
Love Your Body Scan

Let's begin.

Get comfortable by taking a deep breath. Breathe out as you let all tension disappear. Take another deep breath. Breathe out and relax your whole body. Take a third deep breath. With every breath you take, you go deeper and deeper into a tranquil meditative state. This scan is to inform you of what energies are aligned to each body part.

With each segment, think about this concept, release any energy that no longer serves you and draw in what does serve you to change your body, to love your body.

Start to bring awareness and breath to:

The Feet: Representing how we stand up for ourselves. How we show up and walk forward in life. This also includes our Toes and Ankles: Representing flexibility or inflexibility.

The Knees: Representing our being needed.

The Legs: Representing how we move through our day – through life itself.

The Hips: Which carries our beliefs from our mother and father figures.

The Sciatica: Holding fear from those parental beliefs.

The Lower Back: Holding onto fear of non-support in any manner.

The Solar Plexus: Representing our true power or our ego power.

The Stomach: Housing our fears and connection to our growth.

The Bladder: Holding anxiety and fear.

The Kidneys: Holding anxiety, fear, but also anger.

The Liver: The home of anger within the body.

The Arms and Elbows: Represents holding onto the steering wheel of life.

The Hands: Holding that steering wheel with a grasp of not letting go.

The Fingers: Representing the details of your control issues.

The Lungs: The breath of life itself.

The Breasts: Representing how you nurture, either yourself or others.

The Heart: Representing the center of infinite unconditional love.

Heart Issues: Identifies feelings of not enough, there is not enough, I am not enough. Heart Problems: Long-standing feeling of not good enough, non-worth, no self-love. Lack of joy.

The Upper Back: Lack of support from outside of self. The taking on of others' issues and problems.

The Face: Representing how we show up to others in this world.

The Eyes: Representing what we do and do not want to see.

The Ears and Nose: Representing what we do and do not want to hear.

The Neck: Representing flexibility or inflexibility. Also outside programming from others.

The Throat: Representing our version of sharing or not sharing our truths. Can also stuff or harbor anger in holding back. Unable to express oneself. Lump in the throat: Fear of not ingesting life overall.

The Teeth: Representing taking a bite out of life, holding on or not to decisions.

The Jaw: Can hold anger, fear, resentment.

The Brain: This is our inner narration or our inner computer, and its programs. Tumor: Stuffed or blocked beliefs or belief systems that are not aligned.

The Muscles: Resistance to change, or to new experiences. Representing how we move through life with ease or stubbornness.

The Bones: Representing the structure of our beliefs and how we build ourselves.

The Skin and the Facia: Housing our individuality but also stores anxiety and fear including stored memories.

Aches and Pains: Fear of movement forward.

The Arteries: Moves the energies of how we embrace life.

Blood Pressure: High: Ignored ongoing emotional and mental issues. Low: Lack of love or attention.

Cholesterol: Clogging, slowing or cutting off bliss or joy.

Circulation: Representing how our body embraces and infuses emotion.

Fat or Weight Issues: Holding fear or need to protect one's self.

Fatigue: Resistance to change or failure. Boredom of life.

Let's Heal and Love Our Body Now

I now go from my listening brain to my heart. I let my heart take control. My heart knows. My heart has wisdom. And as I sit or lie here, I once again scan my human body, my vehicle of God/Source. I now begin to feel this infinite bliss filling up my heart, giving me this wonderful tranquil state where I know that everything is OK.

Everything is perfect right now, right here in this time and space. And as I feel this, I feel all parts of my body healing.

My feet are healing. My toes, ankles, calves, and legs are healing. My hips and hip flexors are healing. All my internal organs are healing. My intestines, colon, and liver are healing. My kidneys are healing. My stomach and digestion are healing. My back is healing. My chest, lungs, and heart are healing. My immune system is healing. My circulation is healing. My teeth are healing. My eyes are healing. My ears and my hearing are healing. My throat, neck, and voice are healing. My back is healing. My joints, tendons, and muscles are healing. My hands, arms, and shoulders are healing. My head and brain are healing. My skin and facia are healing. All parts of my body are healing. And they are filling up with this great blissful Light. I am OK. All of us are OK just as we are. I know that everything is OK. Everything is perfect just the way it is. I love and accept myself and my body. My body is perfect. And I take care of it. I feed it with nourishing food. Green, life-giving food. Food that is alive. Colorful and fresh. I give it water. And I thank my body for holding me up and strengthening me on my path through this life. I thank my legs. My steady legs. I thank my arms. My strong arms. And I thank my back. My flexible, straight back. And I thank my teeth for being healthy and strong; being able to chew my food in order to nourish my body. And I thank my digestion and all the necessary bacteria in my digestive system for taking care of me and all the food that I eat, extracting all the nutrients that I need and releasing what I don't. I thank my heart for pumping the blood around in my body. And I thank my cells for receiving all the oxygen in my heart and from the air around me. And I also thank this planet and this earth for nourishing me in infinite ways each and every day. And I thank this Universe. I am thankful for everything in my life with my heart, mind, and body as I breathe deeply. I feel so happy and content. I have this deep gratitude for everything. Everything this Universe and this life has given me. I thank this body for supporting me. I love this body as it moves me throughout my day, every day. Allowing me wonderful experiences and creating memories. I thank the Universe for the way I look. And I accept and I love the way I look right now at this time. I look perfect. I am beautiful. My body is wondrous. Everything

created is magnificent. I am a part of this Universe. This magnificent
and beautiful Universe. And I can be nothing but beautiful and
magnificent myself. I will make choices that maximize the energy
within my body. My body is my connection to the infinite supply of
energy in the Universe. If I am feeling a lack of energy in any way, it
means that I am resisting the flow of this infinite supply and blocking
assistance from Source. I will ask my body what it needs and will
sincerely follow its advice. The ideal state is to experience a lightness,
that I do not feel bound by my body. My body and the world are one.
The lightness of being in my body will be my indicator of happiness. If
I feel heavy, dull or stuck within my body, I will pay attention because
these feelings are signs that I am in need of something fresh and
new. The best way to replenish my body is to give it what it needs
most, whether it's sleep, rest, water, life-giving nourishment, the
joy of movement or communion with nature. Before I act on any
emotion, I will consult my heart. My heart is a reliable guide when
I trust it. It monitors the emotions of others around me. This helps
me experience true empathy, compassion, and love. I do not empath
what I do not own. The heart is the seat of emotional intelligence.
Emotional intelligence allows me to get in touch with my deepest
and truest self. It nurtures all relationships by reminding me to see
myself in the other. I love my body. I Love My Body. My body is a
glorious place to live. I rejoice that I have chosen this particular body
because it is perfect for me in this lifetime as a vehicle for Source to
experience itself. It is the perfect size, shape, and color. It serves me
so well. I marvel at the miracle that is my body. I choose the healing
thoughts that create and maintain my healthy body and make me
feel good. I love and appreciate my beautiful body!

I am slowly beginning to come back to my body now. Back to
this moment and back to this place. I am feeling my body, from
top to bottom, from inside to outside. Physically, emotionally, and
mentally. I am coming back to this moment. As I return—I hear this
message: Self-love is about acceptance and seeing yourself as the
gift you are. Today, I am in love with myself because I respect my
body. I see my body as a divine vehicle. My body helps me live my full
potential. I listen to it and honor what it needs. Each day, every day.
So be it.

Meditations Endnote

A majority of humans are sensing something is changing; they feel the emotion in their hearts and desire something more meaningful, yet they are not quite sure what it is or how to find it. Our imagination is a tool for higher consciousness. Each of us is experiencing an awakening of ourselves and of our planet. We are the awakening presence on Earth, and we carry this deep knowing within our spirit. Consider meditation and clear intention as an instrument to spark your spiritual awakening. The more you work with and practice these meditations the more you will align with the energies and intentions of this book. And remember, sometimes life gets busy and when this happens, I suggest to my clients to simplify their efforts, just focus on being present, being meditative throughout the day. Notice and gratify your connection to the everyday, down-to-earth blessings that surround you. I call these mini-meditative-moments. We can do this anywhere from in the car, to the line at the supermarket, to before bed.

There is no right or wrong way to meditate.

+ ✦ +

Prayer for DNA and Lineage Release

I release any family history and DNA challenges that no longer serve me or anyone in my lineage.

I send back all energy and information for any and all DNA-related dysfunction or disease back to Source.

I place any victim-mode mentality and frequencies in the hands of spirit and open my heart to accept the details of any and all Akashic Records and soul contracts affecting me in the past, the present and the future timelines.

I shift my attention to release fear and send home the feel-centered emotions held within me, plus I request genetic healing from past to present to future.

I humbly offer the release and healing through all time–space continuums, to generations before me as well as after me.

My prayer offers them the chance to release this issue, if they so choose, in their next incoming incarnation with no conditions attached.

I am no longer bound by this. I let go of any possessive holds to this, physically, emotionally, mentally, and spiritually.

I lift my thoughts, emotions, and actions now above the personal level and release them into the Source level.

I now free myself fully to love my life according to the highest and best of my personal and collective Akashic Record and the collective of God.

I place this lovingly in the care of the Creator of the Akash and Source energy.

And So It Is.

Index

Acknowledgments

I am so grateful for the opportunity to offer the world another book and would like to first thank Findhorn Press and Inner Traditions International for their encouragement, trust, and support. The individuals within these organizations that have shared their wisdom with me are beautiful souls, and I could not have produced this work without them.

I again thank Kelsey, Tracie, and Annie for their gifts of words, editing skills, vision, and reassurance, and Gisele's keen eye for detail. You are my grounding and my continued inspiration.

To my clients, friends, family, and soul-sisters that consistently present me with content to share, I thank you as well. Your experiences are the foundation of my client stories and assist me to be the practitioner I am today.

Eternal Cosmic Hugs to each and every one of you!

About the Author

Photo by Nicolle Danús

Suzanne Worthley has been an energy healing practitioner, intuitive, and psychic empath for more than two decades. She offers personal healings, space healings, spirit work, crossing over work, clearing work, and vigil/death and dying work. Suzanne's work includes teaching individuals and groups and counseling clients on the subjects of energy, healing, personal power, protection, and the Higher Self. She hosts many metaphysical and healing events, including spiritual tours of Peru and Sedona, AZ, and offers webinars, meditations, workshops, and products on consciousness studies and energy. She has a monthly membership-based online community, Vibe Tribe, that offers ongoing training and forums for learning, discussion, and support.

The author of *An Energy Healer's Book of Dying*, Suzanne lives in White Bear Lake, Minnesota.

Visit Suzanne online at **www.sworthley.com**

FINDHORN PRESS

Life-Changing Books

Learn more about us and our books at
www.findhornpress.com

For information on the Findhorn Foundation:
www.findhorn.org